TOP 100

Simplified®

TIPS & TRICKS

Photoshop® CS6

by Lynette Kent

Visual

CALGARY PUBLIC LIBRARY

OCT   2012

WILEY

Photoshop® CS6: Top 100 Simplified®
Tips & Tricks

Published by
John Wiley & Sons, Inc.
10475 Crosspoint Boulevard
Indianapolis, IN 46256

www.wiley.com

Published simultaneously in Canada

Copyright © 2012 by John Wiley & Sons, Inc., Indianapolis, Indiana

Library of Congress Control Number: 2012936421

ISBN: 978-1-118-20498-6

Manufactured in the United States of America

10 9 8 7 6 5 4 3 2 1

No part of this publication may be reproduced, stored in a retrieval system or transmitted in any form or by any means, electronic, mechanical, photocopying, recording, scanning or otherwise, except as permitted under Sections 107 or 108 of the 1976 United States Copyright Act, without either the prior written permission of the Publisher, or authorization through payment of the appropriate per-copy fee to the Copyright Clearance Center, 222 Rosewood Drive, Danvers, MA 01923, 978-750-8400, fax 978-646-8600. Requests to the Publisher for permission should be addressed to the Permissions Department, John Wiley & Sons, Inc., 111 River Street, Hoboken, NJ 07030, 201-748-6011, fax 201-748-6008, or online at www.wiley.com/go/permissions.

Wiley publishes in a variety of print and electronic formats and by print-on-demand. Some material included with standard print versions of this book may not be included in e-books or in print-on-demand. If this book refers to media such as a CD or DVD that is not included in the version you purchased, you may download this material at http://booksupport.wiley.com. For more information about Wiley products, visit www.wiley.com.

Trademark Acknowledgments

Wiley, the Wiley logo, Visual, the Visual logo, Simplified, Read Less - Learn More and related trade dress are trademarks or registered trademarks of John Wiley & Sons, Inc. and/or its affiliates. Adobe and Photoshop are registered trademarks of Adobe Systems, Inc. All other trademarks are the property of their respective owners. John Wiley & Sons, Inc. is not associated with any product or vendor mentioned in this book.

Contact Us

For general information on our other products and services contact our Customer Care Department within the U.S. at 877-762-2974, outside the U.S. at 317-572-3993 or fax 317-572-4002.

For technical support please visit www.wiley.com/techsupport.

LIMIT OF LIABILITY/DISCLAIMER OF WARRANTY: THE PUBLISHER AND THE AUTHOR MAKE NO REPRESENTATIONS OR WARRANTIES WITH RESPECT TO THE ACCURACY OR COMPLETENESS OF THE CONTENTS OF THIS WORK AND SPECIFICALLY DISCLAIM ALL WARRANTIES, INCLUDING WITHOUT LIMITATION WARRANTIES OF FITNESS FOR A PARTICULAR PURPOSE. NO WARRANTY MAY BE CREATED OR EXTENDED BY SALES OR PROMOTIONAL MATERIALS. THE ADVICE AND STRATEGIES CONTAINED HEREIN MAY NOT BE SUITABLE FOR EVERY SITUATION. THIS WORK IS SOLD WITH THE UNDERSTANDING THAT THE PUBLISHER IS NOT ENGAGED IN RENDERING LEGAL, ACCOUNTING, OR OTHER PROFESSIONAL SERVICES. IF PROFESSIONAL ASSISTANCE IS REQUIRED, THE SERVICES OF A COMPETENT PROFESSIONAL PERSON SHOULD BE SOUGHT. NEITHER THE PUBLISHER NOR THE AUTHOR SHALL BE LIABLE FOR DAMAGES ARISING HEREFROM. THE FACT THAT AN ORGANIZATION OR WEBSITE IS REFERRED TO IN THIS WORK AS A CITATION AND/OR A POTENTIAL SOURCE OF FURTHER INFORMATION DOES NOT MEAN THAT THE AUTHOR OR THE PUBLISHER ENDORSES THE INFORMATION THE ORGANIZATION OR WEBSITE MAY PROVIDE OR RECOMMENDATIONS IT MAY MAKE. FURTHER, READERS SHOULD BE AWARE THAT INTERNET WEBSITES LISTED IN THIS WORK MAY HAVE CHANGED OR DISAPPEARED BETWEEN WHEN THIS WORK WAS WRITTEN AND WHEN IT IS READ.

FOR PURPOSES OF ILLUSTRATING THE CONCEPTS AND TECHNIQUES DESCRIBED IN THIS BOOK, THE AUTHOR HAS CREATED VARIOUS NAMES, COMPANY NAMES, MAILING, E-MAIL AND INTERNET ADDRESSES, PHONE AND FAX NUMBERS AND SIMILAR INFORMATION, ALL OF WHICH ARE FICTITIOUS. ANY RESEMBLANCE OF THESE FICTITIOUS NAMES, ADDRESSES, PHONE AND FAX NUMBERS AND SIMILAR INFORMATION TO ANY ACTUAL PERSON, COMPANY AND/OR ORGANIZATION IS UNINTENTIONAL AND PURELY COINCIDENTAL.

WILEY

John Wiley & Sons, Inc.

U.S. Sales

Contact Wiley at
(877) 762-2974 or
fax (317) 572-4002.

CREDITS

Sr. Acquisitions Editor
Stephanie McComb

Sr. Project Editor
Sarah Hellert

Technical Editor
Dennis R. Cohen

Copy Editor
Scott Tullis

Editorial Director
Robyn Siesky

Business Manager
Amy Knies

Sr. Marketing Manager
Sandy Smith

Vice President and Executive Group
Publisher
Richard Swadley

Vice President and Executive
Publisher
Barry Pruett

Project Coordinator
Sheree Montgomery

Graphics and Production Specialists
Jennifer Henry
Andrea Hornberger
Jennifer Mayberry

Quality Control Technician
John Greenough

Proofreader
Mildred Rosenzweig

Indexer
Potomac Indexing, LLC

Vertical Websites Project Manager
Laura Moss

Vertical Websites Assistant Project
Manager
Jenny Swisher

Vertical Websites Associate
Producer
Rich Graves

Screen Artists
Ronda David-Burroughs
Sennett Vaughan Johnson
Jill A. Proll
Sarah Wright

ABOUT THE AUTHOR

Lynette Kent (Huntington Beach, CA) studied art and French at Stanford University, where she received a master's degree. She taught at the high school and community college level before becoming an unconventional computer guru when she adopted the Mac in 1987. Lynette now writes books for John Wiley & Sons, articles on digital imaging and photography for ShootSmarter.com, and reviews for *Design Tools Monthly*. She also teaches and presents graphics-related hardware and software for technology companies, including Wacom, Adobe, G-Technology, and Digital Foci. Both a photographer and artist, Lynette enjoys traditional and digital painting and often blends these techniques with her photographs to create images. Lynette has written the *Top 100 Simplified Tips & Tricks* titles for Photoshop CS2, CS3, CS4, and CS5; *Teach Yourself VISUALLY Adobe Photoshop Lightroom 2*; *Teach Yourself VISUALLY Mac OS X Leopard*; and *Teach Yourself VISUALLY Digital Photography*, 3rd Edition. In her nonexistent spare time, Lynette helps run the Adobe Technology Exchange of Southern California, a professional organization for photographers, graphic designers, and fine artists.

ACKNOWLEDGEMENTS

Special thanks go out to project editor Sarah Hellert for her literal and meticulous unscrambling of chapters and tireless attention to detail; to copy editor Scott Tullis for making sure the text was understandable and legible; to tech editor Dennis Cohen for overseeing the accuracy of the steps and technical terminology. Thank you to graphics technicians Ronda David-Burroughs, Sennett Vaughan Johnson, Jill Proll, and Sarah Wright, and to the project coordinator, Sheree Montgomery. And thank you, Stephanie McComb, acquisitions editor at John Wiley & Sons, for asking me to write this book.

I also want to thank John Derry for his time-consuming and thoughtful answers to all my questions on mixer brushes. Many thanks also go to Val Gelineau of Photospin.com for allowing me to use some great Photospin images to illustrate several tasks. And of course thanks go to the Adobe team for always being so responsive to all the questions from the beta testers.

How to Use This Book

Who This Book Is For

This book is for readers who know the basics and want to expand their knowledge of this particular technology or software application.

The Conventions in This Book

1 Steps

This book uses a step-by-step format to guide you easily through each task. Numbered steps are actions you must do; bulleted steps clarify a point, step, or optional feature; and indented steps give you the result.

2 Notes

Notes give additional information — special conditions that may occur during an operation, a situation that you want to avoid, or a cross reference to a related area of the book.

3 Icons and Buttons

Icons and buttons show you exactly what you need to click to perform a step.

4 Tips

Tips offer additional information, including warnings and shortcuts.

5 Bold

Bold type shows text or numbers you must type.

6 Italics

Italic type introduces and defines a new term.

7 Difficulty Levels

For quick reference, these symbols mark the difficulty level of each task.

Demonstrates a new spin on a common task

Introduces a new skill or a new task

Combines multiple skills requiring in-depth knowledge

Requires extensive skill and may involve other technologies

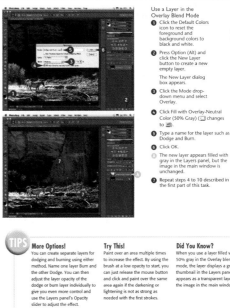

Improve exposure with a DODGE AND BURN LAYER

Dodging and burning are photographic techniques describing the traditional darkroom methods for brightening and darkening tones in an image. You can effectively dodge and burn a digital image in Photoshop.

Although Photoshop includes digital dodge and burn tools, these tools directly affect the pixels on the layer, making your edits permanent and destructive. Using a separate layer and the Brush tool to dodge and burn not only adjusts the image nondestructively, it also gives you greater control over the adjustment.

You can digitally dodge and burn on a separate layer with two different methods. One uses a separate

empty layer in the Soft Light blend mode. The other uses a separate layer filled with neutral gray in the Overlay blend mode. You can use the method that you prefer or that works best on your particular image. With either type of layer, you dodge by painting with white and burn by painting with black on the layer. By setting the brush opacity to about 30% to start, you can increase the effect as you work by brushing over an area multiple times.

Both methods give you complete control over dodging and burning digitally.

Use a Layer in the Soft Light Blend Mode

1 Click the Default Colors icon to reset the foreground and background colors to black and white.

2 Click the New Layer button to create a new empty layer.

3 Click the blend mode drop-down menu and select Soft Light.

4 Click the Brush tool (🖌).

5 Click the Brush Preset drop-down menu to open the Brush picker.

6 Select the soft-edged brush.

7 Double-click the Opacity field in the Options bar and type **30** to set the brush opacity to 30%.

8 Click and drag to paint with black in the light areas of the image to darken, or digitally burn them.

9 Click the Switch Colors icon to reverse the foreground and background colors, making the foreground color white.

Note: You can also press X to reverse the foreground and background colors.

10 Click and drag to paint with white in the dark areas of the image to lighten, or digitally dodge them.

Use a Layer in the Overlay Blend Mode

1 Click the Default Colors icon to reset the foreground and background colors to black and white.

2 Press Option (Alt) and click the New Layer button to create a new empty layer.

The New Layer dialog box appears.

3 Click the Mode drop-down menu and select Overlay.

4 Click Fill with Overlay-Neutral Color (50% Gray) (☐ changes to ☑).

5 Type a name for the layer such as Dodge and Burn.

6 Click OK.

The new layer appears filled with gray in the Layers panel, but the image in the main window is unchanged.

7 Repeat steps 4 to 10 described in the first part of this task.

 # 57

DIFFICULTY LEVEL

● ● ● ○

TIPS

More Options!

You can create separate layers for dodging and burning using either method. Name one layer Burn and the other Dodge. You can then adjust the layer opacity of the dodge or burn layer individually to give you even more control and use the Layers panel's Opacity slider to adjust the effect.

Try This!

Paint over an area multiple times to increase the effect. By using the brush at a low opacity to start, you can just release the mouse button and click and paint over the same area again if the darkening or lightening is not as strong as needed with the first strokes.

Did You Know?

When you use a layer filled with 50% gray in the Overlay blend mode, the layer displays a gray thumbnail in the Layers panel, but appears as a transparent layer over the image in the main window.

Table of Contents

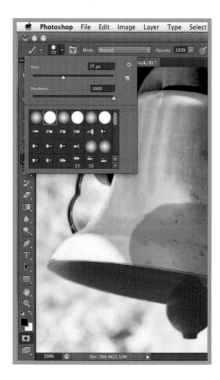

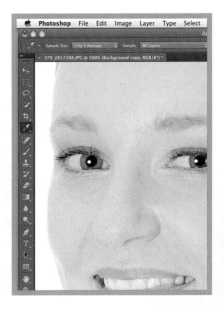

Table of Contents

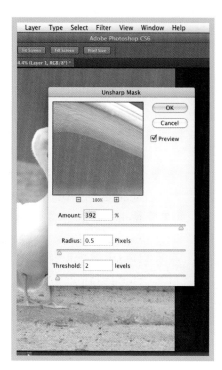

Table of Contents

(11) Plug In to Photoshop

Chapter

1

Make Photoshop Work for You

Photoshop can be used for different types of projects from graphic design to digital photography, from basic photo editing to fine art painting. With each new version, Photoshop becomes more powerful and includes more tools. The key to using Photoshop is learning where the tools are located, how they can be customized, and how to set up Photoshop's interface to suit you.

With so many tools and panels, your screen can become cluttered. You may prefer to see only some panels and not others. You may also prefer certain tool settings to others. Customizing Photoshop's menus and tools to work for you makes the program more useful and fun.

Photoshop CS6 adds new options for customizing the interface. You can now select the color of the background for viewing your projects. You can simplify your screen and keep only the tools you need available. You can make your own gradients, set up your own shortcuts, and load and save your own brushes. You can set up your workspace with only the panels and the tools you want for one project. You can also set up multiple workspaces, each with different tools for different projects, and then switch between workspaces.

By learning to customize the interface, setting your monitor to reflect more accurate colors, and exploring the range of tools in Photoshop, you not only gain familiarity with the application, you also become more productive as you work through different projects.

Using Photoshop, you can improve photographs, repurpose them, or start with a blank canvas to create original graphic designs or paintings. Because different types of output have different limits on the range of colors that they can represent, you should start by setting the working color space that matches your project's intended output, such as for print or the web. Photoshop's default color space is set to sRGB, a limited color space intended for web images to be viewable on even the lowest-quality monitor. sRGB is a small color space. Designers and photographers

who plan to print their work with inkjet printers generally prefer to work in the larger color space called Adobe RGB (1998).

In Photoshop, you can easily choose your working color space and save it. When you work on a project you intend to print, start by selecting the North America Prepress 2 settings and Adobe RGB (1998). You can then select different options depending on your intended output. Alternatively, you can select the ProPhoto working space if you prefer to use the widest color gamut possible for photographic editing.

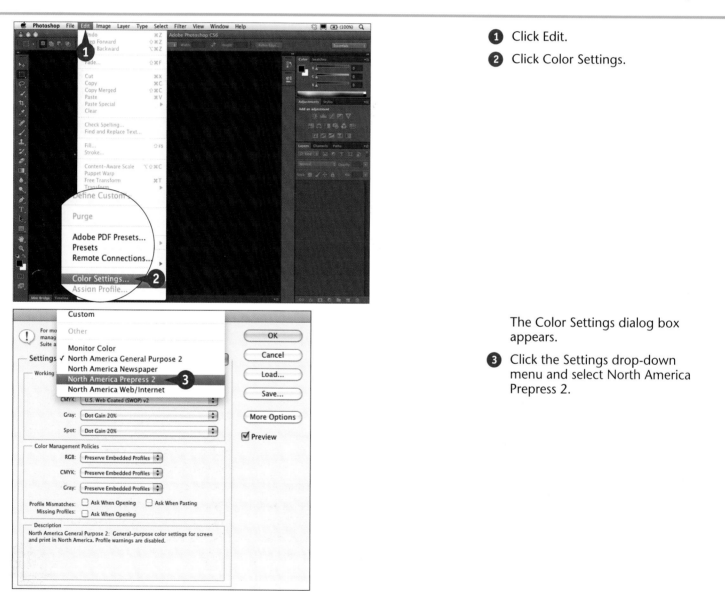

① Click Edit.

② Click Color Settings.

The Color Settings dialog box appears.

③ Click the Settings drop-down menu and select North America Prepress 2.

A The RGB setting changes to Adobe RGB (1998).

Note: *ProPhoto RGB is an even larger color space often preferred by professional photographers because it includes a wider range of tones and allows for fine detail editing.*

The rest of the Color Settings dialog box changes to reflect the preferred working space for images that you print.

4 Click More Options.

The dialog box expands.

5 Click the Intent drop-down menu and select Perceptual for most photographic projects or Relative Colorimetric for graphic design projects.

6 Click OK.

Your color settings are saved until you reset your preferences.

#1

DIFFICULTY LEVEL

TIPS

Important!

Photoshop is all about interacting with what you see on your screen. Wallpapers and bright backgrounds interfere with how you judge colors in your images. You should set your desktop background to a medium neutral gray using System Preferences on a Mac, or the Appearance and Personalization settings in the Control Panel in Windows.

Customize It!

You can save your own Color Settings preset. The name of the preset changes to Custom when you deselect any check box or make any other changes. Click Save after customizing your settings. Type a name in the Save dialog box and click Save. Your customized preset appears in the Settings menu, ready for you to choose.

Try This!

If you have other Creative Suite CS6 applications, you can synchronize the color settings to match your saved custom Photoshop CS6 color settings. In Photoshop, click File ➪ Browse in Bridge. In Bridge, click Edit ➪ Creative Suite Color Settings. Click North America Prepress 2 and click Apply.

CHOOSE YOUR PREFERRED COLOR for the interface and screen modes

In previous versions of Photoshop, you were able to change the color of the background behind the image you were working on, with the tools and panels remaining a light color. Photoshop CS6 now gives you color options for the interface. The color themes include four different shades from light gray through dark gray, and the changes take place immediately when you select a different Appearance Color Theme from the Preferences Interface window.

Viewing your images against darker or lighter backgrounds acts like a traditional matte surrounding your central image, and helps the eye see the colors and contrast more accurately. When the tools and panels around your image are too light, it can distract your eye. You can even match the tools and panels with the background color of your selected screen mode, giving you a more uniform backdrop for viewing and editing.

Darkening the user interface is particularly useful for photographers and those working in both Photoshop and Lightroom, or another application with a dark appearance, because less of a visual shift occurs when switching applications.

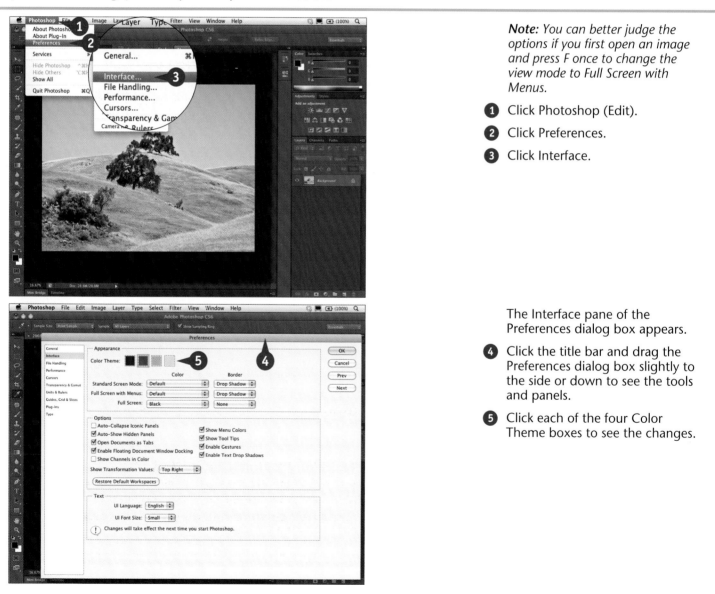

Note: You can better judge the options if you first open an image and press F once to change the view mode to Full Screen with Menus.

1 Click Photoshop (Edit).

2 Click Preferences.

3 Click Interface.

The Interface pane of the Preferences dialog box appears.

4 Click the title bar and drag the Preferences dialog box slightly to the side or down to see the tools and panels.

5 Click each of the four Color Theme boxes to see the changes.

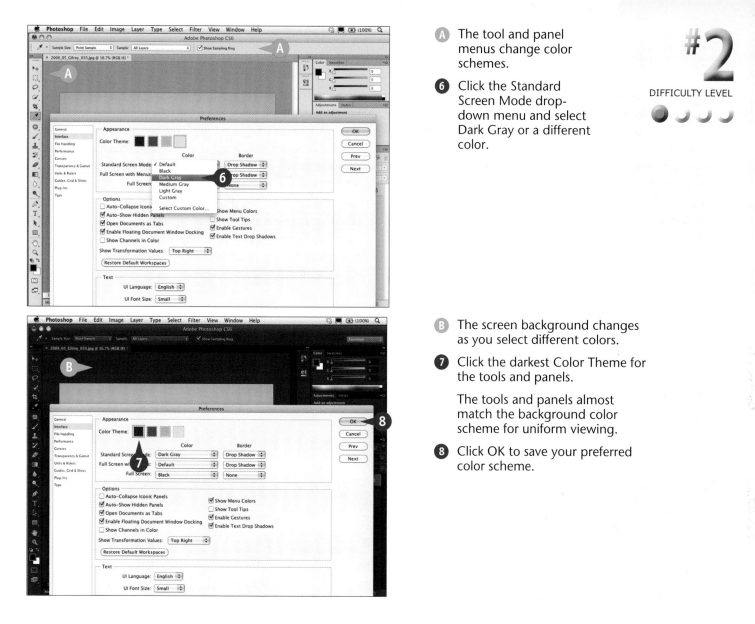

A The tool and panel menus change color schemes.

6 Click the Standard Screen Mode drop-down menu and select Dark Gray or a different color.

B The screen background changes as you select different colors.

7 Click the darkest Color Theme for the tools and panels.

The tools and panels almost match the background color scheme for uniform viewing.

8 Click OK to save your preferred color scheme.

TIPS

Did You Know?
Pressing the F key toggles the screen modes from Standard, to Full Screen with Menus, and then to Full Screen.

Try This!
You can use the F1 and F2 keys to toggle the darkness levels of the user interface. By default, the F1 and F2 keys are secondary shortcuts to other functions. On a Mac, F1 is bound to Edit ⇨ Undo/Redo and F2 is set to Edit ⇨ Cut. In Windows, F1 is set to Help and F2 is set to Edit ⇨ Cut. You can delete these default settings, as in task #8, because those tools have other keyboard shortcuts. You can then quickly darken the user interface by pressing F1, and lighten it by pressing F2.

SET THE PREFERENCES for the way you work

Even if your computer meets the minimum requirements to run Photoshop, you should set up the Preferences to fit the type of tasks you regularly work on. Optimizing Photoshop's performance not only makes your computer run more efficiently, it also makes working with your projects faster and easier. For example, by default, Photoshop is set to use more than half of the available RAM. You can adjust this setting to fit not only the amount of RAM installed in the computer but also the number of applications you need to run at the same time. You can also set a separate scratch disk to speed up your work.

Using the Preferences settings, you can customize other default settings such as the colors for the guides and grid so they are distinct from those in your image and designate an additional plug-ins folder to keep third-party items separate from those included with Photoshop. You can also select the Camera Raw Preferences to change those default settings. Each option under the Preferences menu opens different panes to customize so you can make Photoshop work for you.

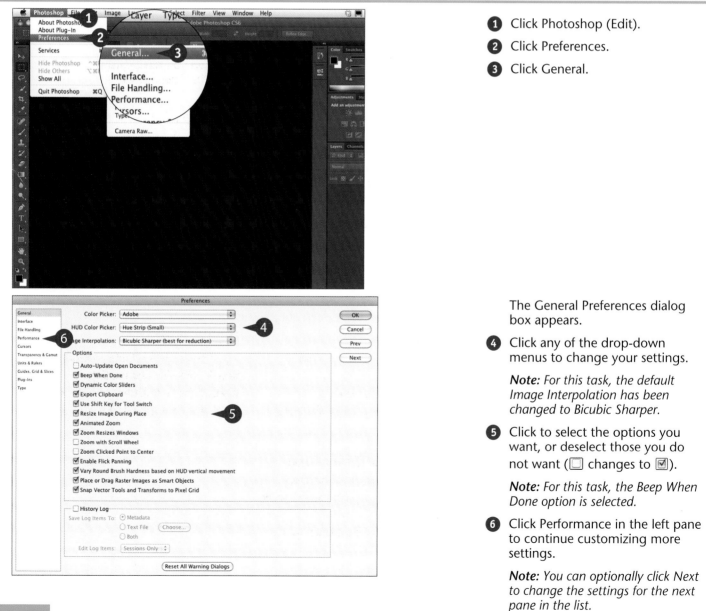

1 Click Photoshop (Edit).

2 Click Preferences.

3 Click General.

The General Preferences dialog box appears.

4 Click any of the drop-down menus to change your settings.

Note: *For this task, the default Image Interpolation has been changed to Bicubic Sharper.*

5 Click to select the options you want, or deselect those you do not want (☐ changes to ☑).

Note: *For this task, the Beep When Done option is selected.*

6 Click Performance in the left pane to continue customizing more settings.

Note: *You can optionally click Next to change the settings for the next pane in the list.*

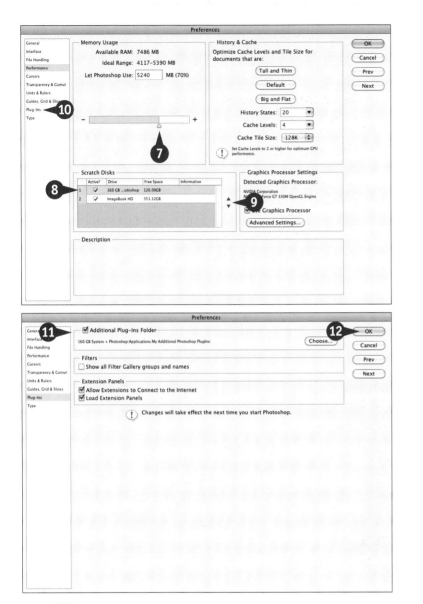

The dialog box changes to the Performance Preferences.

7 Click and drag the slider to adjust the maximum amount of RAM available to Photoshop.

8 Click a different scratch disk (□ changes to ☑).

9 Click the up or down arrow to change the order of scratch disks.

10 Click Plug-Ins or another preference option in the left pane.

11 Make any other changes that you prefer in the other Preferences panes.

12 Click OK when you have cycled through all the Preferences panes.

13 Click Photoshop (File).

14 Click Quit Photoshop (Exit).

The next time you start the application, your custom settings take effect.

TIPS

Optimize Photoshop Performance!

● Set the Memory Usage preference to about 70% or stay within the listed ideal range.

● Close other applications and run Photoshop by itself.

● Keep open only files that you are currently working with. Close other open files.

● Reduce the number of History states.

● Load only the patterns and brush tips you need. Each loaded pattern and tip increases the RAM required to run Photoshop.

● Merge layers that no longer need to be kept separate as you work.

● Add more RAM to your computer.

● Use a separate scratch disk and set the Preferences order to use that disk first.

● Defragment your drives regularly.

Did You Know?

You can restore the Preferences any time by pressing and holding ⌘+Option+Shift (Ctrl+Alt+Shift) as you launch the application.

Create your own CUSTOMIZED WORKSPACE

The workspace in Photoshop refers to the layout of the different panels and tools on your screen. With all the functionality built into Photoshop, your screen area can easily become cluttered. You can design and save a workspace to fit your needs for a particular project, with only the items that you use most. You can hide others or collapse them into buttons to save space. You can even create multiple workspaces with different tools for different types of projects, such as one for painting, one for design, and one for photography.

You can move and resize individual panels. You can move the single-column toolbar, undock it, or change it to a two-column panel. When you select Full Screen Mode With Menu Bar from the View menu, your image appears as large as possible with all the tool panels available.

You can save a custom workspace and even save the keyboard shortcuts and/or menus for that workspace.

You can start from scratch or you can modify any of the Photoshop preconfigured workspaces. When you alter any existing workspace, your changes are automatically saved.

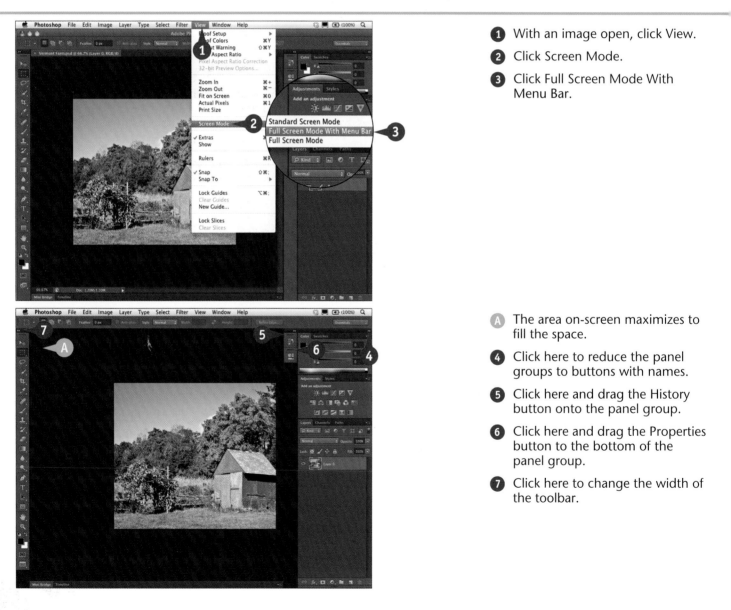

① With an image open, click View.

② Click Screen Mode.

③ Click Full Screen Mode With Menu Bar.

Ⓐ The area on-screen maximizes to fill the space.

④ Click here to reduce the panel groups to buttons with names.

⑤ Click here and drag the History button onto the panel group.

⑥ Click here and drag the Properties button to the bottom of the panel group.

⑦ Click here to change the width of the toolbar.

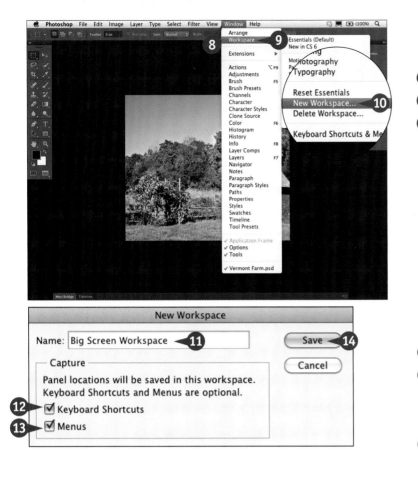

Note: *You can make any changes you prefer for your custom workspace.*

⑧ Click Window.

⑨ Click Workspace.

⑩ Click New Workspace.

The New Workspace dialog box appears.

⑪ Type a name for your workspace.

⑫ Click to save the keyboard shortcuts with the new workspace if you changed these (☐ changes to ☑).

⑬ Click to save the menu changes with the new workspace if you changed these (☐ changes to ☑).

⑭ Click Save.

Your custom workspace is saved.

TIPS

Did You Know?

You can delete any workspaces you do not need. First select a different workspace as in the task to make it active. Then click Window ➪ Workspace ➪ Delete Workspace. Click the Workspace drop-down menu in the Delete Workspace window that appears. Select the name of the workspace to delete and click Delete. Click Yes in the warning dialog box that appears.

Try This!

You can revert any changes to a workspace back to the original default settings. With the workspace you want to revert active, click Window ➪ Workspace ➪ Reset *Workspace Name*.

Important!

Restarting Photoshop while pressing and holding ⌘+Option+Shift (Ctrl+Alt+Shift) as you launch the application also resets all the original workspaces. However, this action also deletes all your personalized workspaces as well as any other custom settings.

Photoshop enables you to open one image or multiple images at one time on the screen. You can then view and compare your images to see which one is the best of the group.

The default setting for Photoshop automatically opens multiple images as separate tabs in one window. Tabs are useful to quickly change from one image to the next, by simply clicking the named tab. You can select one image and open it in a separate window while leaving all the others as tabs in the group, or view all the images as cascading individual windows.

You can also tile multiple windows so they all fit on the screen at once.

You can have two windows of the same image open. Then you can view an enlarged version in one window and the full photo in the other, so you can edit a particular area while still viewing the overall effect on the entire image.

If you need to compare specific areas on similar photos, open all the photos in one of the multiple views. You can then match the areas displayed in each of the images and even match a zoomed-in location.

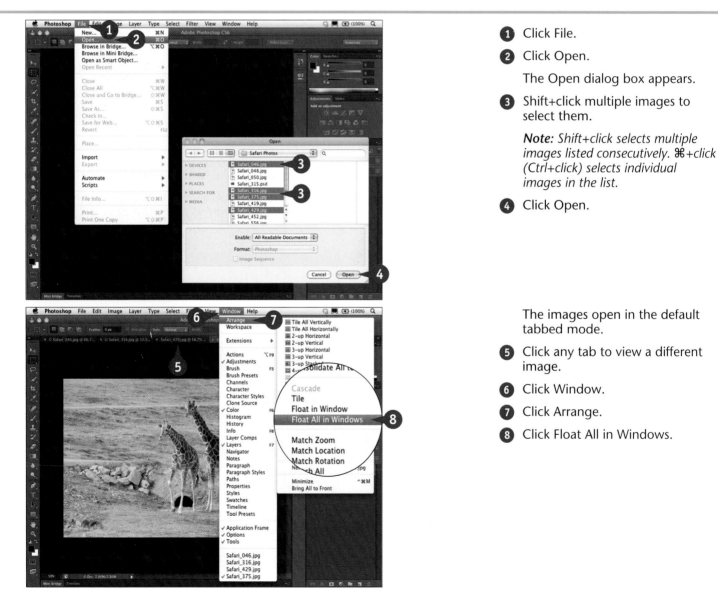

① Click File.

② Click Open.

The Open dialog box appears.

③ Shift+click multiple images to select them.

Note: Shift+click selects multiple images listed consecutively. ⌘+click (Ctrl+click) selects individual images in the list.

④ Click Open.

The images open in the default tabbed mode.

⑤ Click any tab to view a different image.

⑥ Click Window.

⑦ Click Arrange.

⑧ Click Float All in Windows.

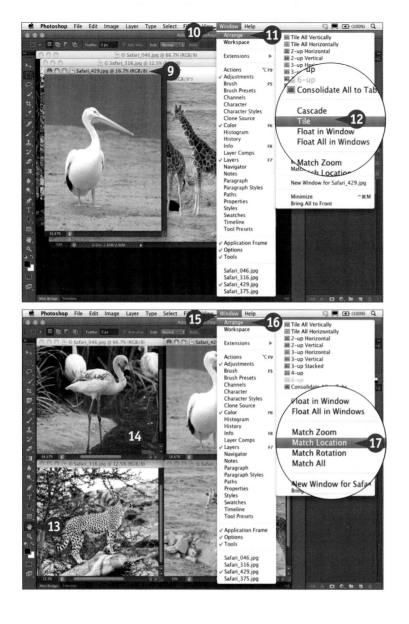

The images open in separate windows cascading down the screen.

9 Click the title bar of one photo to bring it forward.

10 Click Window.

11 Click Arrange.

12 Click Tile.

The images tile across the screen.

13 Click the Hand tool.

14 Click and drag inside one image to move to the bottom right corner.

15 Click Window.

16 Click Arrange.

17 Click Match Location.

All the windows move their contents to display the bottom right corner of each image.

TIPS

Try This!

With multiple images open, click Window ⇨ Arrange ⇨ Tile. Photoshop automatically tiles all the open images at a size to best fit the screen.

Did You Know?

If you zoom in on one image when you have multiple images open, and then tile the windows, you can click Window ⇨ Arrange ⇨ Match Zoom to zoom the same amount on all the windows.

More Options!

You can drag one or more windows to a second monitor. You can then have all your tools and panels on one monitor and all your images on the other, or one version of an image on one monitor and an edited version on the other.

CUSTOMIZE YOUR VIEW of Bridge

Bridge, which ships with Photoshop, acts as a power browser and central hub for all the Creative Suite applications and shows all types of available files and folders. You can even see thumbnails of documents and files from other applications, such as Word or Acrobat files. When you double-click a thumbnail from Bridge, the associated application launches. You can open Bridge from within Photoshop or as a separate application.

Bridge offers different ways to search, categorize, and view your files, options for adding information, and

automation for various repetitive tasks. As with Photoshop, you can customize your Bridge workspace so you can review and compare images more efficiently. And because Bridge adds more functionality, such as creating PDF files and web galleries, you can set up your Bridge workspace to fit your own project.

To launch Bridge from within Photoshop, click File and Browse in Bridge. You can also press the keyboard shortcut ⌘+Option+O (Ctrl+Alt+O).

❶ Launch Bridge.

Note: You can make any changes you prefer for your custom workspace.

❷ Click the Folders tab to navigate to a different folder of images.

❸ Click and drag the Metadata and Keywords tabs to the center of the left panel.

❹ Click and drag the Preview tab to the center pane.

❺ Click and drag the Content tab to the right pane.

The Content images align vertically on the right.

❻ Click an image to see it in the Preview tab.

❼ Click the right separator bar and drag to the right.

The Preview tab enlarges and the content tab narrows.

Ⓐ You can also click the left separator bar and drag to the left to enlarge the Preview tab more.

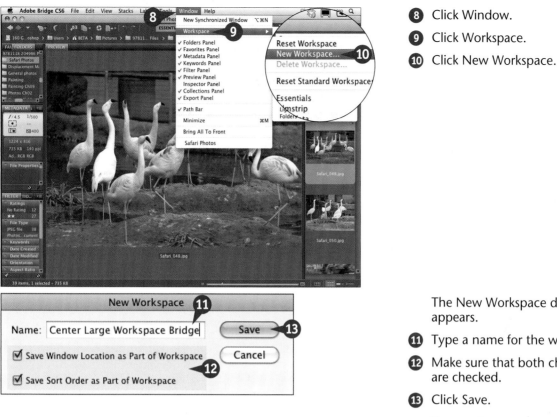

8 Click Window.

9 Click Workspace.

10 Click New Workspace.

#6

DIFFICULTY LEVEL

The New Workspace dialog box appears.

11 Type a name for the workspace.

12 Make sure that both check boxes are checked.

13 Click Save.

Your custom workspace is saved and appears in the top panel.

TIPS

More Options!

You can change the user interface and background to different shades for viewing images by clicking Adobe Bridge CS6 (Edit) ➪ Preferences. Use the User Interface Brightness slider under the General Preferences to vary the interface color, and the Image Backdrop slider to vary the backdrop color from black to gray to white, and click OK to apply the new color.

Enlarge It!

Press Tab to make the Preview window, or whatever center window you designate, fill the screen as the other panels slide away on the sides. Press Tab again to return to your custom Bridge workspace.

Try This!

⌘+click (Ctrl+click) multiple images in the Content pane to compare them in the Preview pane. You can also stack the selected images by clicking Stacks ➪ Group as Stack, or by pressing ⌘+G (Ctrl+G).

SAVE TIME FINDING YOUR IMAGES with the Mini Bridge

The Mini Bridge panel in Photoshop is a time-and space-saving feature. You can quickly find an image from within the Photoshop interface, without having Bridge completely take over your screen.

The Mini Bridge actually launches Bridge in the background; however, the Bridge window does not open until you click the Bridge icon. You can set the preferences for the way the Mini Bridge displays information. Then with a click of the Mini Bridge icon

you can browse the contents of your computer, find an image, preview it in a mini preview window, and zoom in to check details, all without leaving Photoshop. You can even sort multiple images and rate them in a mini review mode window, and then filter the images you want to view in the Mini Bridge.

Finding a specific image or a group of images to work on using the Mini Bridge is the quickest way to improve your Photoshop workflow.

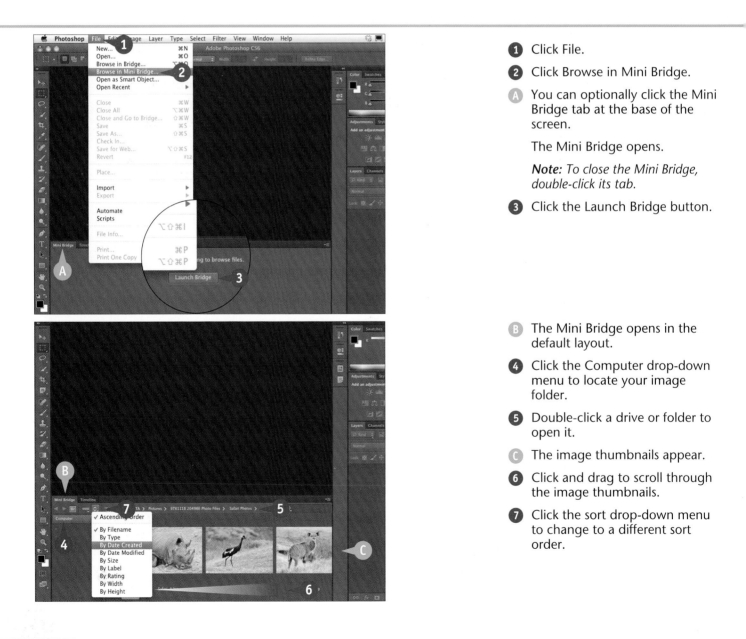

① Click File.

② Click Browse in Mini Bridge.

Ⓐ You can optionally click the Mini Bridge tab at the base of the screen.

The Mini Bridge opens.

Note: To close the Mini Bridge, double-click its tab.

③ Click the Launch Bridge button.

Ⓑ The Mini Bridge opens in the default layout.

④ Click the Computer drop-down menu to locate your image folder.

⑤ Double-click a drive or folder to open it.

Ⓒ The image thumbnails appear.

⑥ Click and drag to scroll through the image thumbnails.

⑦ Click the sort drop-down menu to change to a different sort order.

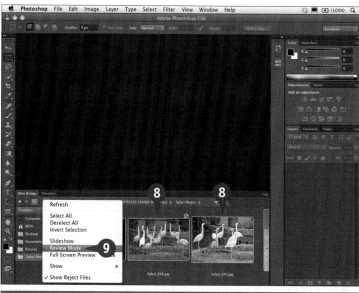

8 ⌘+click (Ctrl+click) multiple images to select them.

9 Click the View drop-down menu (▦) and select Review Mode from the menu.

The screen fills with the selected images in Carousel view.

10 Click any of the smaller images to bring it to the front.

The image carousel rotates to that image.

11 Click here to close the Review Mode window and return to Photoshop.

TIPS

Did You Know?

You can quickly return to Photoshop from the full Bridge CS6 window by clicking the Boomerang icon (🔄) in the Options bar of the Bridge application.

Try This!

When in Review mode in the Mini Bridge content window, click in the front image to get a 100% preview of that section of the image.

More Options!

You can play a mini slide show inside the Mini Bridge panel or in full screen mode, and quickly return to the Photoshop interface. ⌘+click (Ctrl+click) a number of images in the content pane of the Mini Bridge. Click the View button (▦) at the top on the Mini Bridge and click Slideshow in the drop-down list. A slide show of the selected images fills the screen. Press Esc to return to the Photoshop window.

Photoshop includes keyboard shortcuts for the tools that you use most often. Many of the tools already have keyboard shortcuts assigned. Still, you may find yourself going to the menu to select an item, such as the Smart Sharpen or Gaussian Blur filter, so often that a personalized keyboard shortcut becomes a huge timesaver.

You can create your own custom keyboard shortcuts or even change some Photoshop keystrokes to something that you can remember better. If the

keyboard shortcut that you choose is already assigned by Photoshop for another function, a warning appears. Although you should generally avoid keyboard shortcuts that your operating system uses, you can change Photoshop's default shortcuts, or you can apply a different set of keystrokes not already assigned.

Learning and using custom keyboard shortcuts can streamline your workflow, leaving you more time for designing and photo editing.

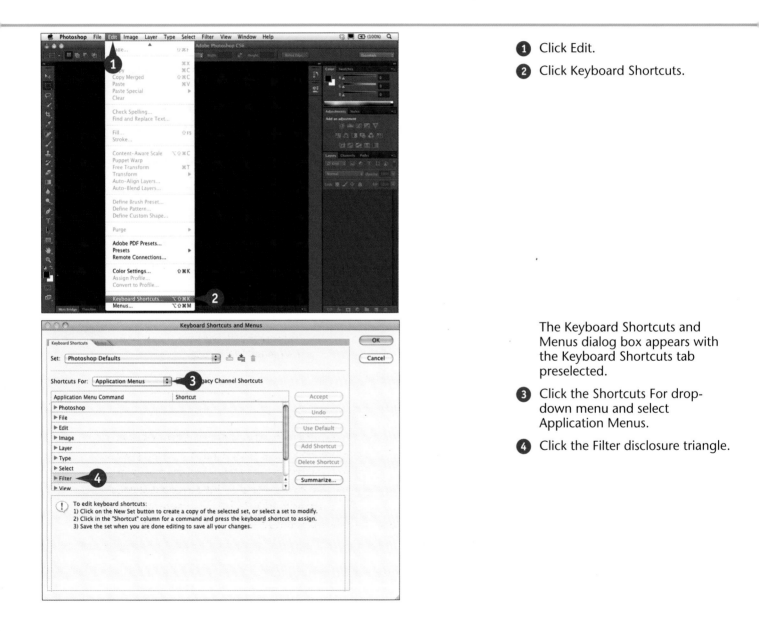

1 Click Edit.

2 Click Keyboard Shortcuts.

The Keyboard Shortcuts and Menus dialog box appears with the Keyboard Shortcuts tab preselected.

3 Click the Shortcuts For drop-down menu and select Application Menus.

4 Click the Filter disclosure triangle.

Saddletowne Library
Self Checkout

9065122641507   7/2/2019
Photoshop CS6 top 100 simplified tips &
tricks

Total   1 item(s)

You have 0 item(s) ready for pickup

Register for the Ultimate Summer Challenge

Starts on May 15

http://calgarylibrary.ca/summer

To check your card and renew items

go to www.calgarylibrary.ca

or call 403-262-2928

CALGARY
PUBLIC
LIBRARY

Saddletowne Library
Self Checkout
June 1, 2019 11:17

30651264150?   7/2/2019
Photoshop CS6 top 100 simplified tips &
tricks

Total   1 item(s)

You have 0 item(s) ready for pickup

Register for the Ultimate Summer Challenge

Starts on May 15

http://calgarylibrary.ca/summer

To check your card and renew items
go to www.calgarylibrary.ca
or call 403-262-2928

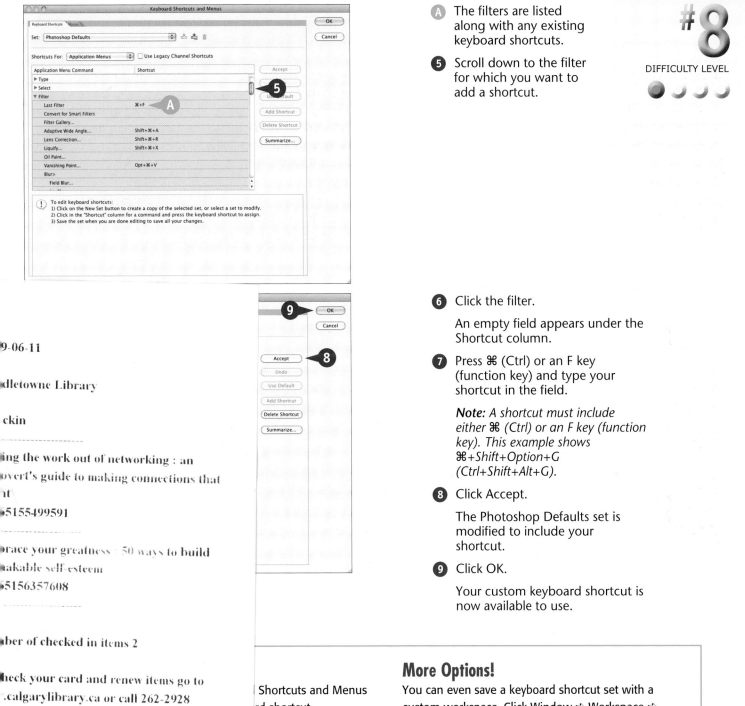

9-06-11

dletowne Library

ckin

ing the work out of networking : an
overt's guide to making connections that
at
5155499591

race your greatness : 50 ways to build
akable self-esteem
5156357608

ber of checked in items 2

heck your card and renew items go to
.calgarylibrary.ca or call 262-2928

A The filters are listed along with any existing keyboard shortcuts.

5 Scroll down to the filter for which you want to add a shortcut.

6 Click the filter.

An empty field appears under the Shortcut column.

7 Press ⌘ (Ctrl) or an F key (function key) and type your shortcut in the field.

Note: A shortcut must include either ⌘ (Ctrl) or an F key (function key). This example shows ⌘+Shift+Option+G (Ctrl+Shift+Alt+G).

8 Click Accept.

The Photoshop Defaults set is modified to include your shortcut.

9 Click OK.

Your custom keyboard shortcut is now available to use.

Shortcuts and Menus
rd shortcut —
ift+Alt+K).

Try This!

You can save and print a list of all keyboard shortcuts. Click Summarize in the Keyboard Shortcuts and Menus dialog box and save the file as Photoshop Defaults.htm. Open the file and print the list for reference.

More Options!

You can even save a keyboard shortcut set with a custom workspace. Click Window ➪ Workspace ➪ New Workspace. In the New Workspace window, name the workspace and click Keyboard Shortcuts (☐ changes to ☑). Click Save to save the current Keyboard Shortcuts set with the workspace.

CREATE A CUSTOM ACTION to increase your efficiency

Actions help you perform repeated steps quickly. An *action* is a series of commands that you can apply to an image with one click of the mouse. Unlike a keyboard shortcut, which can only invoke a command, an action can open a command, apply changes to an image, step through another command, apply it, and even save a file in a particular way. Photoshop includes many predesigned actions, and you can also create your own for steps that you do over and over and add them to the Actions panel.

Using the Actions panel, you record a sequence of steps and save your new action. When you need to apply the same steps to a different image, even to an entire folder of files, you play the action, and Photoshop automatically applies the steps. You can record any number of steps and even create complex actions that include steps requiring specific information in dialog boxes. Actions become particularly useful when you do repetitive projects with many steps.

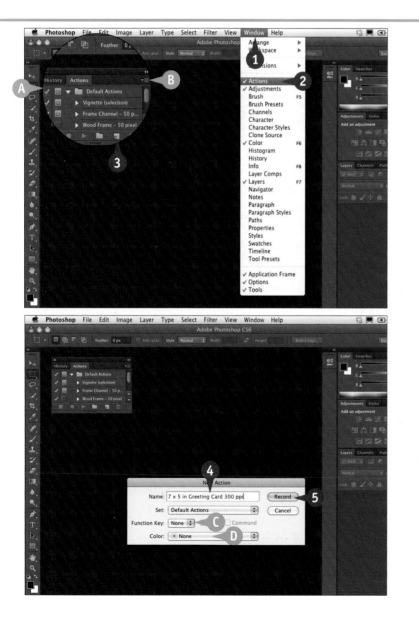

Note: *The steps in this task create a simple action for setting up a new 7-×-5-inch document at 300 pixels/inch for a greeting card.*

1 Click Window.

2 Click Actions.

A The Actions panel appears.

3 Click the Create New Action button.

B Alternatively, you can click the panel menu button and select New Action.

The New Action dialog box appears.

4 Type the name of your action.

C You can click the Function Key drop-down menu and select a function key for a keyboard shortcut.

D You can click the Color drop-down menu and select a color for the action.

5 Click Record.

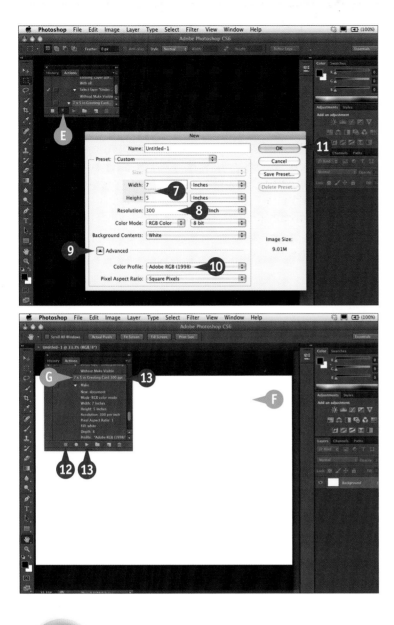

E The Record button in the Actions panel turns red.

Perform the steps that you want to record as an action:

6 Press ⌘+N (Ctrl+N) to open a new file.

The New dialog box appears.

7 Type **7** in the Width field and **5** in the Height field.

8 Type **300** in the Resolution field.

9 Click the Advanced disclosure triangle.

The window expands with more options.

10 Click the Color Profile drop-down menu and click Adobe RGB 1998.

11 Click OK.

F A new untitled document appears.

12 Click the Stop Recording button.

G Your custom action to create a 7 × 5 greeting card is now recorded and listed in the Actions panel.

13 Test your action by clicking the Action name in the Actions panel and clicking the Play button.

TIPS

More Options!

You can apply an action to a folder of files by clicking File ⇨ Automate ⇨ Batch and selecting the action and a source folder. Or you can apply an action to a group of images from Bridge by clicking Tools ⇨ Photoshop ⇨ Batch.

Try This!

Assign colors to your actions and turn them into buttons. With an action highlighted, click the panel menu button (▤) on the actions panel and click Action Options. Click the Color drop-down menu in the Action Options dialog box, select a color, and click OK. Then click the panel menu button (▤) again and select Button Mode. Your actions appear with color-coded labels.

Did You Know?

Photoshop actions are saved in a folder called Actions inside the Presets folder of the Photoshop application folder.

DESIGN A CUSTOM BRUSH with your settings

Many of the tools in Photoshop have modifiable brush options, and whether you retouch photographs, design brochures, or paint from scratch, you often need to vary the shape, size, and hardness of the brushes to fit your project.

The Brush picker includes a variety of brushes you can select from a menu. You can also modify the attributes of any of these preset brushes and save the modified brush as your own custom brush preset so that you can readily use it for your next design. You can name and save any number of custom brushes as presets.

Many other tools also have modifiable brush options, including the Pencil tool, the Eraser tool, the Clone Stamp tool, the Pattern Stamp tool, the History Brush, the Art History Brush, the Blur tool, the Sharpen tool, the Smudge tool, the Dodge tool, the Burn tool, and the Sponge tool.

Customizing tools for your projects and saving your presets can save time for repetitive tasks and also open up more creative possibilities for your drawing, painting, and retouching.

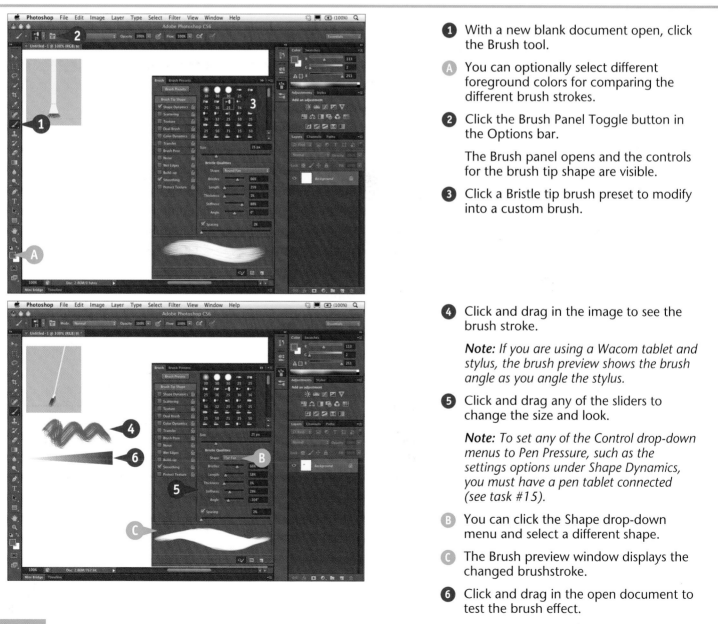

① With a new blank document open, click the Brush tool.

Ⓐ You can optionally select different foreground colors for comparing the different brush strokes.

② Click the Brush Panel Toggle button in the Options bar.

The Brush panel opens and the controls for the brush tip shape are visible.

③ Click a Bristle tip brush preset to modify into a custom brush.

④ Click and drag in the image to see the brush stroke.

Note: If you are using a Wacom tablet and stylus, the brush preview shows the brush angle as you angle the stylus.

⑤ Click and drag any of the sliders to change the size and look.

Note: To set any of the Control drop-down menus to Pen Pressure, such as the settings options under Shape Dynamics, you must have a pen tablet connected (see task #15).

Ⓑ You can click the Shape drop-down menu and select a different shape.

Ⓒ The Brush preview window displays the changed brushstroke.

⑥ Click and drag in the open document to test the brush effect.

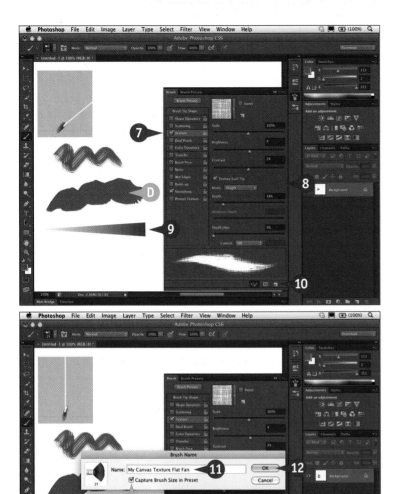

D Your customized brush stroke appears on the document.

7 Click any of the other options, such as Texture, in the left section of the Brush pane (■ changes to ☑).

8 Click and drag any of the sliders or drop-down menus to change the size and look.

9 Click and drag in the document to test the changed brushstroke.

10 Click the Create New Brush button.

The Brush Name dialog box appears.

11 Type a name for your brush.

E You can optionally click Capture Brush Size in Preset to save the brush size (☐ changes to ☑).

12 Click OK.

Your customized brush is now available in the Brush panel and stored in the default brush set.

Note: If you later reset the brushes without saving the changes, you will lose your custom brush preset.

TIPS

Important!

You should save custom brushes in a set so they are available the next time you open Photoshop. Click the Brush Preset drop-down menu in the Options bar. Click the gear menu button (⚙) and click Save Brushes. Type a name for the current set, including your custom brushes, in the dialog box and click Save. The brush set with the custom brushes is saved in the Photoshop Brushes folder in the Presets folder.

Did You Know?

The Brush Tip Shape options available with the Bristle tip brushes are different than those for the Standard brushes. You can change the Standard Brush Tip shapes by clicking and dragging the sides of the brush shape circle in the Brush Tip Shape pane.

More Options!

The Bristle tip brushes display an animated preview on-screen. You can see what a corresponding physical brush would look like, and also see how the bristles splay as you paint on the digital canvas. You can toggle the preview on and off by clicking the Live Tip Brush Preview button (▣) on the bottom of the Brush panel.

Brushes are essential for working with Photoshop. When you customize a brush and create a new preset, you can use that brush with not only the Brush tool but also a number of Photoshop tools, such as the History brush, the Eraser tool, the Pencil tool, and other tools. Adding brushes gives you more options for editing photographs and many more variations for painting with Photoshop. You can view the brushes in the Brush picker and change the default view from small thumbnail to any of the other view options listed.

When you first install and open Photoshop, only the default brushes appear in the Brush picker. The optional brushes are stored in sets in the Presets folder. You can load any set and have the additional brushes replace the default brushes or be appended to the existing brush set using the Preset manager. Once loaded the additional brushes appear in the Brush picker.

You should only add the brushes you need because loading more brushes requires more resources, or memory. At any time, you can append different brush sets to see your options, save different sets, and delete the ones you do not need.

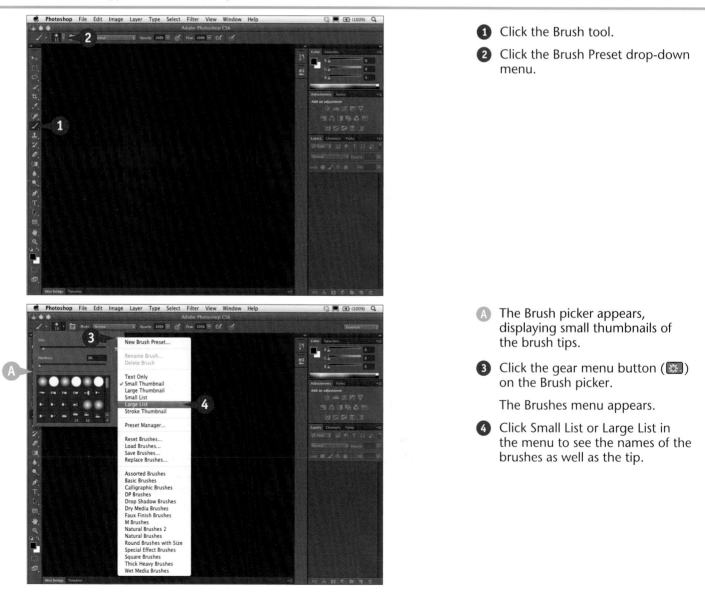

① Click the Brush tool.

② Click the Brush Preset drop-down menu.

Ⓐ The Brush picker appears, displaying small thumbnails of the brush tips.

③ Click the gear menu button (⚙) on the Brush picker.

The Brushes menu appears.

④ Click Small List or Large List in the menu to see the names of the brushes as well as the tip.

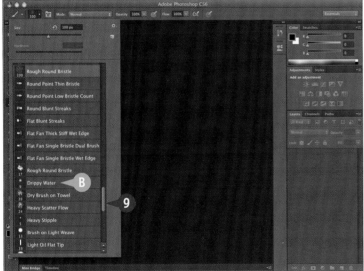

The Brush picker changes to show the brush names.

⑤ Click here and drag down to expand the Brush picker.

⑥ Click the gear menu button (⚙) on the Brush picker again.

⑦ Click Wet Media Brushes in the bottom section of the picker.

Note: You can select any of the brush sets listed.

⑧ Click Append in the dialog box that appears.

Ⓑ The Wet Media Brushes are added to the bottom of the Brush picker.

⑨ Scroll down the Brush picker to see all of the new added brushes.

#️⃣**11**

DIFFICULTY LEVEL

● ◡ ◡ ◡

TIPS

Try This!

You can save a copy of the Brushes folder to another location on your hard drive. Your custom brush set and any brush sets you download can then be transferred to another computer or reloaded if you have to reinstall Photoshop. By default, the Brushes folder is in /Applications/Adobe Photoshop CS6/ Presets/ (on Mac OS X) or C:\Program Files\Adobe\ PhotoshopCS6\Presets\ (in Windows).

Did You Know?

You can find a large number of predesigned brush sets both free and for a fee on the web.

Try This!

You can add patterns the same way you add brush presets. Click and hold the Gradient tool on the toolbar and select the Paint Bucket tool. Click Foreground in the Options bar and select Pattern. Click the pattern icon to open the Pattern picker. Click the gear menu button (⚙) on the Pattern picker and select a different pattern set at the bottom of the menu. Click Append in the dialog box that appears.

You can use the Gradient tool to blend colors and fill text with soft gradations of color, to fill backgrounds or selections with a colored gradient, to apply gradient layers, or to work with masks when making composite images. As with the brushes, Photoshop installs but does not automatically load a number of different gradient color sets, which you can find by opening the Gradient picker menu and loading these using the same steps as in task #11.

You can also create your own custom gradient by sampling colors from areas in your image or choosing different colors altogether. You can add intermediate colors and design a blend among multiple colors in any order that you want. You can design gradients that fade from any color to transparent, and you can choose different styles for the gradient, such as linear, radial, angled, reflected, or diamond. With the Gradient Editor you can start with any existing gradient, and then modify the colors, the color stops, and other options in the dialog box before naming and saving your custom gradient. The creative variations are almost endless!

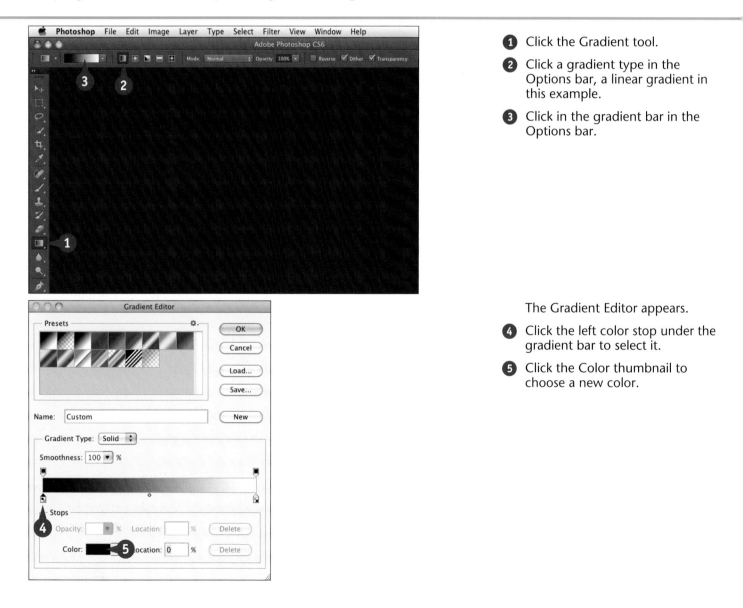

① Click the Gradient tool.

② Click a gradient type in the Options bar, a linear gradient in this example.

③ Click in the gradient bar in the Options bar.

The Gradient Editor appears.

④ Click the left color stop under the gradient bar to select it.

⑤ Click the Color thumbnail to choose a new color.

Color Picker (Stop Color)

OK 7

new

Cancel

Add to Swatches

Color Libraries

- H: 240 °
- S: 91 %
- B: 84 %
- R: 18
- G: 18
- B: 214
- # 1212d6

- L: 26
- a: 56
- b: -95

- C: 90 %
- M: 83 %
- Y: 0 %
- K: 0 %

☐ Only Web Colors

6

6

Gradient Editor

Presets

OK 12

Cancel

Load...

Save... D

Name: Blue Teal Violet 10

New 11

Gradient Type: Solid

Smoothness: 100 %

Stops

A Opacity: % B ion: %

Delete 8

Color: Location: %

Delete

C

#12

DIFFICULTY LEVEL

The Color Picker dialog box appears.

6 Select a color range and a shade in the dialog box.

Note: If you have an image open, you can position the mouse pointer over the image to select a color.

7 Click OK.

Ⓐ The selected color fills the left color stop in the Gradient Editor.

8 Click the right color stop under the gradient bar to select it.

9 Repeat steps 5 to 7 to select the colors for the right color stop.

Ⓑ You can click along the gradient to add more color stops; repeat steps 5 to 7.

10 Type a name for your custom gradient.

11 Click New.

Ⓒ The custom gradient appears in the presets.

Ⓓ You can click Save to save your custom gradient in the Gradients folder. Type the gradient name in the Save dialog box that appears.

12 Click OK to close the dialog box.

Your custom gradient remains in the gradient presets.

TIPS

Caution!

You must save your custom gradients in a preset library to avoid losing them when you reset Photoshop's preferences. Click Save in the Gradient Editor dialog box or choose Save Gradients from the menu in the Gradient picker. Type a name for your gradient library with the suffix .grd. Click Save, and your gradients are saved in Photoshop's presets.

More Options!

Try varying your custom gradient on an open sample file with the gradient applied to see the changes. Add color stops, and then press Option (Alt) and drag the first color stop to another location. Drag a new color stop over other color stops. To remove a color stop, click the color stop and drag straight down.

Make Photoshop TAKE NOTES FOR YOU

Some projects in Photoshop require only a few steps, and if you repeat the project multiple times, you will probably memorize the steps. Most tasks, however, require many steps, and the order in which to apply them is crucial to the function of the tools. Even if you follow the steps in this book, you will often try a new tool, apply a different option, or add multiple changes to complete your vision. When you succeed in creating a particular look, the most difficult part is remembering how you did it.

Photoshop's History log can automatically record every tool you select and each option you click, so you can refer to it for a future project. And the Notes tool lets you add sticky notes and write comments or your own instructions. Notes are great for collaborative projects because you can specify the author and color-code them.

You can activate the History log and select the amount of detail to record in Photoshop's General Preferences window. The Notes tool is grouped under the Eyedropper tool in the toolbar.

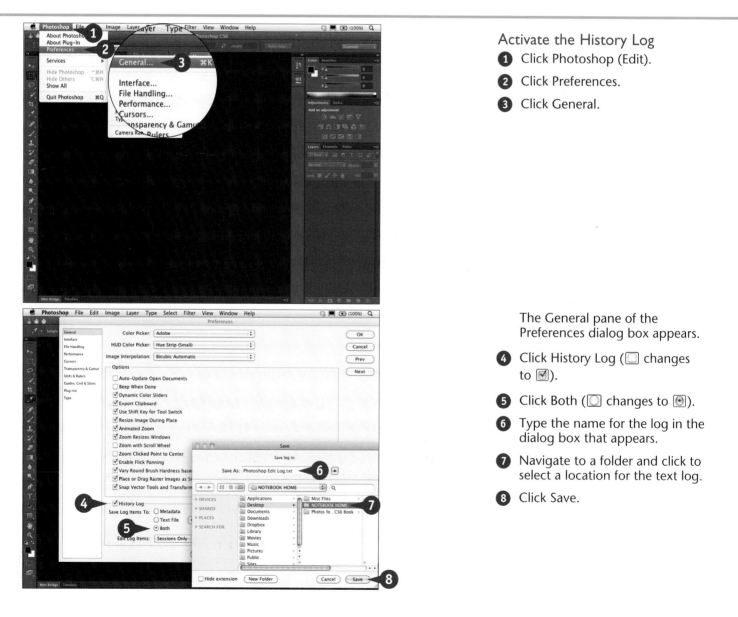

Activate the History Log

① Click Photoshop (Edit).

② Click Preferences.

③ Click General.

The General pane of the Preferences dialog box appears.

④ Click History Log (☐ changes to ☑).

⑤ Click Both (◯ changes to ◉).

⑥ Type the name for the log in the dialog box that appears.

⑦ Navigate to a folder and click to select a location for the text log.

⑧ Click Save.

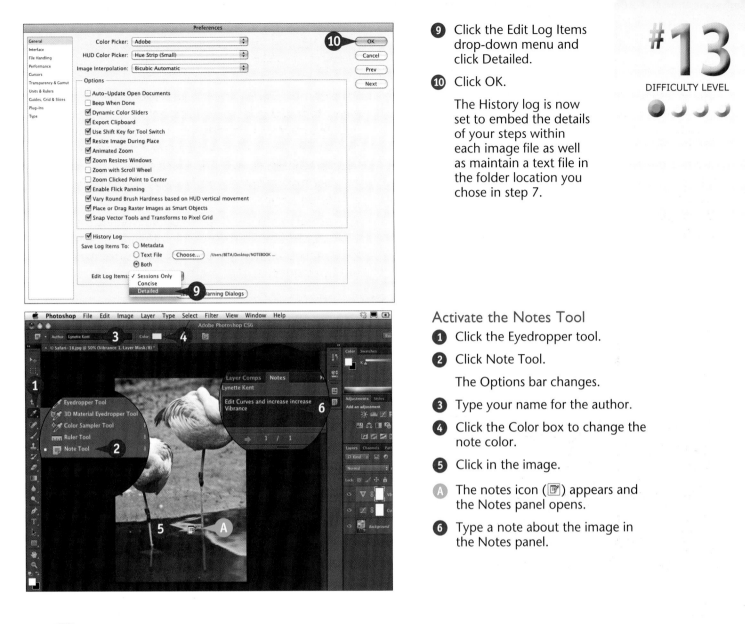

9 Click the Edit Log Items drop-down menu and click Detailed.

10 Click OK.

The History log is now set to embed the details of your steps within each image file as well as maintain a text file in the folder location you chose in step 7.

Activate the Notes Tool

1 Click the Eyedropper tool.

2 Click Note Tool.

The Options bar changes.

3 Type your name for the author.

4 Click the Color box to change the note color.

5 Click in the image.

A The notes icon (📝) appears and the Notes panel opens.

6 Type a note about the image in the Notes panel.

TIPS

More Options!

Metadata saves the details within the image file. You can see it by clicking File ➪ File Info. Click the History tab in the window that appears. **Text File** records the data to a separate text file which is cumulative across all the files until you rename the History text file in the Preferences dialog box. **Sessions Only** records only the time you open and close each file and when you start and quit Photoshop. **Concise** adds some details similar to those that appear in the History panel but without the limit of states. **Detailed** adds all the information including settings used in each step.

Did You Know?

You can toggle the notes on an off by clicking View ➪ Show ➪ Notes. To view the contents of a note, click its icon on the image. The text appears in the notes panel that opens.

All the work you do in Photoshop is based on what you see on the screen, so the color accuracy of your monitor is very important. Because each monitor displays color differently and because a monitor's characteristics change over time, you should calibrate and profile your monitor regularly to make sure that you are viewing the colors that are actually in your files.

Calibration is the process of setting your monitor to an established color standard. *Profiling* is the process of creating a data file describing how your monitor reproduces color.

The software-only methods included with the operating system are subjective and vary greatly with each user.

Using a hardware calibration device called a colorimeter or spectrophotometer is the most accurate way of adjusting your monitor. A colorimeter measures and adjusts the colors as they are displayed on-screen or projected. A spectrophotometer can also create profiles for other peripherals such as your printer.

The following steps are those used with an X-Rite ColorMunki Display. You can follow similar steps for an X-Rite i1Display, the ColorMunki Photo, ColorMunki Design, or another device. Various manufacturers make devices with different options and in various price ranges.

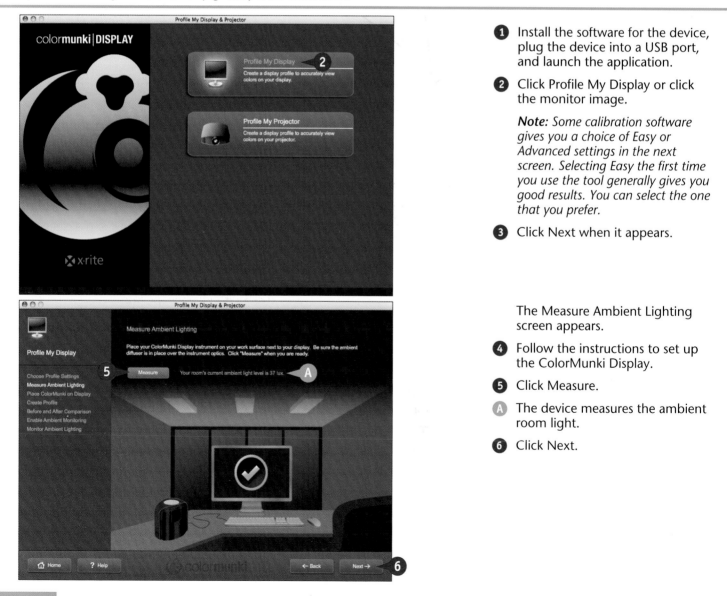

① Install the software for the device, plug the device into a USB port, and launch the application.

② Click Profile My Display or click the monitor image.

Note: Some calibration software gives you a choice of Easy or Advanced settings in the next screen. Selecting Easy the first time you use the tool generally gives you good results. You can select the one that you prefer.

③ Click Next when it appears.

The Measure Ambient Lighting screen appears.

④ Follow the instructions to set up the ColorMunki Display.

⑤ Click Measure.

Ⓐ The device measures the ambient room light.

⑥ Click Next.

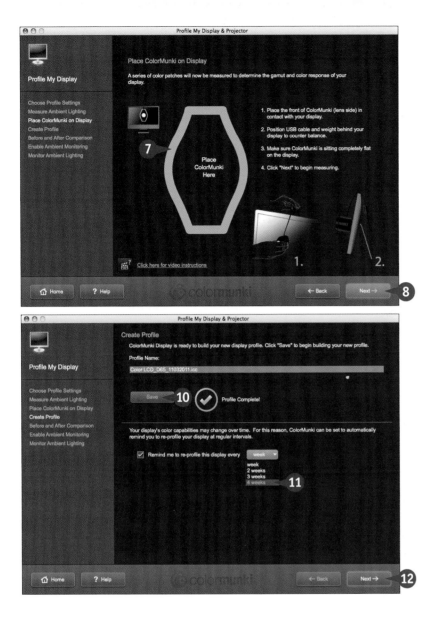

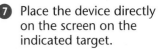

DIFFICULTY LEVEL

7. Place the device directly on the screen on the indicated target.

8. Click Next.

9. Click Measure in the next screen.

The screen fills with a specific sequence of colors as the device automatically measures the color presentation capabilities of your monitor.

Note: *The measuring can take several minutes to complete.*

A new screen appears, showing the name of the monitor profile created by the device.

Note: *Add the date to the profile name to make it easy to know when the profile was created.*

10. Click Save.

The Profile is applied and saved to the appropriate location on your computer.

11. Click a reminder for the next calibration.

12. Click Next.

13. Follow the on-screen directions to enable the device to monitor and correct for changes in the ambient light in the room, and click Finish when it appears.

TIPS

Did You Know?

As monitors age, they lose their color accuracy more quickly. Calibrate and profile regularly — monthly if your monitor is new or weekly if your monitor is over two years old. CRT monitors need to warm up for 30 minutes before you calibrate and create a profile.

Important!

LCD and LED monitors are often set to the maximum brightness at the factory. When you first calibrate and profile a new monitor, it may appear dark by comparison; however, after calibrating and profiling, the monitor displays a more accurate representation of the colors in your images.

More Options!

When you use X-Rite's calibration tools, you can launch a video with step-by-step instruction from most windows. The videos explain each step as you proceed, and they can also help you increase your understanding of color calibration and profiling.

Using a mouse as an input device may work for placing insertion points in text or dragging a rectangular selection in Photoshop, but using a Brush tool or selecting specific areas with a mouse is similar to writing your name with a bar of soap — clunky and inaccurate. You can edit images with greater comfort and control using a pressure-sensitive tablet and pen, such as the Wacom Intuos or Cintiq. More than 20 Photoshop tools, such as the Brushes, the Eraser, the Quick Selection tool, the Clone Stamp, the Dodge and Burn tools, and other tools can be fully customized only when a tablet is connected to the computer. You can then change brush size, roundness, flow, or opacity by applying more or less pressure with the pen.

Instead of scooting the mouse around, you use the pen to place the cursor exactly where you want, and make precise selections or paint digitally as with a traditional paintbrush on paper.

The key to using a tablet and pen and turning on the full power of Photoshop is to start by setting the Tablet Preferences located in the System Preferences or Control Panel.

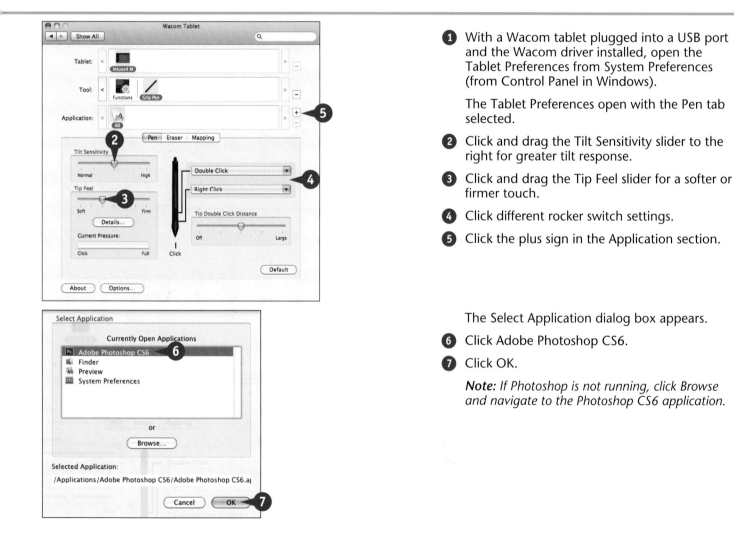

1 With a Wacom tablet plugged into a USB port and the Wacom driver installed, open the Tablet Preferences from System Preferences (from Control Panel in Windows).

The Tablet Preferences open with the Pen tab selected.

2 Click and drag the Tilt Sensitivity slider to the right for greater tilt response.

3 Click and drag the Tip Feel slider for a softer or firmer touch.

4 Click different rocker switch settings.

5 Click the plus sign in the Application section.

The Select Application dialog box appears.

6 Click Adobe Photoshop CS6.

7 Click OK.

Note: If Photoshop is not running, click Browse and navigate to the Photoshop CS6 application.

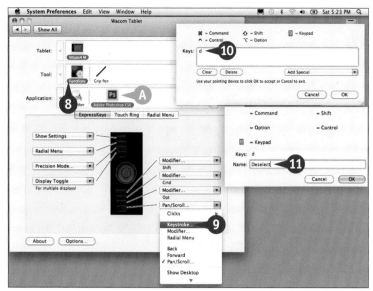

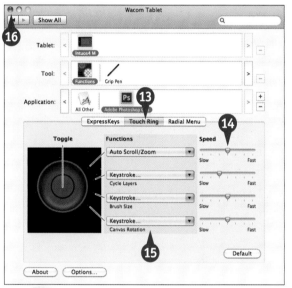

A Photoshop CS6 is listed in the Application section.

8 Click Functions to customize the ExpressKeys, Touch Ring, and Radial Menu.

Note: Make sure that Photoshop CS6 is still highlighted in the Application section.

9 Click any ExpressKey drop-down menu to change the setting to Keystroke.

10 Type a keystroke, such as D for Deselect, and click OK.

11 Type a name for the Keystroke and click OK.

12 Repeat steps 9 to 11 for any other ExpressKey you want to change.

13 Click the Touch Ring tab.

14 Click and drag the Speed slider to change the scrolling speed.

15 Click any of the Functions drop-down menus to select different settings.

Note: If you select Keystroke for any of the Functions drop-down menus, repeat steps 10 and 11.

16 Click the Close button.

Your custom settings are saved in the Wacom Preferences or Wacom Control panel.

TIPS

Did You Know?
Although you can work in Photoshop without a tablet, you will not have access to a large number of tools, which are specifically designed for use with a pressure-sensitive tablet and pen. For example, using a mouse, you can select only Off or Fade for Brush opacity. With a tablet attached to the computer, you can also select Pen Pressure, Pen Tilt, and Stylus Wheel, giving you more natural and responsive control when painting or editing photos.

Try This!
Set one ExpressKey for the Radial menu. Click the Radial Menu tab in the Wacom Tablet Preferences (Control Panel) and click one section of the Radial menu. Click the Function drop-down menu and set your custom settings as in the task steps. Now when you click the ExpressKey, the Radial menu appears on-screen so you can click to launch an application, run an action, or use the keystroke depending on your custom settings.

Important!
Wacom pen tablets come in three basic types: the Bamboo, the Intuos, and the Cintiq, and each comes in multiple sizes. The preferences dialog box varies slightly depending on the type of Wacom tablet you have connected.

Chapter 2

Work with Layers, Selections, and Masks

Layers, selections, and masks are the key to image editing in Photoshop. You improve or enhance photographs and create designs by adding different types of layers to your original file. You can duplicate a layer or build a complex multilayered image combining layers and layer effects with selections and masks.

A *layer* is similar to a transparency sheet with or without an image on it. You can edit, transform, or add filters to a layer independently from other layers. You can make one layer alter the look of a layer above or below it. You can combine different types of layers for creative designs. You can flatten all the layers to finalize an image or save a file with the layers for future editing. You can copy,

paste, or just drag a layer from one document to another.

Selections enable you to isolate areas in your image and apply different effects or filters without affecting the rest of the image. You can even select areas on one layer and create a new layer with that selection. You can make selections and refine them with many Photoshop tools depending on the type of area that you need to isolate or remove. You can copy, move, paste, and save selections.

A *mask* is a selection shown as a grayscale image: The white areas are selected; the black areas are not. You can use masks to block out areas of an image or to prevent edits. You can mask with painting tools or even vectors.

DIFFICULTY LEVEL

Layers are one of Photoshop's most powerful features and essential to editing any image. Layers let you edit nondestructively — that is, work on your images without damaging existing pixels. You can add layers by clicking the New Layer button in the Layers panel or by dragging a layer from another open document; you can also add layers by adding a special type of layer such as a vector layer, type layer, or adjustment layer, or by duplicating another layer. You can even turn on and off the visibility of individual layers to quickly compare your modified image with the original.

By editing a duplicated layer you avoid changing the original, and by applying adjustment layers you not only preserve the original pixels but also keep the overall file size lower. With multiple layers, you can apply different layer blending modes, which control the way the colors in one layer interact with the rest of the colors in the image, without permanently affecting the original image. In addition, you can change the effects of one layer on another by changing the opacity of any layer, or by clicking and dragging layers into different positions in the Layers panel to change their stacking order.

① Open an overexposed image.

Note: This task is intended to help you understand layers. In this example, the exposure in an overexposed photo is adjusted with an adjustment layer and a layer blend mode change. You can accomplish the same effect or the reverse effect in various ways.

② Click Exposure or another adjustment layer.

Note: You can select any of the adjustment layers for this task, because you are only using the layer and not actually applying the adjustment.

Ⓐ Photoshop places an adjustment layer above the Background layer and opens the Properties panel.

③ Click here to close the Properties panel if necessary to see the photo.

④ Click the drop-down menu and change the blend mode to Multiply.

The exposure appears darker.

⑤ Click and drag the adjustment layer over the New Layer button in the Layers panel.

Photoshop duplicates the layer and the exposure appears even darker.

⑥ Click Opacity and drag to the left to lower the opacity of the top layer until the photo appears properly exposed.

Note: You can also double-click the adjustment layer button, Exposure (⬛) in this example, to reopen the Exposure Properties panel and drag the Exposure slider to adjust the image.

The exposure changes.

⑦ Repeat steps 5 and 6 until the exposure appears correct.

⑧ Click the eye icon to toggle the visibility of any layer to compare the effect.

TIPS

Did You Know?

Although duplicating the Background layer and changing the blend mode has the same effect as using an adjustment layer, the duplicate Background layer doubles the file size. Adding an adjustment layer with no adjustments and changing the blend mode adds almost nothing to the file size.

Try This!

With a layer selected, cycle through the blend modes to see which works best. Click the Move tool (⬛) and while pressing Shift, press the plus sign key to go down the list or the minus sign key to go up the list.

Did You Know?

The blend modes are organized by groups according to what they do. The modes in the first group after Normal and Dissolve all darken the image in some way, whereas the modes in the next group all lighten the image. Each mode in the group starting with Overlay varies the contrast of the image in the layer below. The blend modes in the group starting with Difference exaggerate the differences between the images on the two layers, and the modes in the group starting with Hue change the image based on color properties.

Although the tasks in this chapter add only a few layers to each image, depending on the complexity of the project, you will often accumulate many more layers in the Layers panel as you work. You can view all the layers at once by scrolling through the list, or you can expand the Layers panel by clicking and dragging the Layers panel tab to separate it from the other panels on the screen. You can also close any panel tab groups you are not using so the Layers

panel expands automatically to fill the space. You can name individual layers to help you remember which one applied a specific adjustment to an image. You can also color-code your layers to help you visually organize the Layers panel. Whether you work alone or with a group of designers and share projects, organizing your Layers panel with names and colors streamlines the entire editing process.

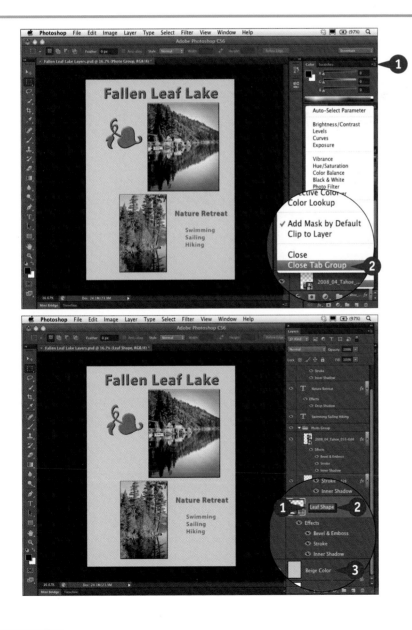

Close Tab Groups

1 Click the panel menu button on any unused tab group.

2 Click Close Tab Group.

The tabbed group disappears and the other tabbed groups expand to fill the space.

Note: You can optionally repeat steps 1 and 2 for other unused groups.

Note: You can also click and drag a panel out of a group to maintain it on the screen before closing the other tabs in the tabbed group.

Rename Layers

1 Double-click the name of a layer.

2 Type a new name in the box.

3 Repeat for any other layers to give each layer a distinctive name.

Color-Code Layers

1 Control+click (right-click) a layer.

2 Click to select a color for the layer.

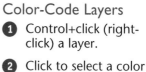

DIFFICULTY LEVEL

A The layer's eye icon box changes color.

3 Repeat steps 1 and 2 to color-code other layers.

TIPS

Try This!

You can group multiple layers into one layer group by selecting the layers and then clicking the New Group button (▢) on the bottom of the Layers panel, or by clicking Layer ➪ Group Layers from the menu. Layer groups can be opened for editing purposes and then collapsed to display a single folder. You can also move a group of layers all at once. Layer groups can be nested more than five levels deep.

More Options!

You can merge any layers that do not need to remain separately editable. Make sure the two layers are one above the other in the Layers panel by clicking and dragging them if necessary. Click the top layer to select it. Click the panel menu button (▤) and select Merge Down, or press ⌘+E (Ctrl+E). You can also merge layers by ⌘+clicking (Ctrl+clicking) two or more layers and then clicking Layers ➪ Merge Selected.

Photoshop CS6 includes a new feature that enables you to filter the layers in the Layers panel based on specific criteria to help you more easily find, select, and organize layers. This is especially important in documents that contain a large number of layers or for workgroups where different people might be working on different parts of a large file.

You can filter the layers by clicking the layer filter drop-down menu at the top of the layers panel and selecting Kind, and then clicking the icon to filter by

pixel layers, adjustment layers, type layers, shape layers, or Smart Object layers. You can also filter layers by selecting a different type of filter in the drop-down menu. You can then filter by the layer name, by a specific type of layer effect, by the blend mode, by an attribute such as locked layers or visible layers, or by the layer color.

The layer filtering switch enables you to view only the filtered layers and then toggle the filter off to view all the layers.

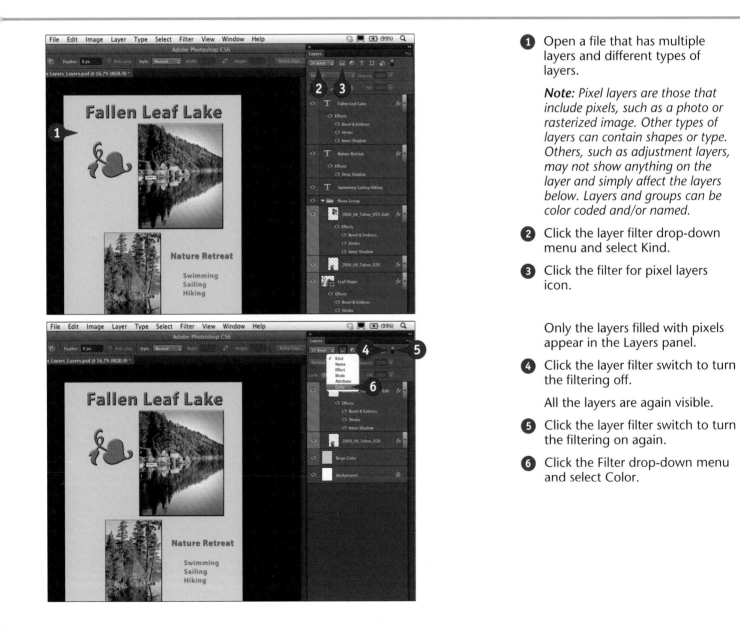

① Open a file that has multiple layers and different types of layers.

Note: Pixel layers are those that include pixels, such as a photo or rasterized image. Other types of layers can contain shapes or type. Others, such as adjustment layers, may not show anything on the layer and simply affect the layers below. Layers and groups can be color coded and/or named.

② Click the layer filter drop-down menu and select Kind.

③ Click the filter for pixel layers icon.

Only the layers filled with pixels appear in the Layers panel.

④ Click the layer filter switch to turn the filtering off.

All the layers are again visible.

⑤ Click the layer filter switch to turn the filtering on again.

⑥ Click the Filter drop-down menu and select Color.

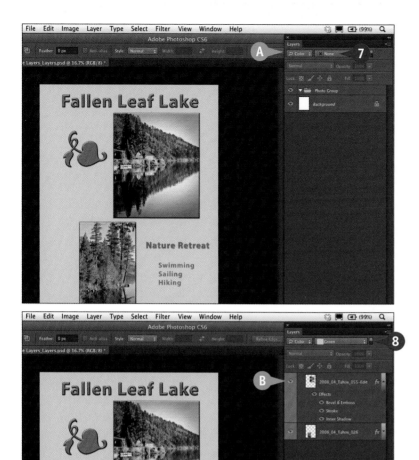

A The Layer Filter bar changes.

7 Click the drop-down menu and select a color such as green.

DIFFICULTY LEVEL

B Only the layers coded with that color appear in the Layers panel.

8 Click layer filter switch to turn layer filtering off.

Layer filtering is temporarily turned off and all the layers appear in the Layers panel again.

Note: *To remove all the filters, click the layer filter drop-down menu and select Kind. Click any of the filter icons, such as pixels or type, to deselect them if necessary.*

TIPS

Important!
The Layer Filter settings remain in effect as long as the document is open. Once you close a document, the filter state is not saved.

Did You Know?
The selected layer is called the *active layer*. You can select multiple layers by pressing ⌘ (Ctrl) and clicking them. You can then color-code them to match, move them together to another open document, or add effects to them all at the same time.

Try This!
To move the Background layer, unlock it by double-clicking its name, type a new name in the dialog box that appears, and click OK. To quickly duplicate the Background layer or any active layer, use the keyboard shortcut ⌘+J (Ctrl+J).

Some adjustment layers include a targeting tool for editing specific areas in an image.

With a Curves adjustment layer, you click in the image using the On-image adjustment tool to set a point on the curve and drag up or down to edit the contrast and tones. The shape of the curve in the Properties panel changes to match. Each time you click another area in the photo, a new point is set and dragging alters the curve.

With a Hue/Saturation adjustment layer, you click a particular color in the image with the On-image adjustment tool and drag left or right to reduce or increase that color's saturation. Each time you click a different area in the image, the corresponding color's saturation decreases or increases in the photo and the color slider moves in the Properties panel.

When you use a Black & White adjustment layer to convert a color photo, you can adjust the range of tones by clicking with the tool and dragging left or right directly on dark or light areas in the photo.

This task applies a Black & White adjustment layer. The steps are basically the same for the other types of adjustment layers with an On-image adjustment tool.

1 Open a color photo.

2 Click the Adjustment Layer button in the Layers panel.

3 Click Black & White.

Note: You can optionally click the Black & White Adjustment Layer button (▦) in the Adjustment Layer panel.

The photo changes to black and white and the Properties panel opens.

4 Click the On-image adjustment tool.

5 Click in the image on an area to lighten and drag to the right.

Note: The mouse pointer changes to an eyedropper.

The grays in the area are lightened and the corresponding sliders in the Properties panel move.

6 Click in the image on an area to darken and drag to the left.

The grays in the area are darkened and the corresponding sliders in the Properties panel move.

7 Repeat steps 5 and 6 for any other tones to adjust.

8 Click the On-image adjustment tool again to return the tool to the Properties panel.

9 Click and drag any sliders to edit other tones.

TIPS

Did You Know?

You can combine multiple adjustment layers on top of one another, and change the parameters for each type of layer. The image remains editable and the original pixels are not permanently changed as long as the layers are not flattened or merged into the Background layer.

Try This!

With all three types of adjustment layers that include the On-image adjustment tool, you can use the tool by itself, or you can start with one of the presets from the drop-down menu in the Properties panel. You can customize the preset visually by using the On-image adjustment tool to click and drag on specific areas on the photograph.

Did You Know?

Adjustment layers affect all the layers below it. Click ⬛ on the Properties panel to clip or limit the adjustment to the one layer below. Click 🔄 to reset the adjustment to the default setting. Click 🗑 on the Properties panel to delete an adjustment layer without going back to the Layers panel.

A Smart Object layer is a special type of layer used for nondestructive editing. This type of layer gives you creative flexibility because the original pixel data of the image, or vector data in some cases, is preserved. You can edit a Smart Object layer and then change the adjustment you applied without altering the image quality.

For example, when you transform or scale a regular image layer to reduce the size, some pixels are removed. If you then transform the layer back again, you lose image quality because your previous changes permanently altered the actual pixels.

However, if you open the same photograph as a Smart Object layer, or convert the layer to a Smart Object layer, you can scale the layer without any image data loss.

You can open a document as a Smart Object, convert one or more layers in Photoshop to Smart Object layers, or move a Smart Object layer into another document, maintaining its quality as a Smart Object. You can also place an Illustrator or other vector file into a document as a Smart Object and maintain the vector's sharp edges or forms even when resizing.

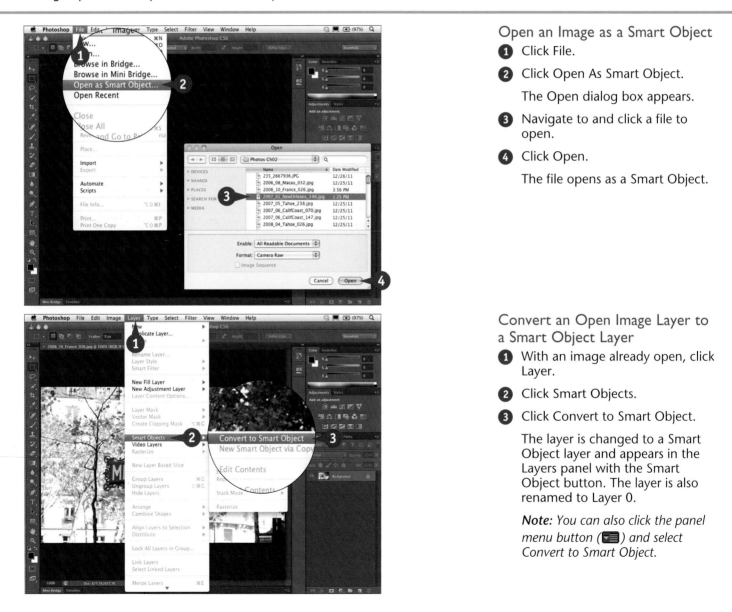

Open an Image as a Smart Object

1 Click File.

2 Click Open As Smart Object.

The Open dialog box appears.

3 Navigate to and click a file to open.

4 Click Open.

The file opens as a Smart Object.

Convert an Open Image Layer to a Smart Object Layer

1 With an image already open, click Layer.

2 Click Smart Objects.

3 Click Convert to Smart Object.

The layer is changed to a Smart Object layer and appears in the Layers panel with the Smart Object button. The layer is also renamed to Layer 0.

Note: *You can also click the panel menu button (*⬛*) and select Convert to Smart Object.*

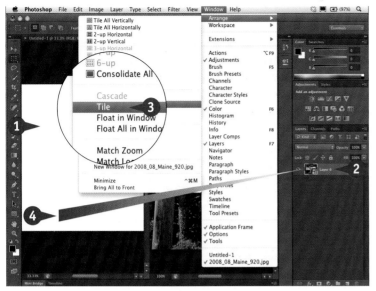

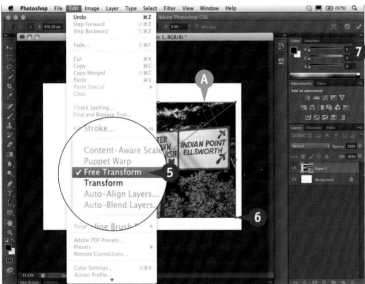

Open an Image as a Smart Object and Copy It to another Document

1 Open a new blank document.

2 Open an image as a Smart Object as in the first section of this task.

3 Click Window ➪ Arrange ➪ Tile so you can view both images on-screen.

4 Click and drag the Smart Object layer from the first document to the blank document.

Note: You can close the Smart Object document after you have moved it.

The Smart Object layer appears in the other document.

5 Click Edit ➪ Free Transform.

A Handles and a bounding box appear on the Smart Object layer.

6 Shift+click and drag an anchor point to reduce the photo size.

7 Click the Commit button to apply the transformation.

The image on the layer is scaled down, but can be resized back up to its original size without any data loss.

TIPS

More Options!

You can edit the contents of any Smart Object layer. Click Layer ➪ Smart Objects ➪ Edit Contents. Click OK in the warning dialog box that appears. Edit the original file and press ⌘+S (Ctrl+S). The Smart Object image is updated.

Try This!

You can create duplicates of a Smart Object layer in a document and link them. When you replace the contents of one Smart Object layer, all the duplicates are automatically updated at the same time.

Did You Know?

You can open a RAW file (such as a DNG, CR2, or NEF file) as a Smart Object by Shift+clicking the Open Image button in Camera Raw. You can then return to Camera Raw even after making edits to the image to make more changes without any data loss.

Filters in Photoshop are used to add blur, reduce noise, sharpen, or style an image. When you apply a regular filter, you permanently alter the pixels. By applying a Smart Filter instead, you can edit and change the settings of the filter at any time, even after the document has been saved and reopened. Any filter applied to a Smart Object layer becomes a *Smart Filter*.

You can apply a Smart Filter to the entire Smart Object layer or to a selection on a Smart Object layer. You can remove or hide Smart Filters at any time.

You can add multiple Smart Filters one on top of another and then change the order of the Smart Filters to change the resulting effect. You can also add a mask to a Smart Filter. You can then paint on the mask with black to hide or white to reveal different areas of the filter and create detailed edits on specific areas, all without altering the image data.

Most Photoshop filters, with the exception of Liquify and Vanishing Point, can be applied as Smart Filters.

1 Open or convert an image as a Smart Object as shown in the previous task.

2 Click Filter.

3 Click Blur.

4 Click Motion Blur.

The Motion Blur dialog box appears.

5 Click and drag the Distance slider and adjust the angle in the dialog box that appears.

6 Click OK.

A The Smart Filter appears below the Smart Object layer in the Layers panel.

B A layer mask is automatically applied to the Smart Filter.

7 Click the Brush tool.

8 Click the Brush Preset drop-down menu to open the Brush picker.

9 Click the first soft-edged brush in the Brush picker.

10 Click and drag the Size slider to adjust the size.

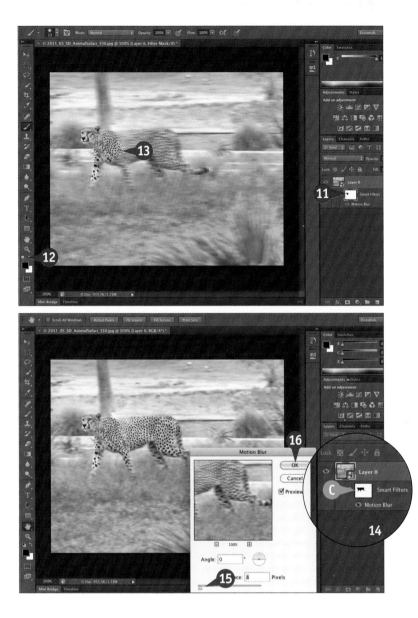

⓫ Click the Smart Filter layer mask thumbnail to select it.

⓬ Click the Default Colors icon to restore the default foreground and background colors, making sure black is the foreground color.

⓭ Click in the image to paint with black to remove the filter from specific areas.

Ⓒ The painted areas appear black in the layer mask, and the filters are removed from those areas in the photo.

⓮ Double-click the filter name to reopen the dialog box.

⓯ Adjust the filter's settings.

⓰ Click OK.

TIPS

Try This!
Click the triangle (▲) by the Smart Object layer to reveal the Smart Filters or any layer effects applied to the layer. Double-click the Edit Blending Options button (▣) next to the Smart Filter. A blending mode dialog box appears. Click Mode to select a different blending mode. Click Opacity to drag the slider to a different percentage.

More Options!
To change the effect when using multiple Smart Filters, click and drag one Smart Filter above or below another one in the Layers panel. To delete an individual Smart Filter, click its name and drag it to the Layers panel trash (🗑). To delete all the Smart Filters on a layer at once, click and drag the text *Smart Filters* on the Smart Object layer to the trash.

Did You Know?
You can copy a Smart Filter or a group of Smart Filters to another Smart Object layer in the Layers panel by pressing Option (Alt) and dragging the Smart Filter. However, you cannot drag a Smart Filter onto a regular layer.

Make a selection with the QUICK SELECTION TOOL

The Quick Selection tool in Photoshop enables you to easily select broad areas of an image by simply painting over them. You can use the Quick Selection tool to remove a background and isolate the main subject.

You can brush over different parts of a photo, varying the brush size as you work, or just click areas for a more limited selection. Once you have made your first selection, the tool automatically changes to the Add to Selection tool, so you can easily add areas without pressing any additional keys. You can subtract from the selection by pressing and holding Option (Alt) as

you paint, or using the Subtract from Selection tool in the Options bar.

This task shows the basic steps for selecting a subject and putting it on a separate layer. You can also select the background on a duplicated layer and press Delete (Backspace) to remove the background from the image, leaving just the subject on the layer. With any active selection you can click Layer in the menu and click Inverse to invert the selection.

For most selections, you will also need to use the tools in task #23 and/or task #25 to improve or refine the selection.

1 Click the Quick Selection tool.

2 Click the Brush Preset drop-down menu to open the Brush picker.

3 Click and drag the Size slider to adjust the brush tip size.

A If you have a pen tablet attached, you can click the Size drop-down menu to set the brush size with Pen Pressure.

4 Press ⌘+spacebar (Ctrl+spacebar) and click to zoom in, or click and drag in the image to dynamically zoom in.

Note: Although on a Mac the Spotlight feature momentarily opens with the same keystrokes, using ⌘+spacebar in Photoshop still zooms in.

5 Click and drag inside the part of the image you want to select.

6 Click and drag in another area to be selected.

B The tool changes to the Add to Selection option.

⑦ Continue changing the brush size and clicking and dragging in the image to select more areas.

⑧ Press and hold Option (Alt).

Ⓒ The tool temporarily changes to the Subtract from Selection tool.

⑨ Click in areas that you want to remove from the selection.

⑩ Press and hold the spacebar and click in the image to move to a different area.

⑪ Click any other areas to remove them from the selection.

⑫ Press ⌘+J (Ctrl+J) to put the selection on its own layer.

The selected area appears on a new layer above the Background layer.

⑬ Click the eye icon to toggle the Background layer's visibility.

TIPS

Enhance It!
You can click the Auto-Enhance option in the Options bar (☐ changes to ☑) to reduce the roughness of the selection boundary and extend the selection toward the edges it detects. Depending on the speed of your computer, adding the Auto-Enhance option may slow the selection process.

Keyboard Shortcuts!
To quickly change the brush size as you work, you can use the keyboard. Press the left bracket key to decrease the brush size or the right bracket key to increase the brush size.

More Options!
Click Sample All Layers (☐ changes to ☑) in the Options bar to make a selection based on all layers instead of just the currently selected layer.

You can select a rectangular or elliptical area with the marquee tools or select free-form or geometric areas with the lasso tools, or make other selections with the Quick Selection tool. You can also use the Brush tool in Quick Mask mode to make a detailed selection or to adjust any previously selected area.

The Quick Mask mode is an editing mode in which protected areas are covered with a translucent colored mask. You paint directly on the areas you want to select, adjusting the brush size as you work to make the selection more precise. The quick mask covers the area with a translucent red so you can see what you are selecting. You can also specify a different masking color if the area you are selecting has a lot of red in it.

Using this masking technique, you are actually masking the areas you paint, so you must invert the selection before making any adjustments. The areas you painted over are then selected, and the remainder of the image is now masked.

1 Click the Zoom tool and click and drag to enlarge the area you want to select.

2 Click the Default Colors icon to set the foreground color to black and the background to white.

3 Click the Quick Mask Mode button.

4 Click the Brush tool.

5 Click the Brush Preset drop-down menu to open the Brush picker.

6 Select a hard-edged brush.

7 Click and drag the Size slider to adjust the size.

8 Paint over the areas you want to select.

The painted areas are covered with a red translucent mask.

Note: Press the left bracket key to reduce the brush size as you work in detailed areas.

9 Click the Switch Colors icon to reverse the foreground and background colors and make white the foreground color.

10 Paint over any areas that you do not want selected.

11 Click the Switch Colors icon to make black the foreground color again.

12 Continue painting until the whole area is covered in red.

13 Click the Quick Mask Mode button to turn off the Quick Mask mode.

A Dashed lines indicate the areas that were covered with the red overlay and are not selected.

Note: You can optionally press Option+spacebar (Alt+spacebar) to zoom back out to see the edges of the image.

14 Click Select.

15 Click Inverse.

The selection now includes only the area you painted in the Quick Mask mode.

TIPS

Caution!

Remember that you are creating a mask, which actually selects the inverse of the area you are painting over. You must invert the selection by clicking Select ⇨ Inverse before you make adjustments to the selected area.

Important!

You may need to feather a selection before you make adjustments. After you invert the selection, click Select ⇨ Refine Edge to adjust the selection using the Refine Edge panel as in task #25.

More Options!

If the image you are painting on is very red, change the masking color. Double-click the Quick Mask Mode button (▣) and click the color box in the Quick Mask Options dialog box to pick a new color. You can also reduce the default mask opacity of 50% if necessary to see the selected area below the mask more clearly.

Portrait retouchers spend a lot time working on faces, improving color and tone, hiding blemishes, enhancing eyes, and more. Yet even everyday snapshots of people can be greatly improved by editing the faces in the image. For example, a Levels adjustment on just the faces can bring the attention of the viewer to the subjects in the image and make an everyday snapshot much more interesting. However, making a selection of just the faces in a photo can be difficult or time consuming.

Photoshop CS6 includes a new tool for limiting a selection to the skin tones in a photograph. When you choose Select ➪ Color Range, Photoshop automatically selects what it sees as skins tones. You can further refine the automatic selection by checking the Detect Faces check box, which appears when the Skin Tones color range menu is open.

You can use this new tool as a starting point and then refine the facial selection with the other selection tools to quickly get a more defined selection.

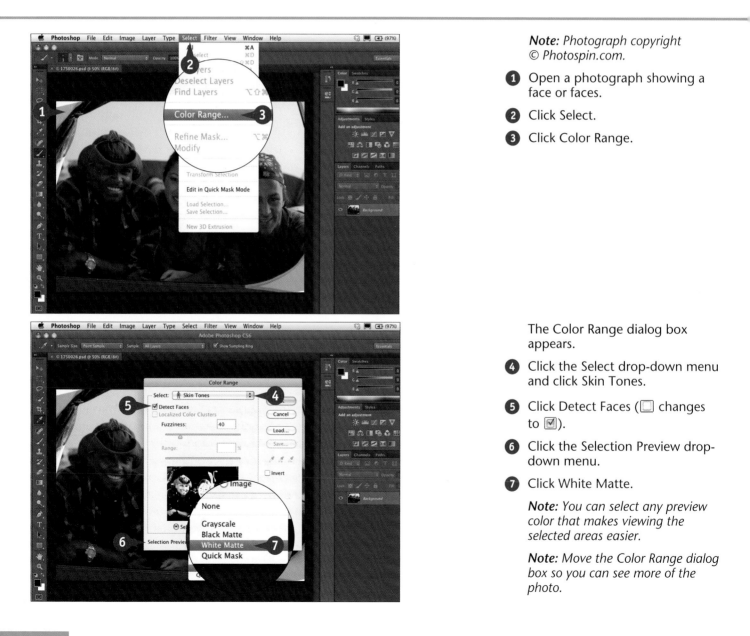

Note: Photograph copyright © Photospin.com.

① Open a photograph showing a face or faces.

② Click Select.

③ Click Color Range.

The Color Range dialog box appears.

④ Click the Select drop-down menu and click Skin Tones.

⑤ Click Detect Faces (☐ changes to ☑).

⑥ Click the Selection Preview drop-down menu.

⑦ Click White Matte.

Note: You can select any preview color that makes viewing the selected areas easier.

Note: Move the Color Range dialog box so you can see more of the photo.

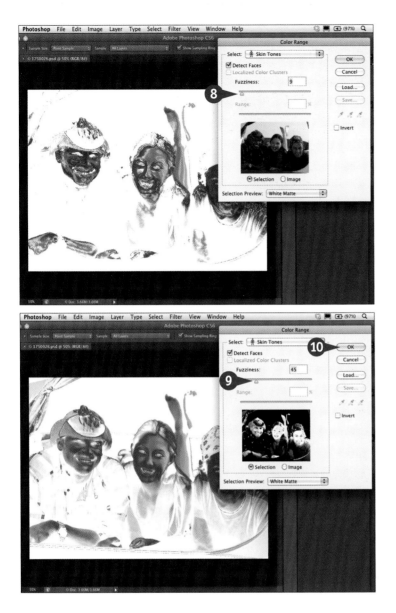

The skin tones appear in color in the image window. Everything else turns white.

⑧ Click and drag the Fuzziness slider all the way to the left.

The image turns completely white and the preview box completely black.

⑨ Click and drag the Fuzziness slider slowly to the right.

The selected area expands.

⑩ Click OK when most of the faces are selected.

TIPS

Did You Know?

You can change the fuzziness by moving the slider or typing a specific number. The fastest way is to start by dragging the slider completely to the left. Then with 0 highlighted in the box, click the up arrow on your keyboard while viewing the changes in the main window.

Try This!

Depending on the colors in the photo, you may want to change the Selection Preview color to any of the other options in the menu. **None** shows the photo. **Grayscale** makes the selected areas white and the deselected areas black. **Black Matte** shows the skin tones in the selected areas with everything else in black. **White Matte** does the opposite, and **Quick Mask** displays the image as it will appear in Quick Mask Mode.

Making selections of skin or faces generally requires refining the selection. You can use the Quick Selection tool or the Lasso to add to or delete from the selection. With these tools, press and hold Option (Alt) as you click to remove areas from the selection or ⌘ (Ctrl) as you click to add areas to the selection.

You can also use the Quick Mask mode to edit the selection by painting on the areas to keep with a white paint brush or painting with a black paint brush to remove areas from the selection.

Once your selection is made, you can then use any tools to edit the area without affecting the surrounding pixels.

You can use the Skin Tones selection option as in this task to quickly brighten faces in a snapshot with a Levels adjustment layer. However, you can also use this Skin Tones selection tool and then invert the selection to adjust the surrounding areas or clothes instead.

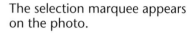

The selection marquee appears on the photo.

Note: You can adjust the selection using any of the selection tools as in previous tasks to more precisely select just the skin tones.

⑪ Click the New Fill or Adjustment Layer button.

⑫ Click the Levels adjustment layer.

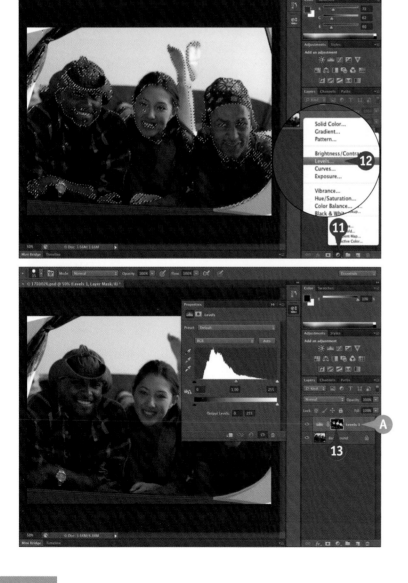

Ⓐ A Levels adjustment layer and a mask are added in the Layers panel.

⑬ Option+click (Alt+click) the layer mask thumbnail on the adjustment layer.

The image shows only the layer mask in black and white.

#24

14 Click the Brush tool.

Note: Make sure that black is the foreground color. Press X if necessary to change it.

15 Paint with black over the white areas in the image that are not faces to remove them from the selection.

16 Option+click (Alt+click) the layer mask thumbnail on the adjustment layer.

The image returns to the normal view.

17 Click the Levels button in the Properties panel.

18 Click and drag the slider to the left until the skin tones are lightened or to the base of the curve.

The adjustments are applied to the selected skin tones only.

TIPS

Did You Know?

You can click Invert (☐ changes to ☑) in the Color Range dialog box to invert the selected area. You can also click Select ➪ Inverse after the selection has been applied.

More Options!

Try clicking the Auto button in the Properties panel of the Levels adjustment layer. You can also click RGB in the Properties panel and adjust the levels for each channel individually.

Important!

The number of pixels required for the Feather Radius depends on the overall dimensions of the photograph. The larger the image, the larger the pixel radius needed to soften the selection edge.

The Refine Edge floating panel is accessible in the Options bar when working with any selection tool. Using Refine Edge, you can clean up selections, soften or feather the edge outlines, and remove edge artifacts, or *jaggies*. The panel offers various previewing options, showing the selection on a white or black background, against a red overlay, or on an empty layer to help you see the edges of the areas you are selecting and the changes you are making.

You can use the Refine Edge panel with any active selection, regardless of the tool used to create the selection. The Refine Edge tool is particularly useful when selecting very irregular edges, such as animal fur. Whenever there is a selection in the image, the Refine Edge button appears in the Options bar.

With the subject selected, you can use the tool to fine-tune the details in the edges of your image to get the best selection possible.

1 Open an image and make a selection using any of the selection tools.

A The foreground subject is selected.

Note: Depending on the image, you might select the background and then invert the selection to show the subject matter in the selection marquee.

2 Click the Refine Edge button in the Options bar.

The subject appears against a solid background.

3 Click the Zoom tool in the Refine Edge panel and click in the image to enlarge certain areas.

Note: Click the Hand tool ( ) in the Refine Edge panel and click and drag to move around the image.

4 Click and drag the Radius slider to refine the edge selection.

5 Click and drag the Contrast slider to remove edge artifacts and to sharpen edges.

6 Click the View drop-down menu to select another view mode.

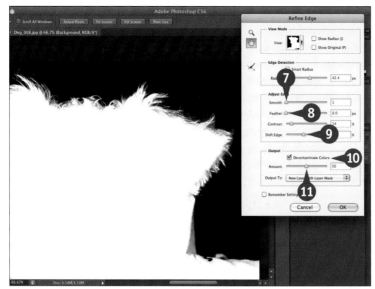

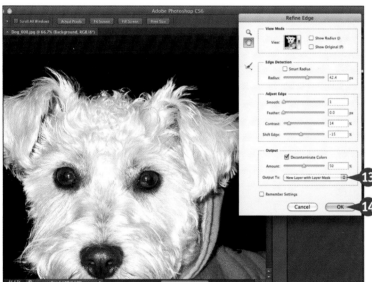

7 Click and drag the Smooth slider to create a smoother selection outline.

8 Click and drag the Feather slider to create a softer-edged transition.

9 Click and drag the Shift Edge slider to adjust the selection edges.

10 Click Decontaminate Colors (☐ changes to ☑).

11 Click and drag the Amount slider to replace the color fringes with the color of the subject.

12 Repeat steps 4 to 11 to make the best selection possible.

13 Click the Output To drop-down menu to have the selected area appear as a selection or a mask on the current layer or placed on a new layer.

14 Click OK to save the selection.

Your refined selection appears on the image as a new layer or as a new layer with a layer mask.

TIPS

Try This!
You can use a keyboard shortcut to quickly change the preview mode when using the Refine Edge panel. Press F to cycle through each preview mode. Press X to temporarily view the original image.

Did You Know?
Moving the Radius slider improves the edge of the selection and helps in areas with more detail. Increasing the Contrast amount sharpens the edges of the selection. The Smooth slider removes jagged edges of a selection, and the Feather slider adds a uniform blur to the selection edge.

Important!
Clicking the Decontaminate Colors option in step 10 (☐ changes to ☑) requires the selection to be placed on a new layer or document because it changes the colors of pixels.

BLEND TWO PHOTOS TOGETHER with an automatic layer mask

Layer masks open a world of imaging possibilities that you cannot create with traditional tools. Using a layer mask to hide parts of an image, you can easily blend one photograph into another and create designs sure to grab a viewer's attention. For example, you can blend a photograph of a wedding couple into a photo of the bride's bouquet, or blend a photo of a potato with a photo of a person lying on a couch.

Generally, to blend a photo on one layer into the photo on the layer below, you add a layer mask to the top layer and paint with black on the layer mask

to blend the images. To hide some of the area you just revealed, simply reverse the colors and paint with white.

You can also have Photoshop create the layer mask for you automatically. By copying one photo to the clipboard and creating a selection on the other photo, you can use Photoshop's Paste Into command. You can then use the Brush tool to add or remove areas if necessary. You can also adjust the way the images blend using the Opacity slider on the Layers panel.

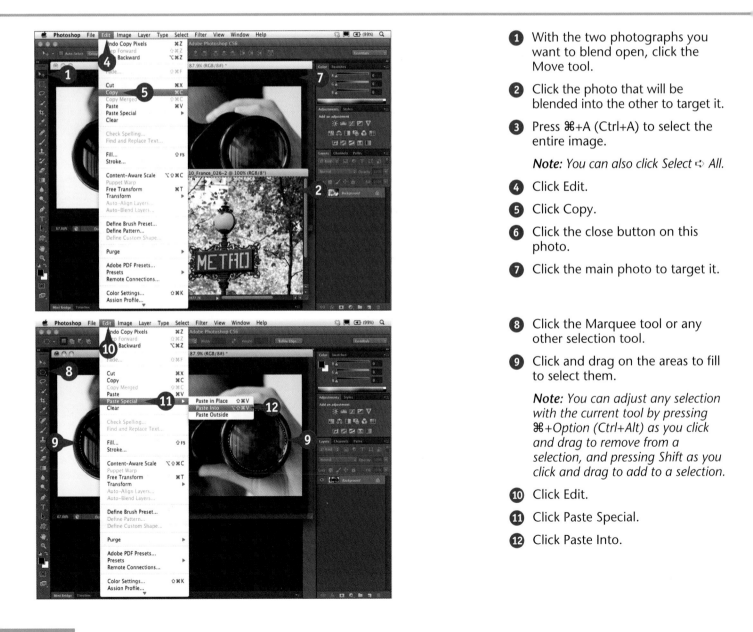

1. With the two photographs you want to blend open, click the Move tool.

2. Click the photo that will be blended into the other to target it.

3. Press ⌘+A (Ctrl+A) to select the entire image.

   Note: You can also click Select ⇨ All.

4. Click Edit.

5. Click Copy.

6. Click the close button on this photo.

7. Click the main photo to target it.

8. Click the Marquee tool or any other selection tool.

9. Click and drag on the areas to fill to select them.

   Note: You can adjust any selection with the current tool by pressing ⌘+Option (Ctrl+Alt) as you click and drag to remove from a selection, and pressing Shift as you click and drag to add to a selection.

10. Click Edit.

11. Click Paste Special.

12. Click Paste Into.

Ⓐ The first photo appears in the active selection.

⑬ Click the Move tool.

⑭ Click and drag in the area to reposition it.

⑮ Press ⌘+T (Ctrl+T) to make the Free Transform anchors appear.

⑯ Shift+click the anchor points to resize the photo.

⑰ Click the layer's Opacity slider and drag to the left to blend the images more naturally.

TIPS

Try This!

You can make two images blend together with a smooth transition by using the Gradient tool (▨) to apply a black-to-white gradient on the layer mask.

Customize It!

When you use a pen tablet to paint on a layer mask, you can easily control how much of the image you reveal with each brush stroke by setting the brush opacity to respond to pen pressure. Click the Brushes thumbnail to open the Brushes Presets. Click Shape Dynamics and set Size Jitter Control to Pen Pressure.

Did You Know?

You can add a layer mask to any layer by clicking the Layer Mask button (▣) in the Layers panel. ⌘+click (Ctrl+click) the Layer Mask button to add a white layer mask that reveals all on that layer. Option+click (Alt+click) the Layer Mask button to add a black layer mask that conceals everything on that layer.

Adjustment layers give you many options for editing and re-editing your images. You can give a scenic photo a more dramatic look or simply increase the colors in a sky with a Gradient Fill adjustment layer. The colors you see are often better than what your camera captures, particularly when you photograph a sunset or a sunrise. You can easily increase the intensity of the sky with a Gradient Fill. You can enhance the existing colors by using a black foreground color, using a more intense version of the

same color, or even selecting another color to create a stylized image. You can adjust how much of the photo to cover with added color. Because you are using a fill layer, you can go back and increase or decrease the amount of color after you apply the Gradient Fill layer. You can even change the color that you applied to get a different effect or to create a more dramatic look. This technique is most effective on a photo with a large sky area and an open horizon.

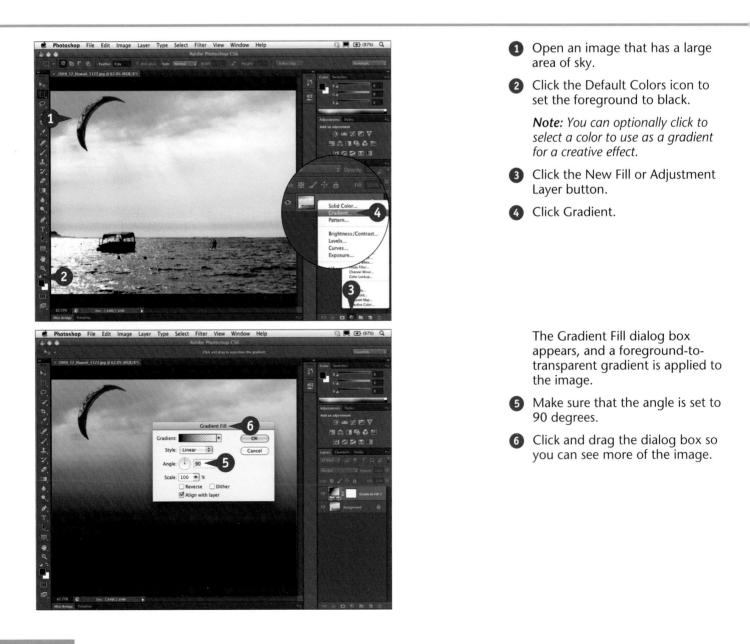

1 Open an image that has a large area of sky.

2 Click the Default Colors icon to set the foreground to black.

Note: You can optionally click to select a color to use as a gradient for a creative effect.

3 Click the New Fill or Adjustment Layer button.

4 Click Gradient.

The Gradient Fill dialog box appears, and a foreground-to-transparent gradient is applied to the image.

5 Make sure that the angle is set to 90 degrees.

6 Click and drag the dialog box so you can see more of the image.

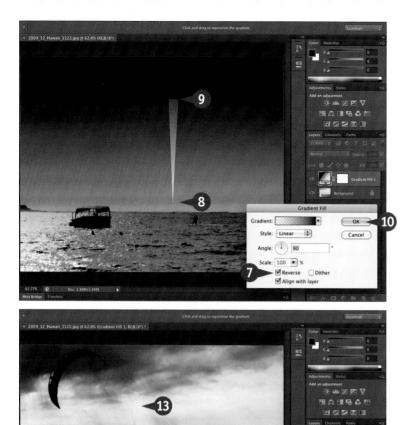

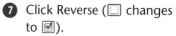

#27

DIFFICULTY LEVEL

7 Click Reverse (changes to).

The gradient reverses to black or the selected color at the top, changing to transparent at the bottom of the image.

8 Position the cursor over the image.

9 Drag upward in the image until the gradient covers only the sky.

10 Click OK.

11 Click the blend mode drop-down menu and click Overlay.

12 Double-click the layer thumbnail for the gradient fill.

The Gradient Fill dialog box reappears.

13 Position the cursor over the image.

14 Drag downward in the image to increase the darkened sky or drag upward to lessen the effect.

Each time that you drag in the image with the Gradient Fill layer selected, the look of the sky changes.

TIPS

Did You Know?

Multiple layers increase the file size of your image. Because Photoshop requires more memory to work on larger files, you should merge layers that will not be changed later. Pressing ⌘+E (Ctrl+E) merges a selected layer with the layer below. Pressing ⌘+Shift+E (Ctrl+Shift+E) merges all the visible layers. Click Layer ⇨ Flatten Image to flatten all the layers into a new Background image.

Try This!

You can apply a Gradient Fill layer on a photo showing a large body of water such as a lake or the ocean. Experiment with different foreground colors for the Gradient Fill for both dramatic and creative effects.

USE AUTO-ALIGN AND AUTO-BLEND LAYERS to combine photos

You can easily combine two or more separate photographs of the same subject and let Photoshop blend these to achieve a better image. You can combine images that do not have identical alignments and Photoshop can automatically align them. You can combine images photographed with different exposures, making some too light and others too dark, and Photoshop blends these to achieve better color and tone.

The Auto-Align Layers command aligns layers based on similar content in different layers, such as corners

and edges, and automatically generates the required masks.

The Auto-Blend Layers command helps you create composites of a scene from multiple images with over- or underexposed areas or even content differences. Auto-Blend Layers creates masks on each layer and to hide or show different areas from each image to create a better and seamless composite image.

Using the Auto-Align and Auto-Blend Layers commands is not the same as creating an HDR (High Dynamic Range) image shown in task #78.

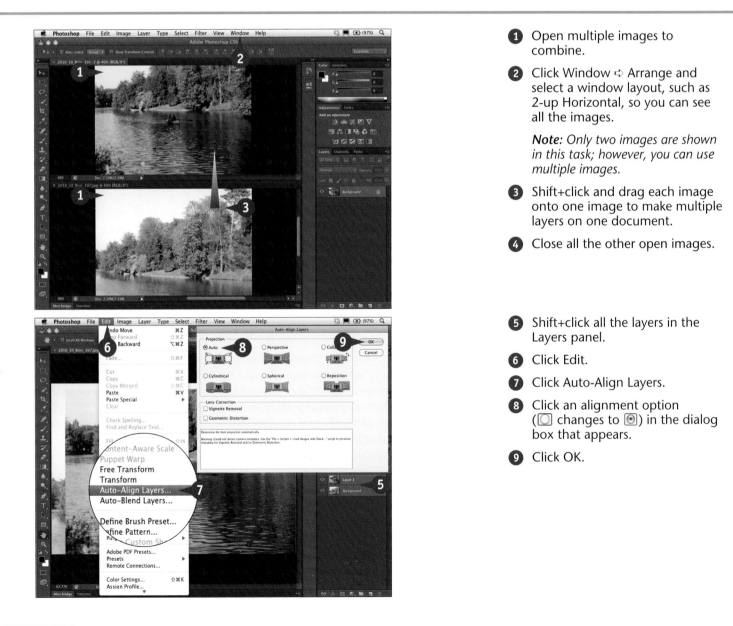

① Open multiple images to combine.

② Click Window ➪ Arrange and select a window layout, such as 2-up Horizontal, so you can see all the images.

Note: Only two images are shown in this task; however, you can use multiple images.

③ Shift+click and drag each image onto one image to make multiple layers on one document.

④ Close all the other open images.

⑤ Shift+click all the layers in the Layers panel.

⑥ Click Edit.

⑦ Click Auto-Align Layers.

⑧ Click an alignment option (☐ changes to ◉) in the dialog box that appears.

⑨ Click OK.

Photoshop automatically aligns the layers based on the content.

⑩ Shift+click all the layers in the Layers panel.

⑪ Click Edit.

⑫ Click Auto-Blend Layers.

⑬ Click Stack Images in the dialog box (◯ changes to ◉).

⑭ Click Seamless Tones and Colors in the dialog box (☐ changes to ☑).

⑮ Click OK.

Photoshop automatically blends the layers.

⑯ Click the Crop tool.

⑰ Click and drag in the image to select the finished composite.

⑱ Click the Commit button to apply the crop.

Note: *You can optionally click Layer ⇨ Flatten Image to combine all the layers into one composite image.*

TIPS

Did You Know?
The Auto-Align command automatically changes the locked Background layer into a regular layer and changes the name to Layer 0.

More Options!
After applying the Auto-Align command, you can click Edit ⇨ Free Transform and then use the anchor points to fine-tune the alignment, or even to make tonal adjustments by changing exposure differences between layers.

Try This!
⌘+click (Ctrl+click) directly on one of the layer masks in the Layers panel to see what areas were added or removed from one layer.

Create photographic designs with VECTOR LAYERS

When you use a shape tool or the Pen tool in Photoshop, you create a vector layer. Vectors are resolution independent — you can scale them at any time and they maintain their sharp edges like the drawings in Illustrator. You can select any of Photoshop predesigned custom shapes for vectors or create your own shape with the Pen tools. You can also load custom shapes you purchase from third-party vendors. You can add shapes alone or in combination with other shapes to create novel designs or logos. When you draw a shape and create a vector layer, you can add to that shape on the same layer or you can create new vector layers with each shape you draw to create new designs. You can fill and stroke the vector shapes independently and still maintain the crisp Illustrator-type edges. You can add vector layers to any image as a design element or use the shape as a mask by clipping the image to the vector layer.

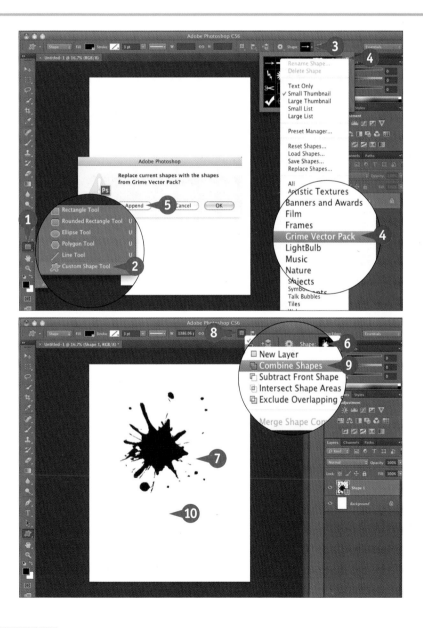

Note: *Photograph copyright © Photospin.com.*

Note: *This task starts with a new white document set to US letter size.*

1. Control+click (right-click) the Rectangle Shape tool.

2. Click the Custom Shape tool.

3. Click the Shape drop-down menu in the Options bar to view the shapes.

4. Click the gear menu button (⚙) and click a set of shapes from the menu such as Grime Vector Pack.

5. Click Append in the dialog box that appears.

   The selected shapes are added to the menu.

6. Double-click a shape in the menu.

7. Click and drag on the document.

   A black shape appears on the white document.

8. Click the Path Operations button in the Options bar.

9. Click Combine Shapes.

10. Click and drag on the document again.

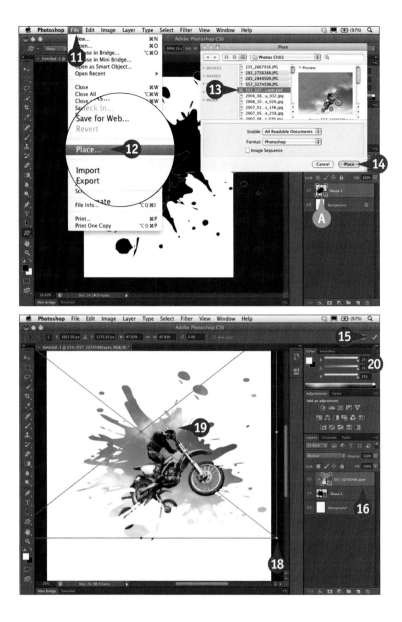

#29

DIFFICULTY LEVEL

Ⓐ The two black shapes are combined on one vector layer.

⑪ Click File.

⑫ Click Place.

⑬ Click a photo in the Place dialog box that appears.

⑭ Click Place.

The photo appears on top of the design.

⑮ Click the Commit button to apply the placed image.

⑯ Opt+click (Alt+click) on the line between the photo layer and the vector shape layer to create a clipping mask.

Note: You can also click Layer and click Create Clipping Mask to clip the photo to the shape.

⑰ Press ⌘+T (Ctrl+T) to make the Free Transform anchors appear.

⑱ Shift+click the anchor points to resize the photo.

⑲ Click and drag on the image to adjust the photo in the shape.

⑳ Click the Commit button to apply the transformation.

The photo fits inside the custom shape.

TIPS

More Options!

Click the Custom Shape tool and click the vector layer to select it. Click the color box for the Stroke in the Options bar and select a color. Then click the word *Stroke* in the Options bar and drag to the left to increase the stroke size.

Try This!

After creating the first shape, click the Path Operations button (▥) in the Options bar and select New Layer. Then each time you click or click and drag in the document, another vector layer is added with that shape in it.

Get Creative!

You can create a grid of different photos by adding multiple vector layers with a rectangular or any other shape, placing one shape just next to the other. Then place one photo layer above each vector layer and repeat steps 16 to 20 for each photo layer.

Chapter 3

Straighten, Crop, and Resize

Whether you work on design projects and professional photographs, or simply use Photoshop to improve your snapshots, your digital photos almost always need to be resized or adjusted to fit your projects. A well-balanced image, free from odd-looking distortions, can mean the difference between a snapshot and a good photograph. The overall layout of the image and where the main subject is placed in relation to the background are essential visual elements in any image. A crooked horizon or unbalanced subject matter can make even a great image look like the work of a beginner.

Photoshop includes a variety of tools and filters to improve the composition of any image. The improved Crop tool makes cropping easier and gives you more visual control. You can choose to delete the cropped pixels, making the crop permanent, or you can leave that option deselected so your crops are nondestructive and can be easily changed. You can crop by selecting a preset aspect ratio, flip the orientation of the crop box, or crop to a specific size and resolution. You can toggle the visibility of the cropped area to better judge your composition, all while keeping your file completely editable.

You can correct perspective or lens distortion with the Crop tool or Lens Correction filter. You can combine images to create a panorama using Photoshop's Photomerge; the software does most of the work for you.

Photoshop makes all such traditionally time-consuming or difficult tasks quick and easy. New tools and resampling algorithms help you straighten, crop, adjust, and resize images, saving hours of tedious work to make all your images look better.

DIFFICULTY LEVEL

CROP YOUR IMAGES USING GUIDES to improve composition

Perfectly composing a photograph in the camera's viewfinder is not always possible; however, you can strengthen the composition of your images by changing the placement of the horizon or the relative position of the main subject using Photoshop's Crop tool.

Designers and photographers use various techniques to balance an image and focus the viewer's attention. They may offset the main subject to guide the viewer into the image, or they may use an overlay, such as the Rule of Thirds principle, as a guide. Photoshop CS6

now includes a number of traditional overlay guides that you can place on your image to help you adjust the composition.

Photoshop's overlay guides are applied by default once you click in the image with the Crop tool. You can use them, change the overlay style, or turn them off to compose your crop visually any way you want.

You can also crop by specifying dimensions in the Options bar, using one of the preset sizes, or by creating and saving your own preset.

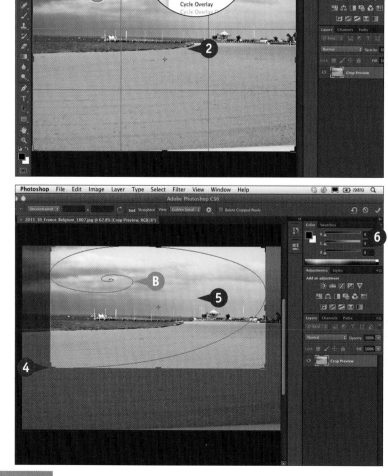

1 With the image you want to crop opened, click the Crop tool.

The crop box is automatically set to the image edges.

2 Click in the image.

Ⓐ The Rule of Thirds overlay is now visible.

3 Click the View drop-down menu in the Options bar to change the view options for the Crop tool.

Ⓑ The overlay changes.

4 Click and drag the side anchors to reposition the crop on the image.

5 Click and drag anywhere inside the crop lines to change the overall area to be cropped.

6 Click the Commit button to apply the crop.

Keeping the horizon perfectly horizontal when you are shooting is not always easy. You can adjust the angle of the horizon line in Photoshop without doing any calculations.

Photoshop CS6 now includes a straighten tool in the Crop tool's Options bar. When you click and drag the Straighten tool along a line that should be horizontal or vertical, the image is rotated, the canvas automatically expands, and the crop box adjusts to fit the maximum size of the straightened image.

At this point the window displays a nondestructive preview of the cropped image. You can click just outside the crop box to go back into crop mode. The canvas then expands and you can re-edit the crop box until you see the final image you want. You can also click the Reset button in the Options bar or press Delete (Backspace) to reset the crop box. And if the Delete Cropped Pixels box in the Options bar is unchecked, you can even change the crop after clicking the Commit button.

① Open an image that has a crooked horizon line.

② Click the Crop tool.

Ⓐ Make sure Delete Cropped Pixels is unchecked.

③ Click the Straighten tool in the Options bar.

④ Click and drag from one side of the image to the other, along what should be a horizontal or vertical line.

The image is rotated and the window displays a preview of the straightened image.

⑤ Click the Commit button to finish the crop.

⑥ Click any of the crop anchors to view the cropped pixels.

Note: The hidden pixels are preserved even after you save the file as cropped.

Expand the canvas with a REVERSE CROP

When you think of cropping, you generally think of reducing the physical size of an image by cutting away areas around the borders. In Photoshop, you can use the Crop tool to expand the canvas, giving your photo a larger border, or giving a design more background area.

Although you can expand the canvas by selecting Image ⇨ Canvas Size and setting the specific dimensions for the canvas, as shown in task #110, using the reverse crop method is quick and gives you

a preview as you work of how your image will appear on the expanded canvas. And Photoshop's Crop tool gives you more flexibility because you can drag the crop marquee handles to create an uneven border.

You can use this technique to enlarge your canvas visually or use precise dimensions for your final image. By specifying the width and height for your finished design in the boxes in the Options bar, you can click and drag out the crop marquee in the image and maintain the exact dimensions you typed.

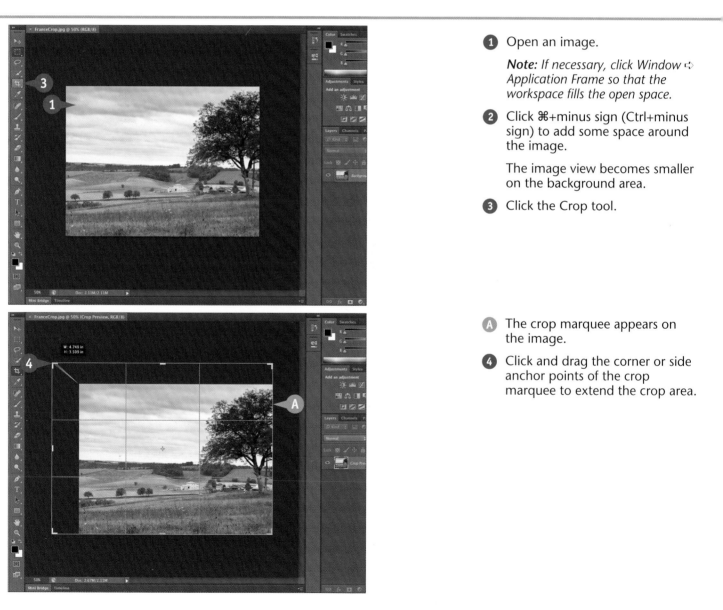

① Open an image.

Note: If necessary, click Window ⇨ Application Frame so that the workspace fills the open space.

② Click ⌘+minus sign (Ctrl+minus sign) to add some space around the image.

The image view becomes smaller on the background area.

③ Click the Crop tool.

Ⓐ The crop marquee appears on the image.

④ Click and drag the corner or side anchor points of the crop marquee to extend the crop area.

The canvas enlarges as you drag and fills with transparency. The current canvas dimensions appear just over the edge of the crop marquee.

5 Repeat step 4 to get the visual proportions you need.

6 Click and drag directly on the image to move it around on the canvas if necessary.

7 Click the Commit button in the Options bar to commit the crop.

The Background layer changes to a regular layer with transparency, named Layer 0.

8 Click the Default Colors icon in the toolbar to reset the background color to white.

9 Click Layer.

10 Click Flatten Image.

Note: You can optionally click the Layers panel drop-down menu and select Flatten Image.

B The transparent area is filled with white and Layer 0 changes into the Background layer.

TIPS

Change It!

Click the Crop tool (⬚) and type the width and height for your finished design in the boxes in the Options bar. You can also click a preset size. Then when you click and drag out the crop marquee in the image, it maintains the exact ratios you typed.

Customize It!

Click Unconstrained from the drop-down menu in the Options bar. Enter specific file dimensions that you use often. Unconstrained changes to Custom. Click the drop-down menu and select Save Preset. Name your custom crop preset in the dialog box that appears and click OK.

Try This!

You can add a colored border instead of white. Before flattening the layers, click the default Background color icon in the Tool bar and select a color in the Color Picker that appears. Then when you flatten the layers, the added border is filled with the new color.

Artwork comprised of two or more photographs, drawings, or paintings normally involves changing width and height, resolution, cropping, and mathematical calculations. With Photoshop, you can easily create such art pieces without any math. The images can be of different sizes and even have different aspect ratios.

You select images whose colors and tone or subject matter will complement each other. Using the Crop tool and a custom size and resolution preset, you crop each image. You then create one document with the different images on layers and move each layer to position it on the final art piece. You can place the images two up, three up, or four up both horizontally or vertically. You can add space between the images, and you can add more canvas all around the artwork as a whole.

The following task uses four images to create a quadriptych. You can also create diptychs and triptychs by moving one image layer to one side or the other.

Start by opening the four images, and tile them across the screen by clicking Window ➪ Arrange ➪ Tile.

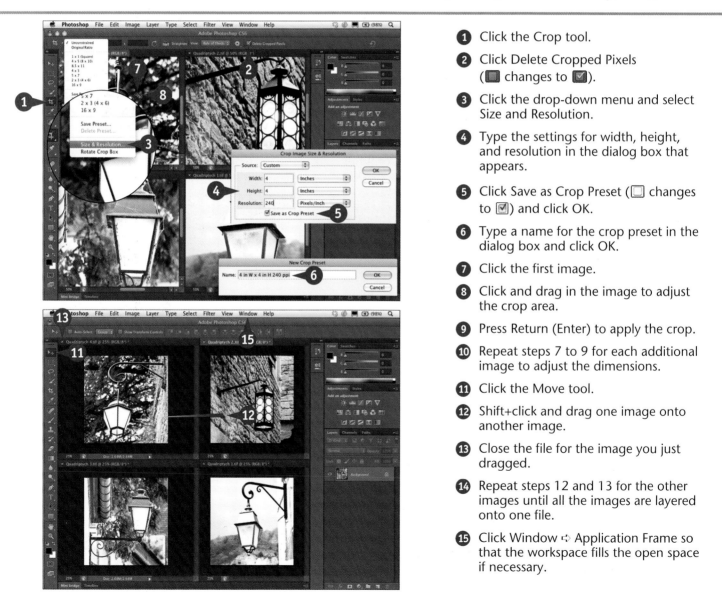

1. Click the Crop tool.

2. Click Delete Cropped Pixels (☐ changes to ☑).

3. Click the drop-down menu and select Size and Resolution.

4. Type the settings for width, height, and resolution in the dialog box that appears.

5. Click Save as Crop Preset (☐ changes to ☑) and click OK.

6. Type a name for the crop preset in the dialog box and click OK.

7. Click the first image.

8. Click and drag in the image to adjust the crop area.

9. Press Return (Enter) to apply the crop.

10. Repeat steps 7 to 9 for each additional image to adjust the dimensions.

11. Click the Move tool.

12. Shift+click and drag one image onto another image.

13. Close the file for the image you just dragged.

14. Repeat steps 12 and 13 for the other images until all the images are layered onto one file.

15. Click Window ➪ Application Frame so that the workspace fills the open space if necessary.

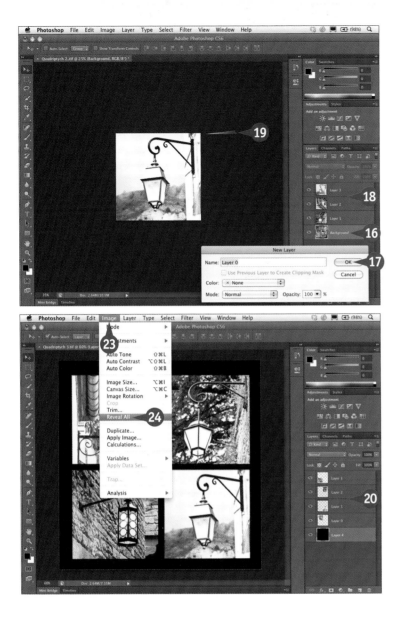

One file with multiple layers remains on the screen.

16 Double-click the bottom Background layer.

The New Layer dialog box appears.

17 Click OK to change the name to Layer 0.

18 Shift+click the top two layers in the Layers panel to select them.

19 Shift+click and drag on the image, dragging to the right until the outline of the two top images snaps to the edge of the underlying image.

Note: You can no longer see the two top image layers on the screen.

20 Shift+click the two middle layers in the Layers panel to select them both.

21 Shift+click and drag on the image, dragging down until the two middle images snap to the bottom edge of the visible image.

22 Press ⌘+minus sign (Ctrl+minus sign) to zoom out.

23 Click Image.

24 Click Reveal All.

The window displays all four images in a quadrant.

TIPS

More Options!

To add space around the images, click the Crop tool (🔲) and select Original Ratio from the drop-down menu. Click and drag to expand the canvas with a reverse crop as in task #32. Then click each layer and use the arrow keys to move the layers individually the same number of steps. Click the New Layer button (🔲) and drag the new blank layer below the four photo layers. Click Edit ➪ Fill and select a color from the Color Picker to fill the layer with color before flattening the image.

Did You Know?

On a Mac, the Application frame groups all the workspace elements into one window. You can move or resize the Application frame or any of its elements, and all the parts correspond, avoiding any overlapping panels and tools.

Did You Know?

When the two images meet as you click and drag one image to the edge of another (in steps 19 and 21) the black arrow of the Move tool changes to a white arrow.

CHANGE YOUR PERSPECTIVE with the Crop tool

When you photograph an object from an angle rather than from a straight-on view, the object appears out of perspective, displaying *keystone distortion*. The top edges of a tall building, for example, photographed from ground level, appear closer to each other at the top than they do at the bottom. If you photograph a window and cannot get directly in front of it to take the shot, the window appears more like a trapezoid. Depending on the photograph, you can correct this type of distortion with a number of Photoshop's tools.

The Crop tool in Photoshop has a special option that enables you to transform the perspective in an image and quickly adjust the keystone distortion. Your image must have an object that was rectangular in the original scene for the Crop tool's perspective function to work properly. You first adjust the cropping marquee to match the rectangular object's edges and then extend the marquee to fit your image. When you click the Commit button, Photoshop crops the image as large as possible while maintaining the angles of the rectangular object.

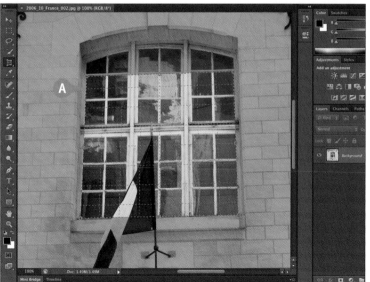

1 Open a photo containing a distorted rectangular object.

2 Press ⌘+spacebar (Ctrl+spacebar) and click and drag in the image to zoom in.

3 Click and hold the Crop tool.

4 Click Perspective Crop Tool.

5 Click each corner of a rectangular object.

Note: The image moves across the window as you drag the Perspective Crop tool, so you can place each perspective anchor on a corner while the image is in the zoomed view.

A A crop marquee surrounds the area to be straightened.

6 Press Option+spacebar (Alt+spacebar) and click and drag in the image to zoom out.

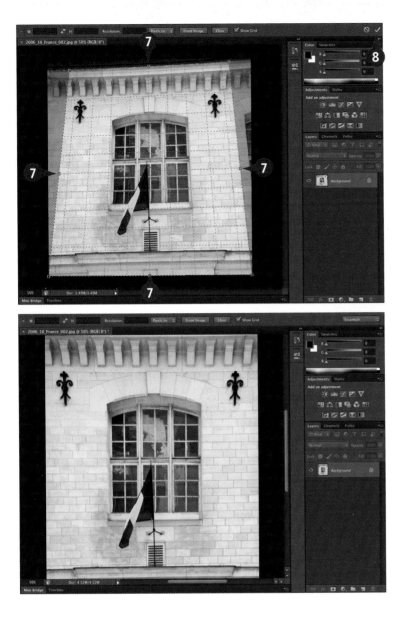

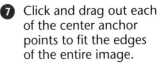

7 Click and drag out each of the center anchor points to fit the edges of the entire image.

8 Click the Commit button in the Options bar to commit the crop.

Photoshop realigns the image and improves the perspective.

TIPS

Attention!

The Crop tool (⬚) may not fix the perspective distortion of an image that has already been cropped for size. Also, if the perspective crop does not look straight, you may not have placed the corner handles precisely. Click the Cancel button (⊘) in the Options bar and try readjusting the cropping marquee.

Keyboard Shortcuts!

Press C to access the Crop tool. Press Return (Enter) to commit the perspective crop or Esc to cancel it, or Control+click (right-click) the image and select Crop or Cancel from the menu.

Important!

If there are any settings for width, height, or resolution in the Options bar with the Perspective Crop tool selected, be sure to click Clear before starting to place the crop corners.

CORRECT GEOMETRIC DISTORTION with the
Lens Correction filter

Depending on the focal length of a camera lens or the f-stop used, a photograph may show common lens flaws such as barrel and pincushion distortion. *Barrel distortion* causes straight lines to bow out toward the edges of the image. *Pincushion distortion* displays the opposite effect, where straight lines bend inward. If the camera tilts up or down or at any angle, the perspective also appears distorted. The Lens Correction filter in Photoshop can help you correct these and other lens defects.

The Lens Correction filter in Photoshop includes an automatic correction based on specific lens profiles. If your lens and camera are listed in the profiles, you can click the option to automatically correct geometric distortion as well as remove a *vignette*, the appearance of darker corners or edges in the image, and any chromatic edge discolorations, called *chromatic aberration*.

You can also choose to correct the distortions manually using the tools on the left of the Lens Correction dialog box. You can line up the perspective of the buildings with a vertical plane and even turn on the filter's image grid to make your adjustments more accurately.

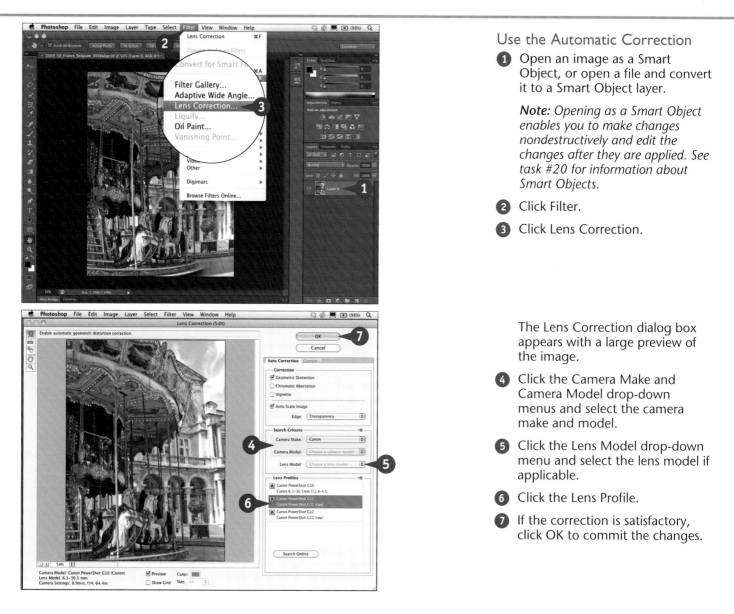

Use the Automatic Correction

1 Open an image as a Smart Object, or open a file and convert it to a Smart Object layer.

Note: *Opening as a Smart Object enables you to make changes nondestructively and edit the changes after they are applied. See task #20 for information about Smart Objects.*

2 Click Filter.

3 Click Lens Correction.

The Lens Correction dialog box appears with a large preview of the image.

4 Click the Camera Make and Camera Model drop-down menus and select the camera make and model.

5 Click the Lens Model drop-down menu and select the lens model if applicable.

6 Click the Lens Profile.

7 If the correction is satisfactory, click OK to commit the changes.

Use the Custom Correction

1. Repeat steps 1 to 3 from the previous set of steps.

2. Click the Custom tab.

3. Click Show Grid (☐ changes to ☑).

4. Drag the Vertical Perspective slider to align the building with the grid.

   Note: The type of distortion in the image determines what sliders to adjust.

5. Click and drag any of the other sliders to adjust the image.

6. Click OK to commit the changes and reopen the photo in Photoshop.

   The image reopens in Photoshop with a changed perspective plane.

A. You can optionally click the Crop tool and crop the image to fit if necessary.

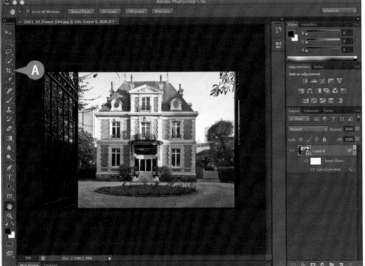

TIPS

Try This!

In the Lens Correction dialog box, click the Auto Scale Image check box (☐ changes to ☑) and select Edge Extension from the drop-down menu. Photoshop automatically tries to fill the empty corrected areas with areas similar to the edges of the photo.

Did You Know?

If your camera or lens model is not listed, you can click the Lens Profiles panel menu button (▼≡) and select Browse Adobe Lens Profile Creator Online. You can then search online for profiles created and uploaded by other photographers, and even try them in an online preview mode before you save the profile locally to your computer.

More Options!

You can also download the Adobe Lens Profile Creator tool from http://labs.adobe.com to generate your own custom camera and lens profiles. You can save the profiles to a folder for use with Photoshop and Camera Raw, as well as Lightroom. You can also send the profiles to Adobe to share with other photographers.

IMPROVE THE FIELD OF VIEW with the Adaptive Wide Angle filter

The Lens Correction filter in the previous task is used to correct lens aberrations and geometric distortion and is applied globally to images. However, using the Lens Correction filter to correct the distortion in a photo taken with a fisheye or a very large field-of-view lens may not always give a visually pleasing result. The Adaptive Wide Angle Correction filter, new in Photoshop CS6, is intended to fix visual distortion on areas near an edge or the bending of straight lines characteristic of photos taken with wide-angle lenses and fisheye lenses.

The filter reads the metadata from the photo file to deduce the focal length and crop factor. You can apply an auto wide-angle lens correction if the filter can find a profile for the specific camera and lens combination used to take the photo. You can also select a lens type, perspective, or fisheye, and specify which lines should be straight by adding both horizontal and vertical constraints. You can continue to adjust the photo until the scene more closely reflects a natural view, and then crop it as necessary in Photoshop.

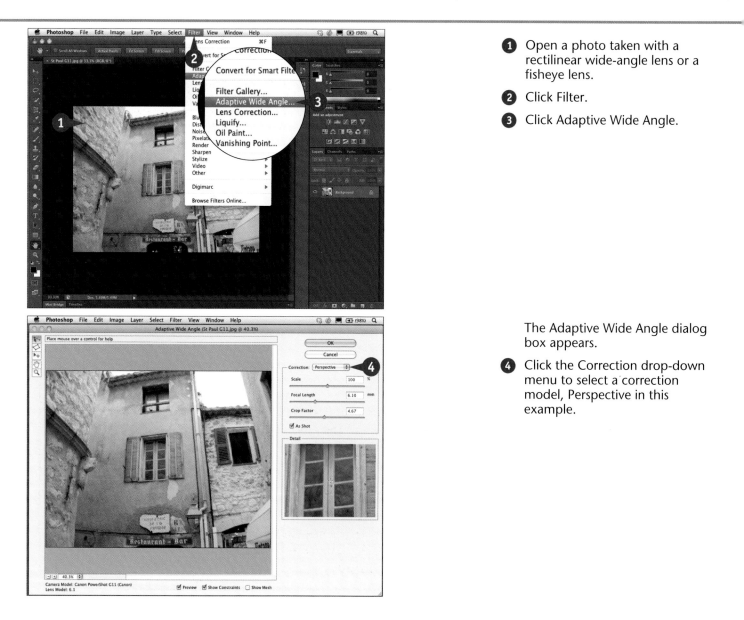

1 Open a photo taken with a rectilinear wide-angle lens or a fisheye lens.

2 Click Filter.

3 Click Adaptive Wide Angle.

The Adaptive Wide Angle dialog box appears.

4 Click the Correction drop-down menu to select a correction model, Perspective in this example.

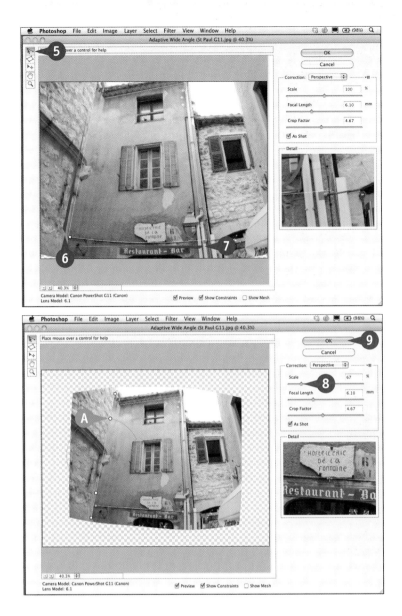

5 Click the Constraint tool.

6 Click and drag along a visually distorted line.

DIFFICULTY LEVEL

The line straightens and the image adjusts in that area.

7 Repeat step 6 on other vertical or horizontal lines.

The image continues to adjust according to the constraint lines.

A Each constraint line also has an angle constraint circle with two anchor points. Click an anchor point and drag to adjust the angle of the line as needed.

8 Click and drag the Scale slider to the left if necessary to view the adjusted photo.

9 Click OK.

The adjusted photo reappears in Photoshop, where you can crop away the excess background area using the Crop tool.

TIPS

Did You Know?

You can click and drag along multiple vertical and horizontal lines with the Constraint tool (🔲) to correct the wide angle distortion. To delete a constraint line, click one of the end points and press Delete (Backspace).

Try This!

Press Shift as you click and drag a constraint line. Or Shift+click any of the constraints you already placed on the image. The constraint forces the line in the photo to be either perfectly vertical or horizontal. Depending on the photo, the correction may look realistic or it may completely distort the perspective.

Important!

The Adaptive Wide Angle filter helps straighten bending lines to make a wide-angle photo more closely resemble human perception. It does not correct for vignetting or chromatic aberrations.

You can combine multiple photographs into one continuous image to create a panorama. For example, you can take two or more overlapping photographs of a scenic horizon, or even a number of scans of parts of a large document, and then assemble them in Photoshop with the Photomerge command. You can combine photos tiled horizontally as well as vertically.

The Photomerge command in Photoshop can automatically position and blend each layer using individual layer masks. You can start with the files open, or you can use the Photomerge dialog box to search for the images to use.

To make any Photomerge project as successful as possible, photos or scans intended for merging should have an overlap of 25 to 40 percent. You should also maintain the same exposure for each photograph or keep the same scanning settings for each scan. If you are shooting the photos, use a tripod to keep the camera level so the photos line up correctly. By shooting in the Portrait mode or vertically, and shooting more images, you have a larger area to crop from for your final image, giving you a better result.

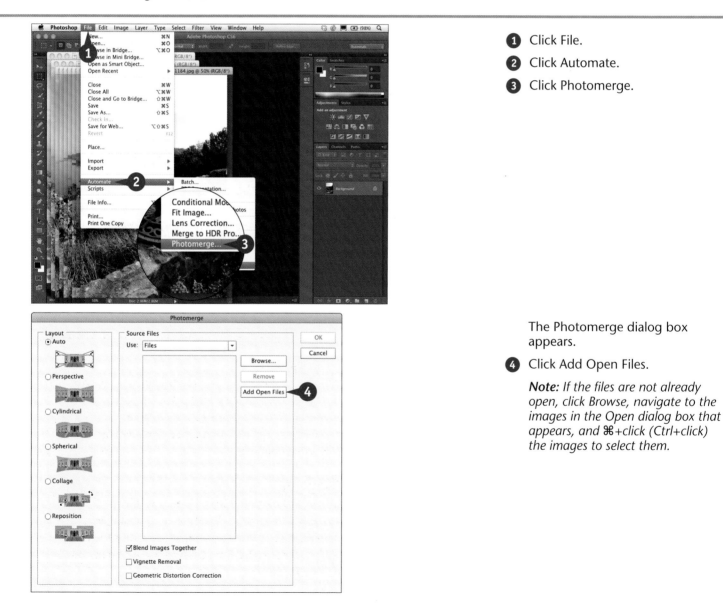

1 Click File.

2 Click Automate.

3 Click Photomerge.

The Photomerge dialog box appears.

4 Click Add Open Files.

Note: If the files are not already open, click Browse, navigate to the images in the Open dialog box that appears, and ⌘+click (Ctrl+click) the images to select them.

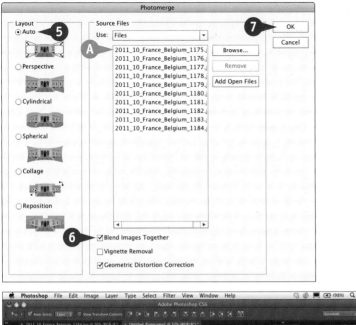

Ⓐ The open files are listed in the dialog box.

❺ Click Auto to select the automatic layout (◻ changes to ◉).

Note: If you shot a series of images that cover 360 degrees, use the Spherical alignment option (◻ changes to ◉).

❻ Make sure that Blend Images Together is selected.

Note: Depending on the images, you can also select Vignette Removal and Geometric Distortion Correction.

❼ Click OK.

Photoshop aligns the images based on content and blends them into a single image.

Note: The new image is a multilayered file.

❽ Click the Crop tool.

❾ Click and drag across the blended image to make your final panorama.

❿ Adjust the corner anchors to fit your image.

⓫ Press Return (Enter) or click the Commit button to complete the crop.

The panorama is cropped to the selected edges.

TIPS

Did You Know?

Each layout option in the Photomerge dialog box (step 5) aligns the merged images in different ways. **Auto** applies either a Perspective, Cylindrical, or Spherical layout based on the overall content. **Perspective** uses one image as a reference and adjusts the perspective of the others by overlapping the content of the reference image. **Cylindrical** reduces the bowed shape that can occur in some merged photos, and **Spherical** has the opposite effect. **Collage** and **Reposition** help Photoshop align uneven images.

More Options!

Select Vignette Removal (◻ changes to ☑) if your images have darkened edges caused by a particular lens. Select Geometric Distortion Correction (◻ changes to ☑) to compensate for barrel or other lens distortions.

Change It!

You can add more files to the merge by clicking the Browse button again in the Photomerge dialog box, and navigating to the new source files to be added. You can remove a file from the list by selecting the file and clicking Remove.

You often need a different size image than the original. You can resize images using the Image Size dialog box.

By deselecting the Resample Image check box in the dialog box, you can adjust the width, height, or resolution without affecting image quality or pixel dimensions. However, to change the overall size of an image, you must check the Resample Image box, and Photoshop resamples by adding or removing pixels to adjust for the changes.

Photoshop's *interpolation algorithm* — the way that it assigns values to added pixels and smoothes transitions between juxtaposing pixels — works well to preserve the quality and detail as long as the size changes are not extreme. Third-party plug-ins such

as Alien Skin's Blow Up, OnOne's Perfect Resize Pro, and AKVIS Magnifier sometimes get better results when enlarging greater than 150 to 200 percent, depending on the image.

The generally recommended resampling method for reducing image size is Bicubic Sharper, and Bicubic Smoother is intended for enlarging. Photoshop CS6 now includes Bicubic Automatic, which selects the best resample method based on the type of resize. However, depending on the image, many photographers find that the Bicubic Sharper resampling method actually works best both for enlarging and reducing photos.

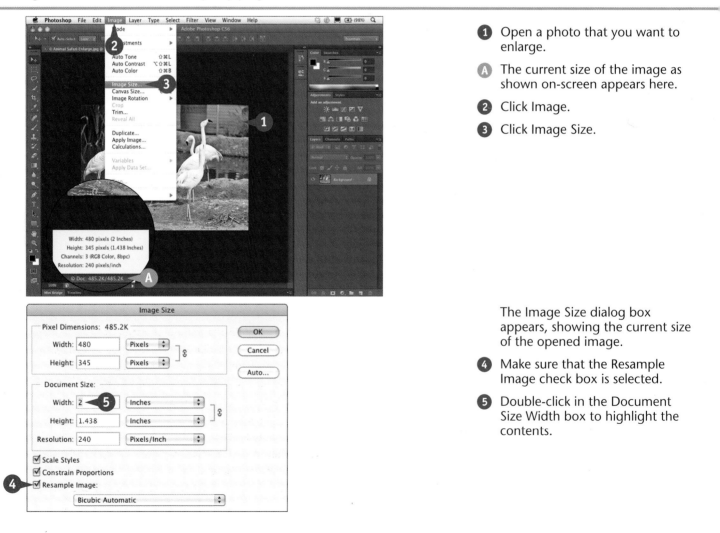

1 Open a photo that you want to enlarge.

A The current size of the image as shown on-screen appears here.

2 Click Image.

3 Click Image Size.

The Image Size dialog box appears, showing the current size of the opened image.

4 Make sure that the Resample Image check box is selected.

5 Double-click in the Document Size Width box to highlight the contents.

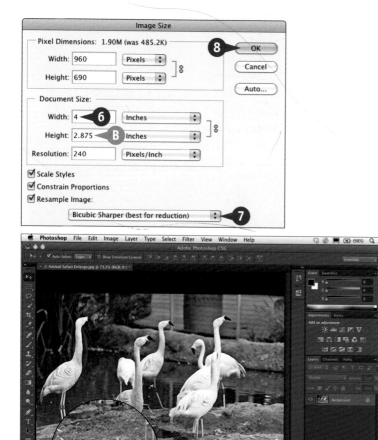

6 Type the width that you want for the final printed image.

B The height automatically adjusts proportionally.

7 Click the drop-down menu and select Bicubic Sharper (best for reduction).

8 Click OK.

A progress bar may appear depending on the speed of the computer's processor and the size of the image as Photoshop processes the enlargement.

The enlarged photo appears.

9 Click here to check the file size in the window frame.

TIPS

Test It!

Make two copies of an image. Enlarge the first using Bicubic Smoother and the second using Bicubic Sharper. Crop the same 4-×-6-inch section on both enlargements and paste these into two new documents. Because resampling may reduce detail and sharpness, you can apply the Smart Sharpen filter with the same settings to each new document and print them for comparison.

Did You Know?

A resolution of 150 to 360 ppi is generally recommended for inkjet printing. Images for on-screen viewing need only a resolution of 72 ppi. Images intended for a printing press require a resolution of twice the *line screen* of the press, referring to the number of lines of dots that appear per linear inch (lpi) on the printed piece. If the line screen is 133 lpi, the resolution should be 266 ppi. Rounding up to 300 ppi is generally recommended.

Retouch Portraits

You can use Photoshop to give your subjects a digital makeover and make them look more beautiful, younger, and healthier. However, altering images in Photoshop is so easy that new users often overdo it and make people look like plastic versions of themselves. You are trying to enhance a person's best features and minimize other areas, not turn him into someone else. If your subject looks at his photo and thinks that he looks good, you have done your job well.

You can use the tools in Photoshop to remove spots and blemishes, enhance the eyes, whiten teeth, soften the face, and more. You can also change a model's eye color to fit a client's request. You can enhance a portrait by adding a catchlight to the eyes, even if the camera did

not capture one. You can even reduce wrinkles and smooth the skin without plastic surgery.

Applying the enhancements on separate layers enables you to preserve the original image as well as blend or reduce the changes, making them appear more natural. You can keep all the layers and continue to make small adjustments. To finalize the image, select Flatten Image from the Layer menu before saving it with a new name. Like a magician, you should not reveal your tricks or show the original unretouched photo to the subject!

Because these enhancements should be subtle, a pen tablet is particularly useful when retouching portraits.

DIFFICULTY LEVEL

You can greatly improve a portrait with some simple steps in Photoshop. You can remove skin imperfections such as blemishes and liver spots. You can remove them all, or leave some while making them less obvious.

As with many other projects in Photoshop, you can use a variety of tools to reduce or remove spots and blemishes. Depending on the areas that need to be retouched, the Clone Stamp tool, the Patch tool, and the Healing Brush can all be used; however, the Spot Healing Brush in content-aware mode is often the most

effective tool for removing small imperfections. The Spot Healing Brush automatically samples the areas around the spot to be removed and blends the pixels so you do not need to specify the source sample. The key to using the Spot Healing Brush on skin is to work in stages on separate layers and to adjust the brush as you work such that the brush size is just slightly larger than the area needing correction.

You can then change the opacity of each layer and make the changes less obvious. If you do not like the changes, you can simply discard the layers.

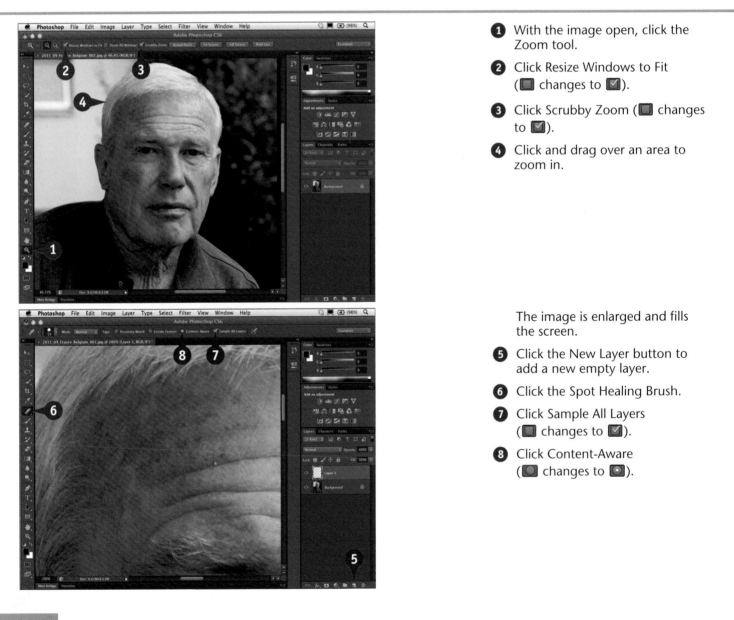

1. With the image open, click the Zoom tool.

2. Click Resize Windows to Fit (🔲 changes to ☑).

3. Click Scrubby Zoom (🔲 changes to ☑).

4. Click and drag over an area to zoom in.

The image is enlarged and fills the screen.

5. Click the New Layer button to add a new empty layer.

6. Click the Spot Healing Brush.

7. Click Sample All Layers (🔲 changes to ☑).

8. Click Content-Aware (⚪ changes to ⚫).

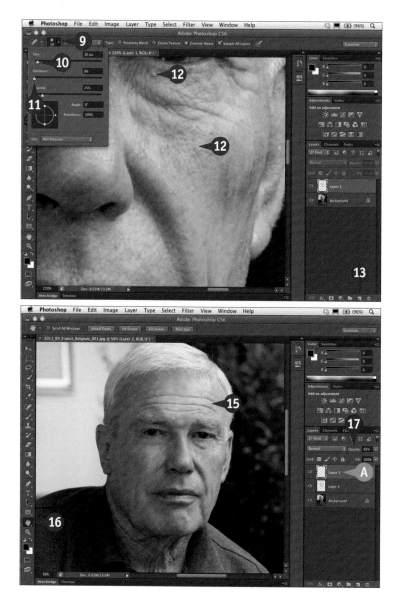

9 Click the Brush Preset drop-down menu to open the Brush picker.

10 Move the Size slider to set a brush just larger than the spot you want to remove.

11 Move the Hardness slider to 0% for a soft brush.

12 Click each of the worst areas of a similar size first.

Photoshop removes the spots and blends the surrounding skin area.

Note: Press the spacebar and click and drag around the photo to repair other areas.

13 Click the New Layer button to add another empty layer.

14 Press the left bracket key to reduce the brush size or the right bracket key to increase the size.

A Layer 2 should be highlighted in the Layers panel.

15 Click the other areas to be corrected.

16 Double-click the Hand tool or use the Zoom tool so the entire face is visible.

17 With Layer 2 selected, click Opacity and drag to the left until the skin looks natural.

#39

DIFFICULTY LEVEL

TIPS

More Options!

Once you have finished removing the spots or blemishes, you can combine the spot-repair layers by selecting the top one and pressing ⌘+E (Ctrl+E), leaving just one spot layer and the original Background layer. You can then quickly compare the before and after images by turning on and off the eye icon (👁) for the spot layer.

Did You Know?

If you use a pen tablet rather than a mouse, you can set the size in the Brush picker to respond to Pen Pressure. Then set the initial brush size to be just larger than the largest spot or blemish. To vary the size as you brush, press harder to remove large areas and press lightly to remove smaller areas.

The Spot Healing Brush generally removes blemishes and imperfections and makes the skin appear cleaner. However, the liver spots and blemishes often discolor the surrounding skin tone, and removing them can leave spots or streaks of mismatched colors on your subject. You can add another layer to smooth any blotches the Healing Brush may have left and improve the overall skin tone at the same time.

You can use many different tools and methods to improve skin. This particular technique enables you to control the amount of tonal adjustment by working on a neutral gray layer in the Overlay blending mode. Painting with white and black on the layer mimics dodging and burning but with much more control, so you can adjust the skin without making the photo appear retouched and without altering your original file.

This skin-smoothing technique was perfected by Jane Conner-ziser, one of the most experienced and well-respected portrait retouching professionals in the industry. You can learn more about Jane's many classes and seminars at www.janeconner-ziser.com.

18 Press Option (Alt) and click the New Layer button.

The New Layer dialog box appears.

19 Type a name such as Skin Tone in the Name field.

20 Click the Mode drop-down menu and select Overlay.

21 Click Fill with Overlay-Neutral Color (50% Gray) (☐ changes to ☑).

22 Click OK.

A A gray layer in Overlay mode appears in the Layers panel.

23 Click the Brush tool (🖌).

24 Click the Brush Preset drop-down menu and click a soft-edged brush.

25 Click Opacity and drag to the left to reduce the brush opacity to about 3%.

26 Click the Default Colors icon to reset the default colors to black and white.

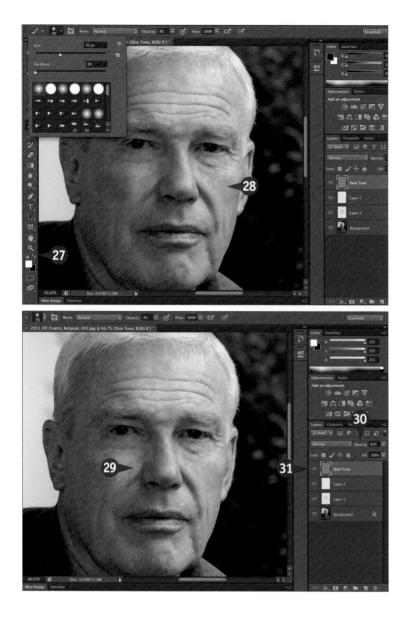

27 Click the Switch Colors icon to reverse the colors, making white the foreground color.

28 Paint over any dark spots in the image to smooth the skin.

The skin tone appears smoother.

Note: The skin tone changes are very subtle and should be more visible on your monitor and on a printed photo than in the photo in this task.

29 Continue painting over any dark areas, adjusting the size of the Brush tool as necessary.

30 Click Opacity and drag to the left to reduce the effect for a more natural look.

31 Click the eye icon for the gray layer multiple times, turning it off and on to compare the image before and after the adjustment.

The skin tone is smoothed and appears natural rather than over-corrected.

TIPS

More Options!
You can press X to reverse the background and foreground colors and paint with black to darken any areas that appear too light. However, if your image starts to appear unnatural, open the History panel and click back several steps to undo the changes. Then continue painting until the skin tone appears natural.

Attention!
You may not see much of a change as you paint with the brush opacity set to 3%; however, when you turn off the eye icon ( ) for the layer, you will definitely see the changes. You can increase or decrease the brush opacity one or two percent, brush over an area, and then check the changes by toggling on and off the eye icon.

REDUCE WRINKLES for a more youthful appearance

You can remove wrinkles with Photoshop in a variety of ways, and with a variety of Photoshop tools. However, if you remove all the wrinkles and give a person perfectly smooth skin, the effect is not believable. By using the Spot Healing Brush in content-aware mode and working on separate layers, you can maintain more control over the corrections and give your subject a rejuvenated yet natural appearance.

You can modify the Spot Healing Brush to a medium softness and change its shape and angle so that your brush strokes are not as visible when you literally paint to reduce the wrinkles. A pressure-sensitive pen tablet is particularly useful for this task because you can set the Spot Healing Brush to respond to pressure and then gently paint over the lines, using multiple light strokes.

You can create multiple layers and remove the wrinkles on one area of the face on each layer. After you brush away the years, you can change the opacity of the altered layers individually to reintroduce just enough wrinkles to appear natural.

Note: Photograph copyright © Photospin.com.

① Click the Zoom tool and zoom in to enlarge the areas with wrinkles.

② Click the New Layer button to add a new empty layer.

③ Click the Spot Healing Brush.

④ Click Sample All Layers (☐ changes to ☑).

⑤ Click Content-Aware (◐ changes to ◉).

⑥ Click the Brush Preset drop-down menu to open the Brush picker.

⑦ Click and drag the Size slider to change the brush width to cover the deepest wrinkles.

⑧ Click and drag the Hardness slider to the midpoint to build a brush with slightly soft edges.

⑨ Click here and drag toward the center to change the roundness of the brush.

⑩ Click and drag the arrowhead to change the angle of the stroke in the direction of the deepest wrinkles.

⑪ Click and drag directly on the deepest wrinkles to paint them away.

⑫ Click the New Layer button to add a new empty layer.

⑬ Repeat steps 6 to 10, changing the brush angle and roundness for smaller wrinkles.

40

DIFFICULTY LEVEL

⑭ Press ⌘+Option (Ctrl+Alt) and click and drag in the image to zoom out.

⑮ With the top layer selected, click Opacity and drag to the left until the wrinkles appear diminished and still natural.

⑯ Repeat step 15 for any other wrinkle layers.

The wrinkles on the face are less pronounced, and the person appears slightly rested and younger.

TIPS

Did You Know?

If you use many small strokes rather than one larger one and change the size and angle of the brush according to the area of the wrinkle, the skin tones match more closely, and the results appear more natural.

More Options!

You can create a special wrinkle-removing brush by changing attributes in the Brush picker in the Options bar and saving your wrinkle remover as a brush preset in the Brush picker.

Try This!

You need to zoom in and out often when removing wrinkles. Instead of changing tools when the Spot Healing Brush is selected, press ⌘+spacebar (Ctrl+spacebar) and click to zoom in. Press Option+spacebar (Alt+spacebar) to zoom out. On a Mac, unless you have previously changed the default keystrokes for the Spotlight feature to something like ⌘+Control+spacebar, the Spotlight momentarily opens with the same keystrokes as those for zooming in (⌘+spacebar). Either way, using ⌘+spacebar in Photoshop still zooms in.

SOFTEN THE SKIN naturally

Even after repairing spots and blemishes, blending the tones, and reducing wrinkles, you may still need to soften skin to make your subjects look their best. Digital cameras are very good at capturing all the details, including rough skin. In theory, skin softening with Photoshop involves a simple blurring of a duplicate layer with a Gaussian Blur filter or a noise reduction filter, and the use of a layer mask so the effect can be brushed on the face where needed. Other techniques start with selections of the face avoiding the eyes, nose, and mouth. The selection is

placed on a separate layer and blurred, and the blurred layer blended into the main photo using layer blend modes.

Too often, the resulting image looks badly retouched, showing blurry skin with sharp sections for the eyes, nose, and mouth.

You can create a custom skin-softening filter using two separate layers with different filter strengths and different opacity settings, and then brush the filter over the skin with much more control. The steps are more involved, but the results are far more natural.

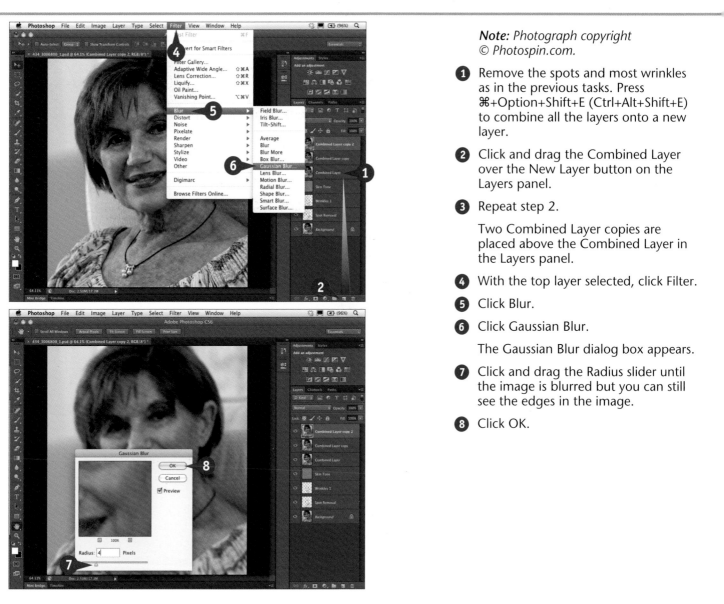

Note: Photograph copyright © Photospin.com.

1 Remove the spots and most wrinkles as in the previous tasks. Press ⌘+Option+Shift+E (Ctrl+Alt+Shift+E) to combine all the layers onto a new layer.

2 Click and drag the Combined Layer over the New Layer button on the Layers panel.

3 Repeat step 2.

Two Combined Layer copies are placed above the Combined Layer in the Layers panel.

4 With the top layer selected, click Filter.

5 Click Blur.

6 Click Gaussian Blur.

The Gaussian Blur dialog box appears.

7 Click and drag the Radius slider until the image is blurred but you can still see the edges in the image.

8 Click OK.

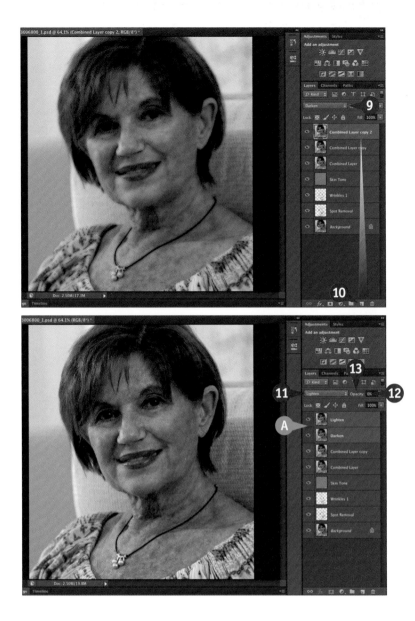

A Gaussian Blur is applied to the Combined Layer copy 2.

9 Click the blend mode drop-down menu and select Darken.

10 Click and drag the Combined Layer copy 2 over the New Layer button on the Layers panel.

The blurred layer is duplicated.

11 Click the blend mode drop-down menu and select Lighten.

A You can optionally rename the top layer Lighten and the next layer down Darken.

12 Click in the Opacity field to reduce the opacity to zero for each of the top two layers.

13 Click and drag the Opacity slider of the top layer slowly to the right.

TIPS

Did You Know?
The Darken blend mode spreads the shadows in the image. The Lighten blend mode spreads the highlights.

More Options!
You can record an action so you can create the skin-softening filter quickly when you need it. Make sure to set the action to stop so you can determine the amount of Gaussian Blur according to the details in the particular photograph. See task #9 for more about actions.

Did You Know?
Each of the layers with the Gaussian Blur applied will probably be at different opacities to get the most natural softening effect.

To create the skin-softening filter, you combine two separate Gaussian Blur layers into a layer group. Layer groups not only make your Layers panel more organized; you can use them to turn off the visibility of multiple layers at once, and move or duplicate all the layers in a group at once. You can also change the opacity of a layer group, thereby altering the opacity of every layer in the group. And you can add a layer mask to a layer group to apply effects by combining the attributes of all the layers in the group.

The settings you use depend on the subject in your particular image and the overall dimensions of the photograph. And depending on the image and how much area you need to soften, you can either brush the effect on the skin by painting with white on a black layer mask, or by applying the filter to the entire image, and then painting with black on a white layer mask to reveal the areas that need to stay sharp.

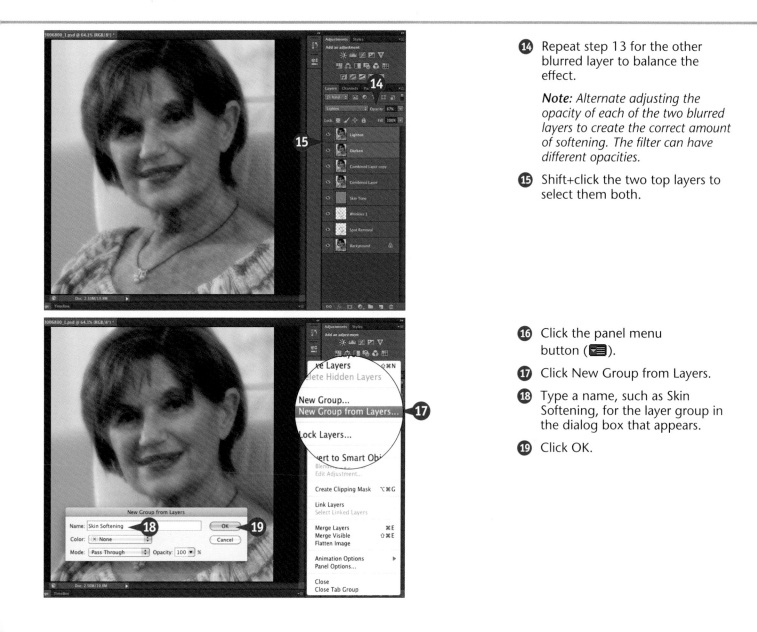

14 Repeat step 13 for the other blurred layer to balance the effect.

Note: Alternate adjusting the opacity of each of the two blurred layers to create the correct amount of softening. The filter can have different opacities.

15 Shift+click the two top layers to select them both.

16 Click the panel menu button (▤).

17 Click New Group from Layers.

18 Type a name, such as Skin Softening, for the layer group in the dialog box that appears.

19 Click OK.

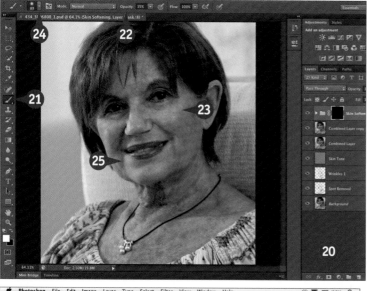

The two blurred layers are combined in a layer group folder.

⑳ Option+click (Alt+click) the Layer Mask button in the Layers panel.

A black-filled layer mask is added to the layer group and the foreground color is set to white.

㉑ Click the Brush tool.

㉒ Click the Brush Opacity slider to 35%.

㉓ Paint over the skin where it needs softening.

㉔ Click the Brush Preset drop-down menu and reduce the brush size.

㉕ Continue painting over smaller areas to soften the skin.

Note: To maintain the sharpness of the image, avoid painting over edges.

The skin is softened as you paint over the areas.

㉖ Click and drag the Opacity for the layer group to 0 and then slowly drag it to the right until the skin appears smoothed.

㉗ Click the panel menu button and select Flatten Image.

#41

TIPS

More Options!
If you accidentally paint over areas in the photo that should be sharp edges, such as the nostrils or eyes, in step 23, you can quickly revert the areas by pressing X to reverse the background and foreground colors. Set the brush to 100% opacity and paint with black over the areas that should remain sharp.

Important!
You should apply the filter delicately just where it is needed and avoid any edges and areas that should remain sharp, such as the eyes, eyebrows, lips, nostrils, hair, and edges of the nose and face.

Try This!
Whenever you need to adjust the Opacity slider for a layer, try moving it first completely to the left to remove the effect, and then slowly move it to the right until just the right amount is applied.

REMOVE THE GLARE *from eyeglasses*

Portraits of people with eyeglasses can be particularly challenging. Even the so called nonglare lenses can cause reflections, glare, and ghosting across the lenses in a photo. Professional photographers try to avoid the glare by repositioning the lights or even angling the eyeglasses slightly by tipping up the earpieces, so the plane of the lens is not pointing directly at the camera and lights. They might also photograph the subject both with and without glasses at every head position, so they can correct the glare in Photoshop by copying

pieces of the eyes without glasses onto the image with the glasses.

If you have only the one photograph, you can use this cloning technique along with a bit of digital dodging and burning to remove the glare. You should work on a duplicated Background layer and zoom in as far as needed, even more than 100% if necessary to sample areas with a small brush from the sides of the glare. By working on small areas on a separate layer you can slowly build up the photo to conceal the glare and then dodge and burn to blend the pixels.

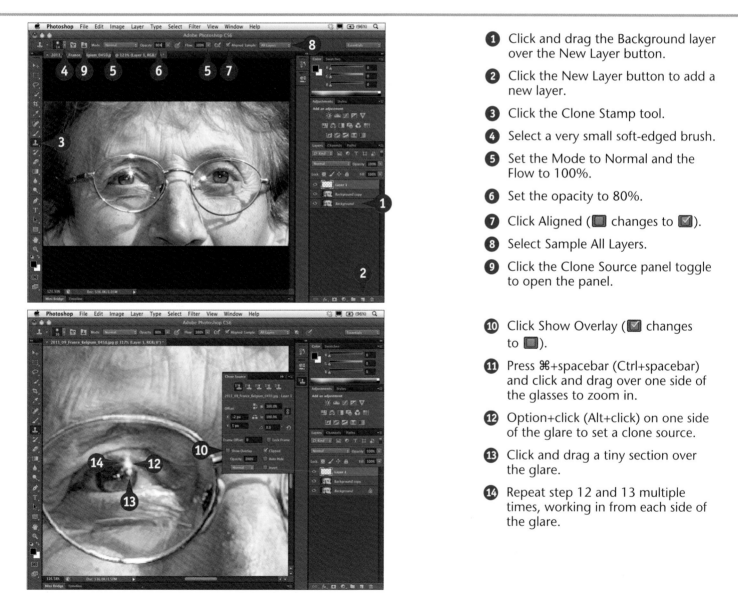

① Click and drag the Background layer over the New Layer button.

② Click the New Layer button to add a new layer.

③ Click the Clone Stamp tool.

④ Select a very small soft-edged brush.

⑤ Set the Mode to Normal and the Flow to 100%.

⑥ Set the opacity to 80%.

⑦ Click Aligned (☐ changes to ☑).

⑧ Select Sample All Layers.

⑨ Click the Clone Source panel toggle to open the panel.

⑩ Click Show Overlay (☑ changes to ☐).

⑪ Press ⌘+spacebar (Ctrl+spacebar) and click and drag over one side of the glasses to zoom in.

⑫ Option+click (Alt+click) on one side of the glare to set a clone source.

⑬ Click and drag a tiny section over the glare.

⑭ Repeat step 12 and 13 multiple times, working in from each side of the glare.

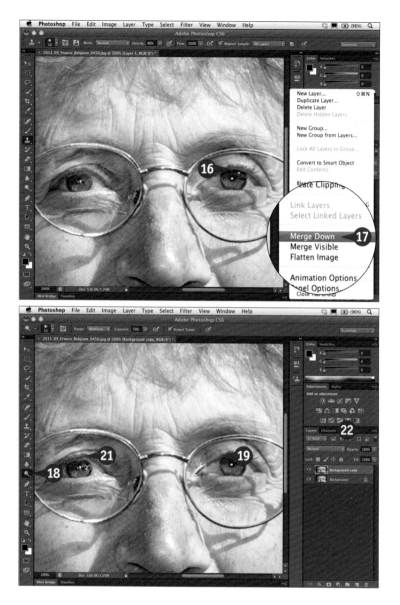

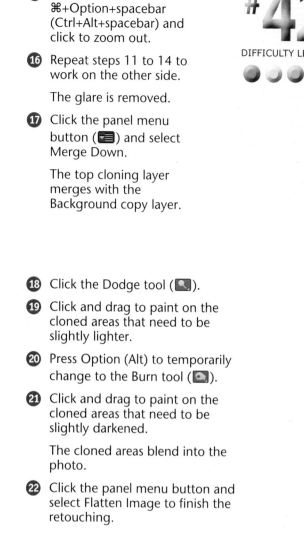

⑮ Press
⌘+Option+spacebar
(Ctrl+Alt+spacebar) and
click to zoom out.

⑯ Repeat steps 11 to 14 to
work on the other side.

The glare is removed.

⑰ Click the panel menu
button (▤) and select
Merge Down.

The top cloning layer
merges with the
Background copy layer.

⑱ Click the Dodge tool (🔍).

⑲ Click and drag to paint on the
cloned areas that need to be
slightly lighter.

⑳ Press Option (Alt) to temporarily
change to the Burn tool (🖐).

㉑ Click and drag to paint on the
cloned areas that need to be
slightly darkened.

The cloned areas blend into the
photo.

㉒ Click the panel menu button and
select Flatten Image to finish the
retouching.

#42

DIFFICULTY LEVEL

⬤ ◯ ◯ ⬤

TIPS

Try This!
You can click the Dodge tool to select it and then
press Option (Alt) to quickly switch back and forth
with the Burn tool.

Did You Know?
Dodging and burning reduce the contrast between
pixels, so the photo gets a little softer. However, in this
project the softness helps to blend the areas. Make
sure you use a very small brush size for the tool so
you do not over-soften the area.

More Options!
If one side has a lot of glare, and the other side is
pretty clear, you can try selecting small areas of the
clear side, copying and pasting them to the glare side,
and then using the Transformation tools to reposition
the areas. Be careful not to reverse the location of any
catchlights or other differences, so the photo looks
realistic.

CHANGE EYE COLOR digitally

Eye color often appears grayer or darker in photos than the actual color of the eyes in real life. You can improve many photos by adding a little color to the iris of the eyes. You can simply add a little more color or you can change the color to a different hue.

When you colorize the eyes, you are looking for a natural eye color. You can also select any color as the foreground color and paint-in the irises. If you have another photo of the same person where the eye color appears more natural, you can sample the eye color from the first photo and paint it into the one

with the grayed eyes. The specific brush options you set in the Options bar are key to colorizing the eyes to appear natural.

You can also use the same technique to apply one person's eye color to another subject's eyes. Agencies often request a specific eye color for a model to better blend into the color scheme of an advertising piece. You can save time by using Photoshop to change the eye color in the original photo and avoid finding and photographing a different model.

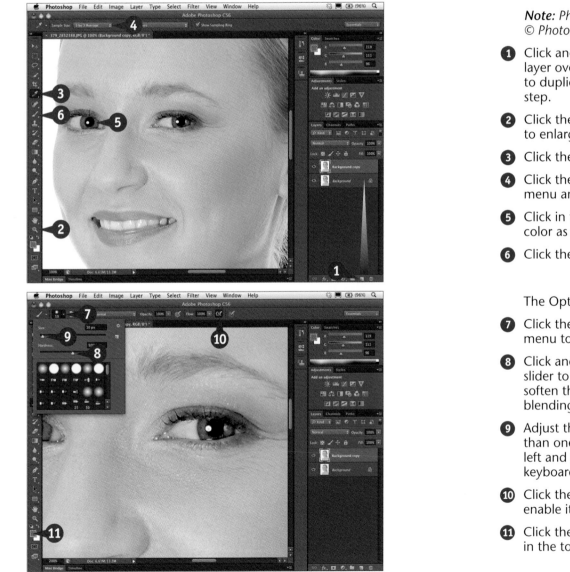

Note: Photograph copyright © Photospin.com.

1 Click and drag the Background layer over the New Layer button to duplicate the layer as a safety step.

2 Click the Zoom tool and zoom in to enlarge the eyes.

3 Click the Eyedropper tool.

4 Click the Sample Size drop-down menu and select 3 by 3 Average.

5 Click in the iris to set a reference color as the foreground color.

6 Click the Brush tool.

The Options bar changes.

7 Click the Brush Preset drop-down menu to open the Brush picker.

8 Click and drag the Hardness slider to 50% to only slightly soften the brush edge for better blending.

9 Adjust the brush size just smaller than one-half the iris using the left and right bracket keys on the keyboard.

10 Click the Airbrush button to enable it.

11 Click the Foreground Color box in the toolbar.

The Color Picker appears.

12 Click and drag the Hue slider to another color.

13 Click OK to close the Color Picker.

#43

DIFFICULTY LEVEL

14 Click the New Layer button to add a new empty layer.

15 Click the blend mode drop-down menu and select Color.

16 Click and drag over both irises to paint-in the new color.

17 Click the Eraser tool and erase if you paint over other areas.

18 Click Opacity and drag to the left until the eye color appears natural.

The irises of the eyes are now a different color.

TIPS

More Options!

If you have another photo with an appropriate eye color, you can use the Color Replacement tool (⬛) instead of the standard Brush tool. The tools are in the same group in the toolbar. Option+click (Alt+click) in the first photo using the Color Replacement tool to sample the color of the eyes that you want to use. Then apply the color on the empty layer of the image you are correcting using a soft-edged brush.

Did You Know?

Dog and cat eyes often show a greenish or white eye when they are photographed with a flash. The Red Eye tool (⬛) does not remove that effect. You can, however, paint-in the eye color using the techniques described in this task.

LIGHTEN THE IRISES with a gradient layer

The eyes are generally considered the most important feature in a portrait. You can add interest to the eyes and draw the viewer in by giving the eyes a digital brightening effect. You can improve the eyes in a variety of ways in Photoshop. Some methods work better on one image than another, so learning and trying various techniques lets you improve your images according to your subject and the project's requirements.

You must apply the gradient on a separate layer, not only to protect the original image and make it easy to undo the effect, but also so you can adjust the strength of the eye brightening to fit your photo and make it look natural. You adjust the layer opacity as you view the effect on-screen before flattening the layers and saving the file. This technique is very quick and often gives just enough sparkle to an otherwise dull eye.

Like all portrait retouching, the effect should be subtle and yet still brighten the subject's eyes.

Note: Photograph copyright © Photospin.com.

1 Click the New Layer button in the Layers panel to add a new layer.

2 Click the Default Colors icon to reset the default colors to black and white.

3 Press X to reverse the default colors, making the foreground color white.

4 Click the Zoom tool and zoom in to enlarge the eyes.

5 Click the Gradient tool.

The Options bar changes.

6 Click the Radial gradient.

7 Click the gradient drop-down menu and select the Foreground (White) to Transparent gradient.

A Reverse should be unchecked; Dither and Transparency should be checked.

8 Click in the center of one pupil and drag to the edge of the iris.

9 Repeat step 8 for the second eye.

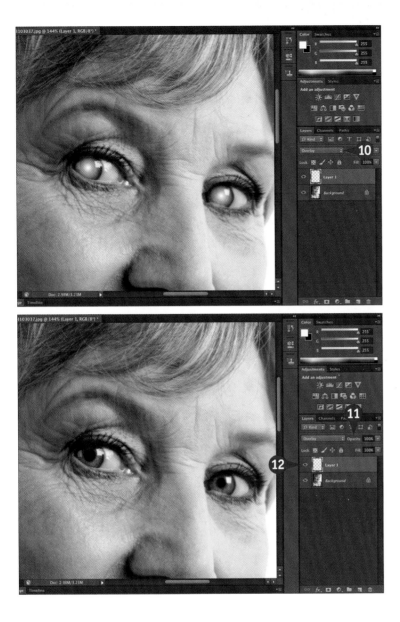

44

10 Click the blend mode drop-down menu and select Overlay.

The bright white spots blend into and lighten the irises.

11 If necessary, click Opacity and drag to the left to reduce the layer opacity until the eye color appears lighter but still natural.

The irises of the eyes are now brighter.

12 Click the eye icon for Layer 1 to turn it off and compare the before and after views.

TIP

Did You Know?

The default gradient always uses the current foreground and background colors in the toolbar. Set the foreground color before you select the Gradient tool and then press G to quickly select the Gradient tool. You can also access the other tools in the toolbar by pressing a specific letter, such as V for the Move tool or Z for the Zoom tool. When multiple tools are grouped together, like the Spot Healing Brush, the Healing Brush, the Patch tool, and the Red Eye tool, you can press the one-letter keyboard shortcut to access the first tool and then repeatedly Shift+press the letter to cycle through all the grouped tools.

BRIGHTEN THE EYES by lightening the whites

You can quickly enhance any portrait by lightening the whites of the eyes. The eyes are the most important feature of the face and the key to a person's individuality. Whether the whites of the eyes are bloodshot or just appear dull, lightening them can enhance the whole face. Lightening and removing red or yellow areas in the white area brightens the subject's eyes.

Lightening the whites of the eyes is a multistep and multilayer process and can be done in various ways. You can paint directly on the whites of the eyes or start by selecting the whites. You can remove the redness or yellow areas using a Hue/Saturation adjustment layer and a layer mask. Then you can lighten the eyes by duplicating the Hue/Saturation adjustment layer and layer mask, adjusting the lightness, and changing the blend mode. You can reduce the adjustment layer opacity to give a more natural look.

The whites of people's eyes are not completely white, so you need to zoom in and out to view the entire photo as you apply the changes. Using adjustment layers, you can easily go back and modify the changes to keep the subject looking natural.

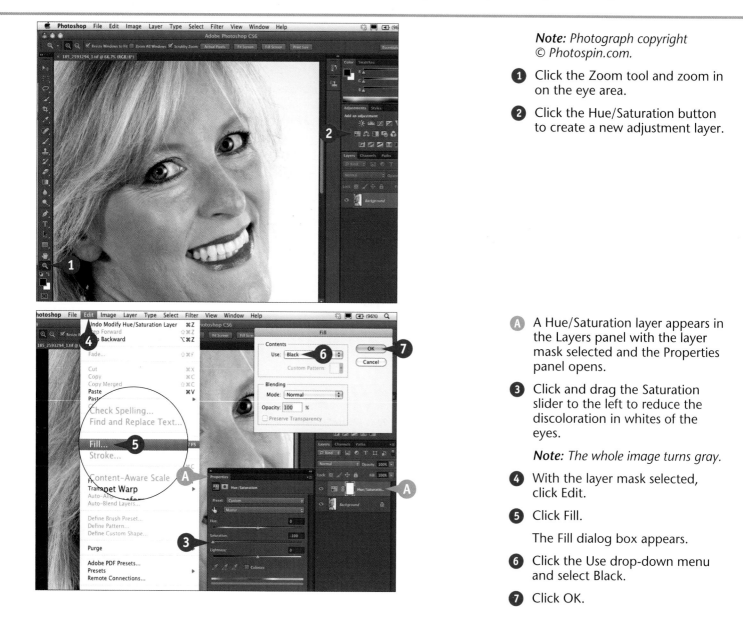

Note: Photograph copyright © Photospin.com.

1 Click the Zoom tool and zoom in on the eye area.

2 Click the Hue/Saturation button to create a new adjustment layer.

A A Hue/Saturation layer appears in the Layers panel with the layer mask selected and the Properties panel opens.

3 Click and drag the Saturation slider to the left to reduce the discoloration in whites of the eyes.

Note: The whole image turns gray.

4 With the layer mask selected, click Edit.

5 Click Fill.

The Fill dialog box appears.

6 Click the Use drop-down menu and select Black.

7 Click OK.

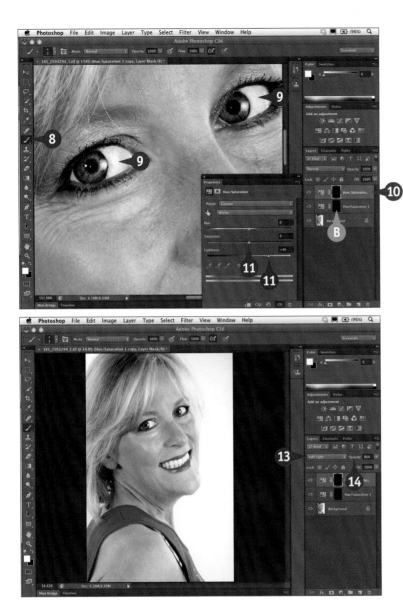

B The layer mask turns black and hides the Saturation adjustment.

8 Click the Brush tool.

9 With white as the foreground color, carefully paint over the whites of the eyes to remove the discoloration.

10 Press ⌘+J (Ctrl+J) to duplicate the Hue/ Saturation layer and layer mask.

11 Click and drag the Lightness slider for this adjustment layer to the right and the Saturation slider to 0.

12 Press ⌘+0 (Ctrl+0) to zoom out and view the whole face.

13 Click the blend mode drop-down menu for the top adjustment layer and select Soft Light.

14 Click Opacity and drag to the left to reduce the effect until the eyes look brighter but still natural.

TIPS **More Options!**

Instead of painting directly over the whites of the eyes on the mask, you can apply the same technique to a selection of the eye whites. Start by selecting the white areas with a selection tool such as the Quick Selection tool ( ) as in task #22. With the selection tool still active, Control+click (right-click) the selection area. A contextual menu appears, listing options such as Feather and Select Inverse. Click Feather, and then apply the first Hue/Saturation adjustment layer as in step 2. The selected area appears on the layer mask automatically.

Try This!

When using any selection tool, press Shift as you click and drag to add to a selection or to add a separate selection. Press Option (Alt) as you click and drag to remove areas from that selection.

Retouching portraits is always tricky. You want to improve the image and still preserve the person's character. Because the eyes can define personality, enhancing the eyes helps the viewer focus on the subject. And adding a little intensity to the lips, particularly on women, can often improve the overall portrait.

You can add depth to the eyes by intensifying the eye color and darkening the natural outline of the iris and the eyelashes. Using a Vibrance adjustment layer and a layer mask lets you control the strength of the enhancement. You can follow the same

Vibrance layer technique to intensify the color of the lips.

And instead of using Photoshop's Dodge and Burn tools directly on the image, you can use the Brush tool to darken lines and add eyelashes on separate empty layers. You can vary the opacity of each layer for complete control. This digital technique is similar to dodging and burning in the darkroom. Painting with black darkens areas, lengthens the eyelashes, and adds definition to the eyes. Using the Opacity setting in the Layers panel, you can fine-tune the adjustments before you finalize the image.

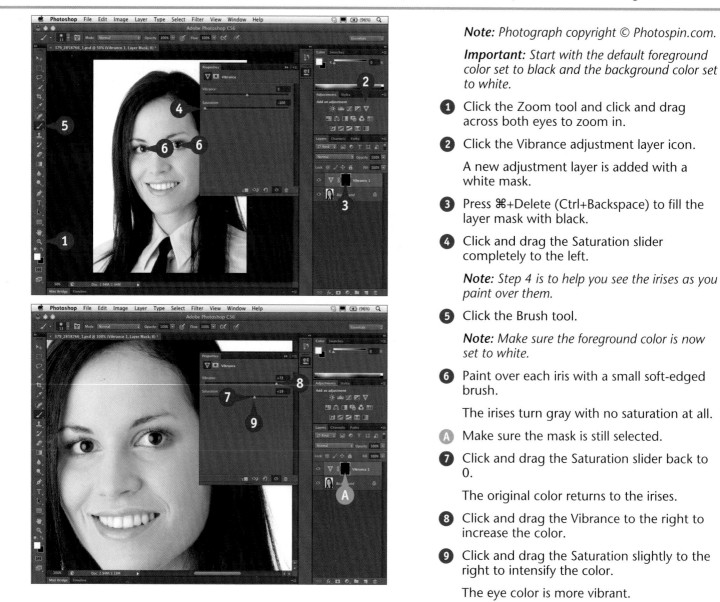

Note: Photograph copyright © Photospin.com.

Important: *Start with the default foreground color set to black and the background color set to white.*

① Click the Zoom tool and click and drag across both eyes to zoom in.

② Click the Vibrance adjustment layer icon.

A new adjustment layer is added with a white mask.

③ Press ⌘+Delete (Ctrl+Backspace) to fill the layer mask with black.

④ Click and drag the Saturation slider completely to the left.

Note: Step 4 is to help you see the irises as you paint over them.

⑤ Click the Brush tool.

Note: Make sure the foreground color is now set to white.

⑥ Paint over each iris with a small soft-edged brush.

The irises turn gray with no saturation at all.

Ⓐ Make sure the mask is still selected.

⑦ Click and drag the Saturation slider back to 0.

The original color returns to the irises.

⑧ Click and drag the Vibrance to the right to increase the color.

⑨ Click and drag the Saturation slightly to the right to intensify the color.

The eye color is more vibrant.

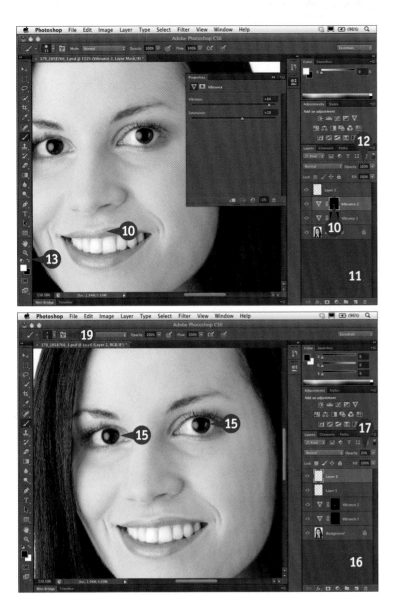

10 Repeat steps 2 to 9, this time painting over the lips.

The lip color is intensified.

11 Click the New Layer button in the Layers panel.

12 Double-click in the Opacity field and type **10**.

13 Click the Switch Colors icon to set the foreground color to black.

14 Press the left bracket key to reduce the brush size.

15 Paint with black around the edges of the irises and in the pupils to darken them.

16 Click the New Layer button to add a second empty layer.

17 Double-click in the Opacity field and type **20** for this new layer.

18 Press ⌘+spacebar (Ctrl+spacebar) and then click in the image to zoom in more to see the eyelashes.

19 Click the Brushes button, or press F5 to open the Brushes panel.

#46
DIFFICULTY LEVEL

TIPS

Try This!

Press D to set the foreground and background colors to the default black and white. Press X to quickly switch the foreground and background colors as you digitally dodge and burn.

Try This!

If the lips look too strong, simply click the Vibrance layer and adjust the sliders, or reduce the layer opacity using the slider on the Layers panel.

Did You Know?

You can save and reuse an eyelash brush. With the settings that you create for Brush Tip Shape (see steps 19 to 23), click the panel menu button (▤) on the right in the Brush panel. Click New Brush Preset. Type a name in the dialog box and click OK.

When you work on any portrait, you need to make small changes. Large changes are too often obvious, and your subjects want to see themselves and be seen at their best, not different. Using multiple layers, you can easily create more variations in brush strokes and color and adjust the opacity of each layer independently. With adjustments on multiple layers, it is also easier to delete enhancements that do not seem natural.

Using a pressure-sensitive pen tablet also gives more variety to brush strokes. Many of the brush options can be set to respond to pressure or tilt, allowing you to alter brush styles with fewer trips to the Brushes panel. Use light brush strokes rather than heavy ones and the Photoshop brushes respond to the pressure.

Making the eyes sparkle by using Vibrance adjustments and variation of digital dodging and burning in Photoshop helps draw the viewers' attention to the eyes and engages them in the photo.

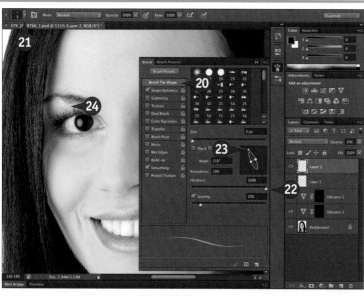

20 Click Brush Tip Shape.

21 Select a very small brush to match the size of the eyelashes.

22 Click and drag the Hardness slider to 100% to build a completely hard-edged brush.

23 Drag the brush angle and the dots on the roundness icon to conform the brush shape to the eyelashes of one eye.

24 Paint over the eyelashes one at a time to darken them.

25 Repeat steps 23 and 24 to adjust the brush for different-angled eyelashes.

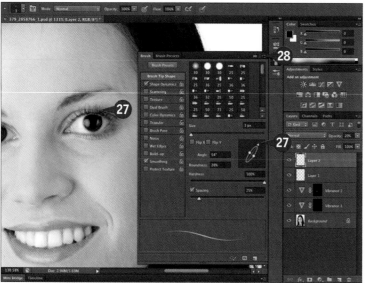

26 Press the spacebar and click and drag in the image to move to the other eye.

27 Repeat steps 23 and 24, adjusting the brush to fit the shape of the lashes of the other eye.

28 Click the Brushes close button to close the Brushes panel.

29 Press Option+spacebar (Alt+spacebar) and click in the image to zoom out to see the whole face.

30 Click Layer 1 to highlight it.

31 Click in the Opacity field.

32 Press the keyboard up or down arrows to increase or decrease the layer opacity until the irises look natural.

33 Click Layer 2 to highlight it.

34 Click in the Opacity field.

35 Press the keyboard up or down arrows to increase or decrease the opacity until the eyelashes look darker but still natural.

The eyes now appear stronger and still natural and help focus the viewer's eyes.

36 Click the panel menu button and select Flatten Image from the menu to finalize the photo.

#46

TIPS

More Options!

You can add eyeliner to the eyes in a photograph. First add another layer. Click Opacity and drag to the left to lower the opacity to about 18%. Paint with black at the edge of the eyelashes on each eye. Click in the Opacity field and use the keyboard up and down arrows to increase or reduce the opacity of the layer until the eyeliner looks natural.

Did You Know?

You can use the same technique shown in this task to enhance light eyebrows. Add a layer and reduce the opacity to 8%. Open the Brushes panel and click Brush Tip Shape. Set the Hardness to 0% and change the size, angle, and roundness to match the shape of the eyebrows. Paint a few smooth strokes over both eyebrows using black. Change the layer's opacity as needed.

Make the eyes come alive with a DIGITAL CATCHLIGHT

When the light source — whether it comes from a camera flash, side lighting, or a natural light source — reflects in the subject's eyes, it forms a catchlight. A *catchlight*, also called a *specular highlight*, in a subject's eyes adds life and sparkle to the subject and brightens the overall photograph. More importantly, it draws attention to the subject's eyes and engages the viewer.

If the subject in a photograph does not have any specular highlights in the eyes or if the subject's eyes

appear somewhat dull, you can use Photoshop to add catchlights. The trick is to make them look real.

Jane Conner-ziser teaches this technique in her classes and instructional videos. Jane creates catchlights with diffused edges and emphasizes the use of two separate layers, one for the glow and the other for the sparkle of catchlights. By placing them on separate layers, you can adjust the catchlights to achieve a natural, realistic look.

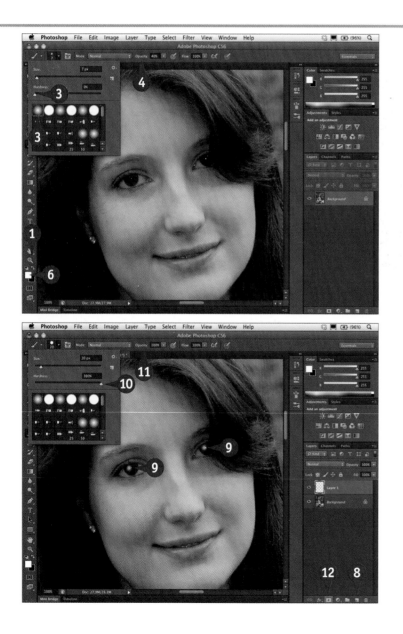

Note: Photograph copyright © Photospin.com.

1 Click the Zoom tool and zoom in on the eye area.

2 Click the Brush tool (✏️).

3 Click the Brush Preset drop-down menu and select a soft-edged brush, with the Hardness slider at 0%.

4 Click Opacity in the Options bar and drag to the left to reduce the brush opacity to 40%.

5 Press D to reset the foreground and background colors.

6 Press X to reverse the colors, making white the foreground color.

7 Press the left or right bracket keys to adjust the brush size to be slightly larger than the final catchlight.

8 Click the New Layer button to add a new empty layer.

9 Click once in each eye to create the catchlights.

10 Click the Brush Preset drop-down menu to change to a hard-edged brush.

11 Click Opacity in the Options bar and drag to the right to 100%.

12 Click the Layer Mask button to add a layer mask.

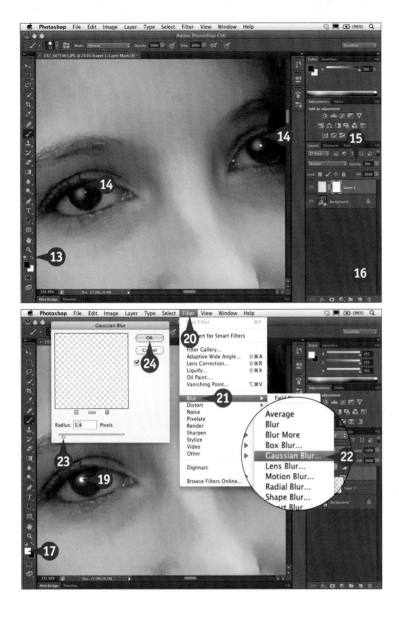

13 Click the Switch Colors icon to make black the foreground color.

14 Paint over the top of the catchlight so that it conforms to the upper eyelid.

15 Click Opacity and drag to the left to reduce the layer opacity to about 70% to slightly better blend the effect.

16 Click the New Layer button.

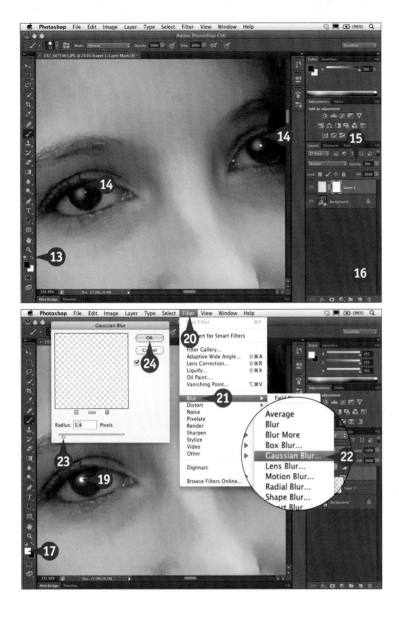

#47

DIFFICULTY LEVEL

17 Press X if necessary, to make white the foreground color.

18 Press the left bracket key multiple times to reduce the brush size to about half the previous size.

19 Click once in the center of each catchlight.

20 Click Filter.

21 Click Blur.

22 Click Gaussian Blur.

The Gaussian Blur dialog box appears.

23 Click and drag the Radius slider to soften the edges.

24 Click OK.

A soft-edged catchlight with a sparkle in the center appears in each eye.

TIPS

More Options!
You can refine the catchlights more by viewing the whole face at once. Press Option+spacebar (Alt+spacebar) and click to zoom out. Click and drag the Opacity slider for each of the catchlight layers until you see a bright sparkle with a natural diffused edge.

Important!
The catchlights must correspond to the natural direction of the light to appear natural. If the light is coming from the right, the catchlights should be on the right side of the pupils, just slightly above the center.

Did You Know?
Studio portrait lighting is often arranged to intentionally create catchlights to help draw attention to the eyes. Different types of photographic lighting produce different styles of catchlights.

The final step to enhancing the eyes in a photograph is to sharpen the eye area. You want to add focus and draw the viewer into the photo, but you may not want to sharpen the rest of the face or the skin. You can selectively sharpen the eyes by using a Sharpen filter and then applying the filter with the History panel and History Brush.

You can use not only the Unsharp Mask filter for sharpening, but also the Smart Sharpen filter. This filter is not only easier to use, but it also has added features including a much larger preview.

After sharpening the entire portrait, you hide the effect using the History panel to go back to a version of the photo before the sharpening was applied. Then, using the History Brush, you can paint the sharpening effect specifically on the eye area where you want to draw the focus.

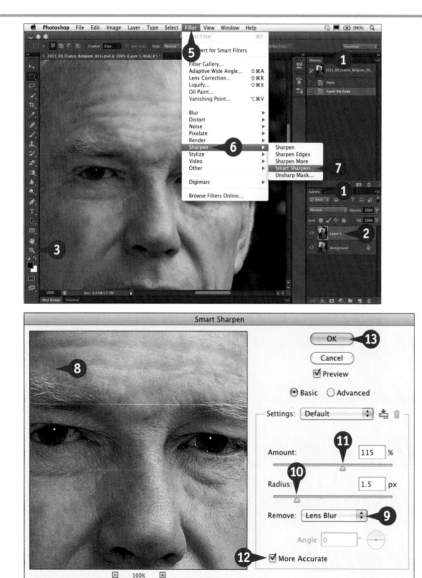

1 Arrange the workspace panels to see both the Layers panel and the History panel.

2 Press ⌘+J (Ctrl+J) to duplicate the Background layer.

3 Double-click the Zoom tool to view the image at 100%.

4 Press the spacebar, click in the image, and move it to see the eyes.

5 Click Filter.

6 Click Sharpen.

7 Click Smart Sharpen.

The Smart Sharpen dialog box appears.

8 Click in the Preview pane and drag to see the eyes area.

9 Click the Remove drop-down menu and select Lens Blur.

10 Click and drag the Radius slider to 1.5 to increase the area to be sharpened.

11 Click and drag the Amount slider to sharpen the eye, generally between 80 and 115 percent.

12 Click More Accurate (☐ changes to ☑).

13 Click OK to apply the sharpening.

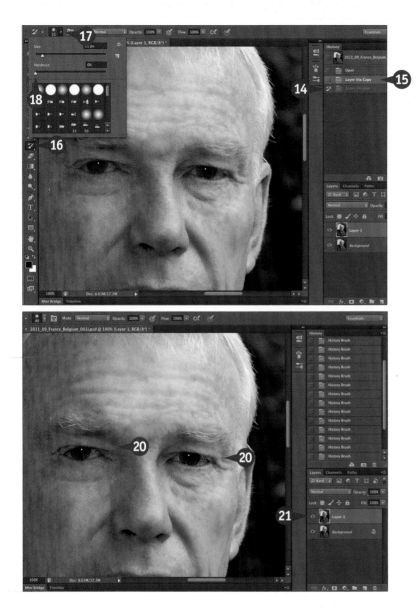

The sharpening is applied to Layer 1.

14 In the History panel, click the box to the left of the Smart Sharpen step to set the source for the History Brush.

15 In the History panel, click the previous state named Layer Via Copy.

16 Click the History Brush tool.

17 Click the Brush Preset drop-down menu.

18 Click to select a soft-edged brush (0%).

19 Press the left or right bracket keys to adjust the brush size to be large enough to cover the edge of the eyes.

20 Paint over the eyes, eyelashes, and eyebrows with the History Brush to apply the sharpening.

21 Click the eye icon for Layer 1 on and off to compare before and after sharpening.

Note: You can reduce the opacity of the sharpened layer if necessary to better blend the image.

The sharpening is applied only to the eye areas.

TIPS

Attention!

The Smart Sharpen filter applies only to one layer. If you have made other adjustment layers, you must merge them before applying the sharpening. Press ⌘+Option+Shift+E (Ctrl+Alt+Shift+E). The adjustment layers and the Background layers merge in the new layer. All the adjustment layers, Background copy or Layer 1, and original Background layers remain unchanged.

Did You Know?

Always view the image at 100% magnification when you use a sharpening filter to get the most accurate view on-screen of your changes. Still, the amount of detail visible in a print may be slightly different than what you see on the screen. The amount of detail can vary depending on the type of printer and paper used.

Improve a smile by WHITENING TEETH

You can greatly improve every portrait in which the subject is smiling by applying a little digital tooth-whitening. Yellow teeth always dull a smile as well as the overall look of the photo.

You first select the teeth and soften the selection, to avoid a visible line between the lightened areas and the rest of the image. Although you can make a selection in Photoshop in many ways, using the Quick Mask mode or the Quick Selection tool as described in Chapter 2 works well when making a detailed selection, such as of a person's teeth.

After the teeth are selected, whitening is a two-step process. You have to remove the yellow and then brighten the teeth by adjusting the saturation. As in previous tasks, zoom in to make the detailed selection, and then zoom out to see the whole image before adjusting the color. Digital tooth-whitening should be a subtle adjustment to keep the smile and the person looking natural.

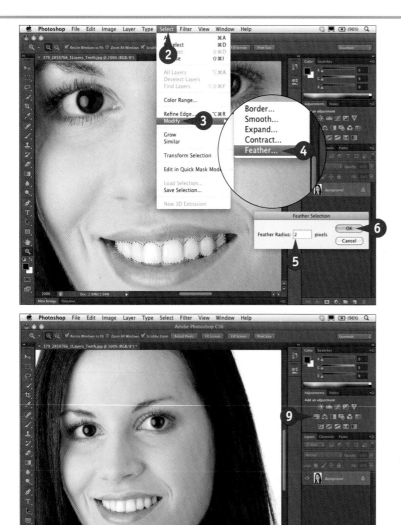

Note: Photograph copyright © Photospin.com.

① Zoom in and make a selection of the teeth using the Quick Mask mode or the Quick Selection tool.

Note: To use the Quick Mask mode, see task #23. To use the Quick Selection tool, see task #22.

② Click Select.

③ Click Modify.

④ Click Feather.

The Feather Selection dialog box appears.

⑤ Type **1** or **2** in the Feather Radius field to slightly soften the edge of the selection.

⑥ Click OK.

⑦ Click the Zoom tool and zoom out to see the whole image.

⑧ Press ⌘+H (Ctrl+H) to hide the selection marquee.

Note: If the dialog box appears, click Hide Extras.

The selection marquee is no longer visible, but the teeth are still selected.

⑨ Click the Hue/Saturation button to create an adjustment layer.

A The Properties panel appears and a Hue/Saturation layer is created in the Layers panel.

10 Click the drop-down menu and select Yellows.

11 Click and drag the Saturation slider slowly to the left to remove the yellow in the teeth.

12 Click the drop-down menu and select Master.

13 Click and drag the Lightness slider slowly to the right to brighten the teeth.

14 Press ⌘+D (Ctrl+D) to deselect the teeth.

15 Press ⌘+Shift+E (Ctrl+Shift+E) to merge all the visible layers into one layer.

TIPS

Try This!

When zooming in on an image, press and hold the spacebar; the pointer temporarily changes to the Hand tool. You can click and drag around your image with the Hand tool and easily move to the area that needs to be adjusted. When you release the spacebar, you change back to the previously selected tool.

Did You Know?

Feathering softens the edge of a selection and smoothes the transition between two distinct areas. You can also click Select and click Refine Edge to feather the selection edge. The default settings of the Refine Edge dialog box include a one-pixel feather. Click OK in the dialog box and continue lightening the teeth as shown here.

Chapter

5

Enhance Colors, Tone, and Sharpness in Photos

Almost every project in Photoshop involves color or the lack of it. Whether you work on a design or a photograph in Photoshop, you often adjust the hue, saturation, and brightness of an image. You can fine-tune shadows and highlights or completely alter the overall tone of a photograph. You can transform a color photograph into a grayscale image, colorize an old grayscale image, or make a color image look like an antique colorized photograph. You can also tone a photo as photographers used to do in the darkroom by digitally dodging and burning. And you can create these effects using many different techniques.

Whenever you make color and tonal adjustments, some pixel information is discarded. By applying your corrections on a duplicate layer, on separate layers, or on a

Smart Object layer, you can edit nondestructively. Using Photoshop's adjustment layers, you can make changes without permanently altering pixel values. And by opening or converting an image or a layer to a new Smart Object, you can apply most filters as Smart Filters, making them continuously editable as well as nondestructive. Smart Filters can even be used when sharpening a photograph, so you can reedit the changes without altering pixels until you complete your edits and flatten the image.

Working on a color calibrated monitor, as shown in task #14, is even more important when working with color or tone. Otherwise, you may be changing colors that are not really in the image, and what you see on your monitor may look very different when it is printed.

When you need to make a quick adjustment to the brightness and contrast of an image, you can first try Photoshop's Auto button correction, found in the Curves and the Levels adjustments and now also in the Brightness and Contrast adjustment. The Auto button in both the Curves and Levels adjustments in Photoshop CS6 applies a completely new and very effective algorithm to enhance brightness and contrast. Although you can apply any of these adjustments to the Background layer, you permanently alter pixels, and if you apply the adjustments to a duplicated layer, you double the file size. You can apply the same new algorithm using the Auto button using adjustment layers, without increasing file size and still making the adjustments nondestructive.

Some images might require more than one adjustment. You can add multiple adjustment layers and still not increase the file size or permanently destroy pixels. Auto may not work in all situations, and you can often improve the image by editing with more precise tools. However, when you need a quick edit, the Auto button can be the fastest solution.

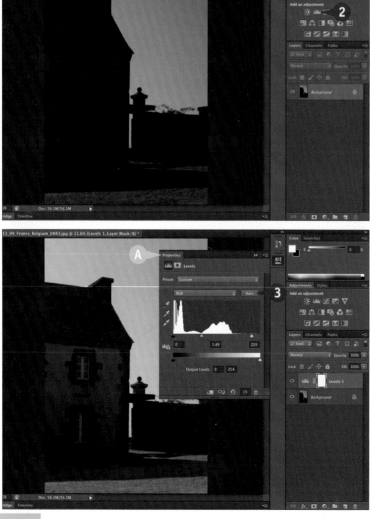

① Open an underexposed photo.

② Click the Levels Adjustment button.

Note: *You can also click the Adjustment Layer button in the Layers panel (⬛) and click Levels.*

Ⓐ The Levels Properties panel opens.

③ Click Auto.

The brightness and contrast change in the photo.

Note: *The photo may look fine this way, or you can continue editing with more adjustments and adjustment layers.*

An overexposed photograph is impossible to salvage with traditional darkroom techniques. Too much light means that there is nothing in the film to print. Digital photography is different. The image sensor in the camera sees more of the lighter values, and it records more tonal differences in the brighter areas, or the right side of the histogram. As long as the highlights are not completely blown out or showing no information, you can improve an overly bright photograph with a variety of tools in Photoshop.

You can use the Shadows/Highlights command in the basic mode to effectively reduce the highlights.

With most dialog boxes in Photoshop, when you move the slider to the right you increase the amount. When you use the Shadows/Highlights adjustment to reduce the highlights, it works in the opposite fashion.

As with every project in Photoshop, you can accomplish the task in a variety of ways. By applying the Shadows/Highlights command on a Smart Object layer, you can continue to adjust the exposure nondestructively. This three-step technique for reducing the highlights and improving an overexposed photo is so easy that it is always worth testing before spending time with other methods or discarding the photo.

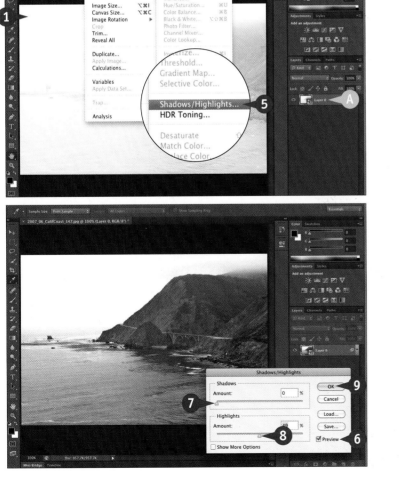

① Open an overexposed photo.

② Click Filter ▷ Convert for Smart Filters.

Ⓐ The Background layer is converted to a Smart Object layer.

③ Click Image.

④ Click Adjustments.

⑤ Click Shadows/Highlights.

The Shadows/Highlights dialog box appears.

⑥ Click Preview (☐ changes to ☑).

⑦ Click and drag the Shadows Amount slider to the left to 0%.

⑧ Click and drag the Highlights Amount slider to the right until the image looks the way you want.

⑨ Click OK.

The image exposure is improved.

Improve contrast with a CURVES ADJUSTMENT LAYER

The Curves adjustment is one of Photoshop's most powerful tools. It can also be quite intimidating. Like the Levels adjustment, Curves adjustments compress or stretch the input tones of the image, affecting the tonal range, contrast, and color balance of the image. Whereas Levels has only three adjustments — white point, black point, and gamma — the Curves adjustment lets you control multiple points along the tonal range curve. Creating an S-curve to add contrast to the midtones, which in turn reduces contrast to the shadows and highlights, is the most

commonly applied Curves adjustment. When applied to the entire RGB image, a Curves adjustment not only changes the contrast but also the hue and saturation.

By using a Curves adjustment layer, you can alter the curve of just the lightness or luminosity of the image. Such a targeted adjustment is not only nondestructive but also protects the existing hue and saturation.

The amount of contrast an image requires depends on the subject matter and the intent of the photographer.

1 Click the Adjustment Layer button in the Layers panel.

2 Click Curves.

Note: You can optionally click the Curves button (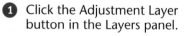) in the Adjustments panel.

A The Curves Properties panel opens.

3 Click the Properties panel title bar and drag it to the left until it disconnects from the other panels.

4 Click and drag the bottom right corner of the Properties panel to enlarge the window.

Note: Enlarging the panel lets you make finer adjustments on the curve.

The Properties panel enlarges, showing a larger curve.

5 Click the layer blend mode drop-down menu and select Luminosity.

6 Click a point on the curve toward the top right intersection of the grid and drag slightly up.

7 Click a point on the curve toward the bottom left intersection of the grid and drag slightly down.

The lightness and contrast values change in the photo.

8 Continue adjusting the two points to increase the tones in the image.

Note: To remove a point, click and drag the point away from the curve until it pops off.

9 Click and drag the Opacity of the adjustment layer to slightly reduce the effect.

TIPS

Important!
Make only small changes to the curve to preserve the natural look of the image. Even small changes in the curve can create major changes in the photo, and strong curves can cause posterization.

Did You Know?
A straight diagonal line spreads the contrast evenly across the image. When you change the curve, you are redistributing the contrast in the image. An S-curve adds contrast to the midtones, while removing that amount of contrast in the highlights and shadows.

Try This!
You can use the Curves adjustment layer in the Normal layer blend mode to affect all the tones, hue, and saturation at the same time. You can also use the Curves adjustment to make precise adjustments to individual color channels in an image.

Whether you have a scanned image or one from a digital camera, your image may show a colorcast due to improper lighting, white balance settings, or other factors. A *colorcast* often appears as a reddish, bluish, or greenish tint over the whole image. Photoshop has many tools that you can use to remove a colorcast, including the White Balance setting in Camera Raw, and sometimes you may need to try different ones, depending on the photograph. Using the Match Color command as shown here to remove a colorcast is simple and often works well.

Intended for matching the colors between two images, the Match Color command uses advanced

algorithms to adjust the brightness, color saturation, and color balance in an image. Because you can adjust the controls in different combinations, using this command on just one image gives you better control over the color and luminance of the image than many other tools.

Using the Match Color command on a duplicated layer, you can protect the original image as you compare the adjustment and also adjust the layer's Opacity slider. Blend the results with the Background layer to achieve the best color for your image.

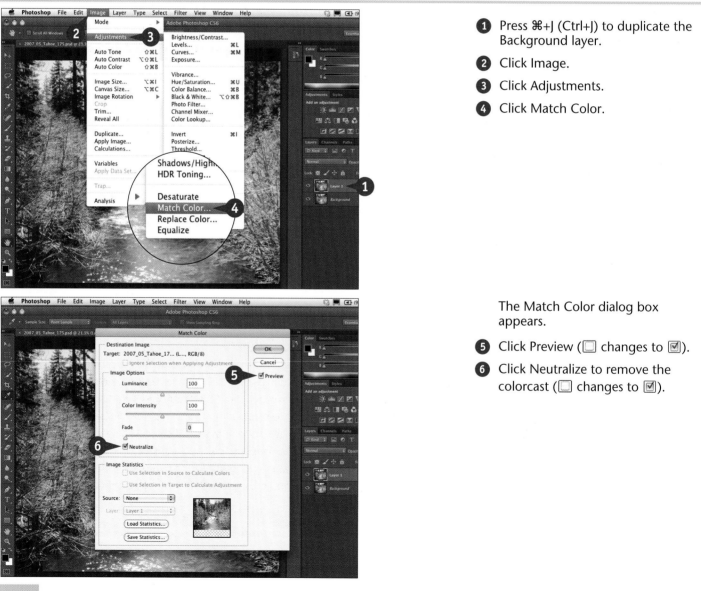

① Press ⌘+J (Ctrl+J) to duplicate the Background layer.

② Click Image.

③ Click Adjustments.

④ Click Match Color.

The Match Color dialog box appears.

⑤ Click Preview (☐ changes to ☑).

⑥ Click Neutralize to remove the colorcast (☐ changes to ☑).

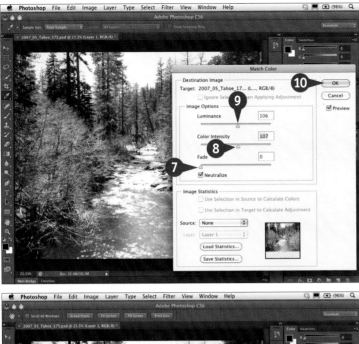

The overall colorcast is removed.

7 Click and drag the Fade slider slowly to the right to reduce the effect, if necessary.

8 Click and drag the Color Intensity slider to the right to increase the color range, if necessary.

9 Click and drag the Luminance slider to the right to increase the luminance, if necessary.

10 Click OK to apply the change.

11 Click Opacity and drag to the left to adjust the overall effect if necessary.

The colorcast is removed and the colors appear more natural.

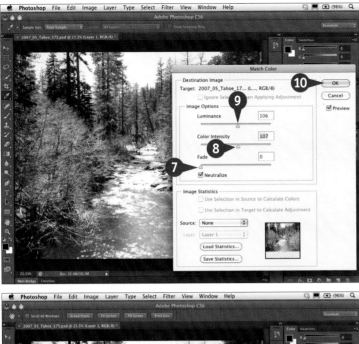

TIPS

Did You Know?

You can view the floating Histogram panel and see the color changes as they are made. Click Window ➪ Histogram to display the Histogram panel. Click and drag the Histogram panel so that you can keep it open and still see the image and your other panels.

More Options!

If an area in the image is normally neutral gray, you can also correct a colorcast using the Levels adjustment panel. Click the Adjustment Layer button (![icon]) to create a new adjustment layer. Click the Gray Point eyedropper, the middle eyedropper in the Levels pane. Click in the part of the image that should be neutral gray to neutralize the colorcast. If necessary, click another area until the colors appear natural.

HAND-TINT a black-and-white photograph

Hand-tinting a photograph using traditional paints and traditional film photos was very difficult. With Photoshop, hand-tinting a black-and-white image is much easier. You can use any black-and-white photo, also called a *grayscale image*, and paint over areas using any colors that you choose.

Hand-tinted photos tend to have very subtle colors. By painting the colors on separate layers, you can easily edit the hues and the intensity of the colors. You can paint directly over areas or you can make selections of detailed areas if you need to be more precise. After the entire image is painted, you can change the opacity of each colored layer as a final touch.

You can vary the size of the Brush tool as you paint using the left and right bracket keys. If you are using a pressure-sensitive stylus and tablet, open the Brush panel, click Shape Dynamics, and set the Control drop-down menu to Pen Pressure. The brush size now varies automatically according to the pressure applied with the stylus.

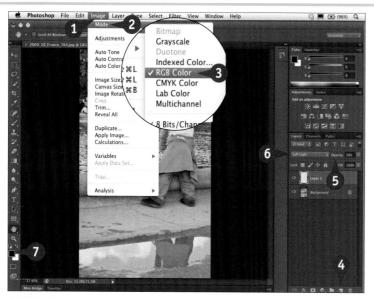

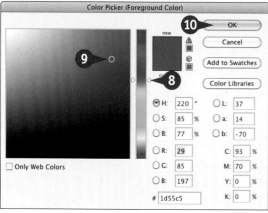

① Click Image.

② Click Mode.

③ Click RGB Color.

The color mode changes, but the image on the screen does not.

④ Click the New Layer button in the Layers panel.

⑤ Click Opacity and set the layer opacity to 30% so you can see the image as you paint on it.

Note: You can change the opacity setting as you work on the tinting.

⑥ Click the blend mode drop-down menu and select Soft Light.

⑦ Click the foreground color in the toolbar.

The Color Picker appears.

⑧ Click and drag the Color slider to select a hue.

⑨ Click in the Color Preview box to select a color.

⑩ Click OK to close the dialog box.

11 Press B to select the Brush tool.

12 Click the Brush Preset drop-down menu to open the Brush picker.

13 Click the soft-edged brush.

14 Press the left or right bracket keys to adjust the brush size.

15 Paint over an area to apply the color.

16 Repeat steps 4 to 15 until the entire image is painted, adding new layers for each color.

The black-and-white photo now appears tinted with color.

17 Click and drag the opacity of individual layers to adjust the look.

TIPS

Try This!

Instead of clicking the foreground color, simply click in the Set Foreground Color box in the Color panel to open the Color Picker without changing tools. You can also position the cursor over the Color panel and click in the color ramp to select a color — all without changing tools. Click and drag the RGB sliders to adjust the colors.

More Options!

You can select realistic colors for a grayscale image by sampling the colors from a color image that has similar subjects. Keep the other image open on the screen while you are colorizing the grayscale photo. With the Color Picker open, position the cursor outside the dialog box to sample real colors from the color image. Then paint in the grayscale image with those colors.

CONVERT A COLOR PHOTO to a black-and-white photo

You can convert a color image to black and white using many different tools and techniques in Photoshop, and because there are no fixed rules on which colors in an image should match specific levels of gray, you can create a variety of different grayscale images from just one color photograph.

Both the Black & White adjustment layer and the Channel Mixer adjustment layer offer powerful conversion methods with complete visual control. You interactively determine what shade of gray is applied to any particular color range in the image by moving the sliders in the Properties panel for either of these types of adjustment layers. And because you are editing using a nondestructive adjustment layer, the original image data is preserved without duplicating the Background layer.

The Black & White and the Channel Mixer Properties panels each include a number of presets that you can use or modify, or you can create and save your own preset. You can also apply a tint to the photos using either of these adjustment layers.

Convert with a Black & White Adjustment Layer

1 Open a color image to convert to grayscale.

2 Click the Black & White button in the Adjustments panel.

Note: You can optionally click the Adjustment Layer button (⬛) on the Layers panel and click Black & White.

The image converts to a default grayscale image.

3 Click Auto to see the changes.

The grays in the image change.

Note: The Auto function in the Black & White Properties panel maps the colors to grays differently from the Default setting.

4 Click and drag any of the color sliders to vary the grays according to the colors in the image.

5 Click the Preset drop-down menu to try a different preset.

Note: To tint the image, click Tint (⬛ changes to ☑) and then click in the color box. Select a color from the Color Picker that appears.

Convert with a Channel Mixer Adjustment Layer

1 Open an image to convert to grayscale.

2 Click the Channel Mixer button in the Adjustments panel.

Note: You can optionally click the Adjustment Layer button ( ) on the Layers panel and click Channel Mixer.

3 Click Monochrome (changes to).

4 Click and drag any of the sliders to customize the preset settings.

5 Click the Preset drop-down menu to try a different preset.

Note: To tint the photo, clear the Monochrome check box (changes to) and move the sliders.

TIPS

Important!

Converting a color image to grayscale is not the same as changing the mode to grayscale, which in effect throws away image data. When you convert a color image to grayscale using one of the adjustment layer methods, you map individual colors to different shades of gray, preserving the same complete tonal range that exists in the color image. The image remains in RGB mode.

More Options!

You can also convert a color image to a grayscale image using the LAB – Black & White Technique action in the Actions panel. Click Window ➪ Actions to open the panel. If the LAB – Black & White action is not available, click the panel menu button ( ) and select LAB – Black & White Technique to load the action. Then click the action in the Actions list and click the Play button ( ) on the Actions panel to automatically convert your image. You can also apply a tint using the LAB – Black & White action.

You can hand-tint any grayscale photograph with Photoshop, as shown in a previous task. You can also start with a color image, convert it to grayscale using any of the methods shown in task #55, and then colorize it or just add color to specific elements to get a very different look. Tinting a photo you just converted to grayscale is much easier to accomplish. You can paint-in the color, giving your photo a watercolor painting like effect by changing the opacity of the brush as you paint. Starting with a low brush

opacity, you add layers to bring back the original color gradually.

If you have already saved a grayscale version of the photo without the original layers, you can still use the method shown here. Open both the original color image and the converted grayscale photo. Using the Move tool, press and hold Shift as you click and drag the grayscale version onto the original color photo. Then follow steps 4 to 14 of this task using the Eraser tool rather than the Brush tool to paint a very creative image.

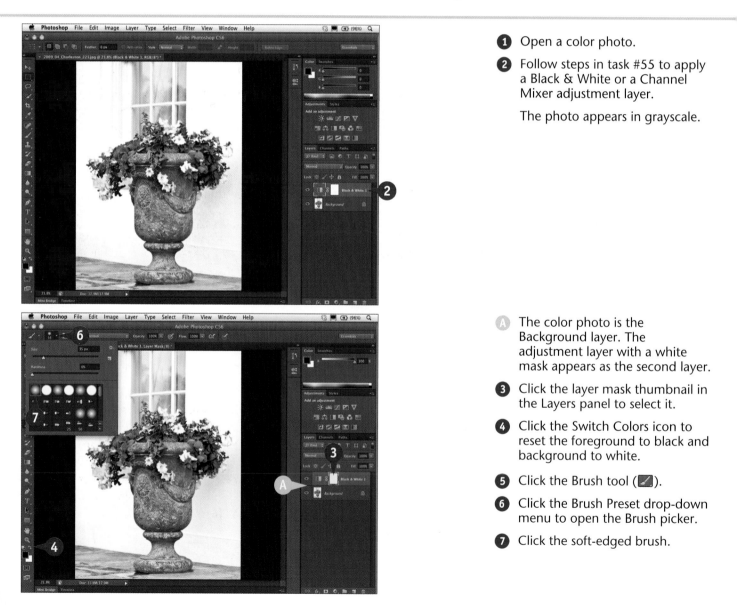

1 Open a color photo.

2 Follow steps in task #55 to apply a Black & White or a Channel Mixer adjustment layer.

The photo appears in grayscale.

A The color photo is the Background layer. The adjustment layer with a white mask appears as the second layer.

3 Click the layer mask thumbnail in the Layers panel to select it.

4 Click the Switch Colors icon to reset the foreground to black and background to white.

5 Click the Brush tool (▨).

6 Click the Brush Preset drop-down menu to open the Brush picker.

7 Click the soft-edged brush.

#56

DIFFICULTY LEVEL

8. Click the Airbrush button.

9. Double-click the Opacity field in the Options bar and type **20**.

10. Paint over the area to be colorized.

11. Double-click the Opacity field in the Options bar again and type **40**.

12. Press the left bracket key several times to reduce the brush size.

13. Paint over parts of the colored area to increase the color.

The image is selectively colorized and the viewer's attention is drawn to the perfect spot.

TIPS

Keyboard Shortcut!

You can change the size of the Brush tool by pressing the right and left bracket keys, or by pressing Control+Option (right-click+Alt) and clicking and dragging right or left. If you use a Wacom pen tablet, you can click the Tablet Pressure Controls Size and/or the Tablet Pressure Controls Opacity buttons in the Options panel (and) and then alter both the brush size and opacity depending on how hard you press down on the stylus.

Did You Know?

You can also vary the hardness or softness of the Eraser or Brush tools using the keyboard rather than the Brush picker. Click the Eraser or Brush tool to select it. Press and hold Shift as you repeatedly press the right or left bracket keys, or press Control+Option (right-click+Alt) while clicking and dragging up or down to increase the hardness or the softness of the tool.

Improve exposure with a DODGE AND BURN LAYER

Dodging and burning are photographic techniques describing the traditional darkroom methods for brightening and darkening tones in an image. You can effectively dodge and burn a digital image in Photoshop.

Although Photoshop includes digital dodge and burn tools, these tools directly affect the pixels on the layer, making your edits permanent and destructive. Using a separate layer and the Brush tool to dodge and burn not only adjusts the image nondestructively, it also gives you greater control over the adjustment.

You can digitally dodge and burn on a separate layer with two different methods. One uses a separate

empty layer in the Soft Light blend mode. The other uses a separate layer filled with neutral gray in the Overlay blend mode. You can use the method that you prefer or that works best on your particular image. With either type of layer, you dodge by painting with white and burn by painting with black on the layer. By setting the brush opacity to about 30% to start, you can increase the effect as you work by brushing over an area multiple times.

Both methods give you complete control over dodging and burning digitally.

Use a Layer in the Soft Light Blend Mode

1 Click the Default Colors icon to reset the foreground and background colors to black and white.

2 Click the New Layer button to create a new empty layer.

3 Click the blend mode drop-down menu and select Soft Light.

4 Click the Brush tool ().

5 Click the Brush Preset drop-down menu to open the Brush picker.

6 Select the soft-edged brush.

7 Double-click the Opacity field in the Options bar and type **30** to set the brush opacity to 30%.

8 Click and drag to paint with black in the light areas of the image to darken, or digitally burn them.

9 Click the Switch Colors icon to reverse the foreground and background colors, making the foreground color white.

> *Note: You can also press X to reverse the foreground and background colors.*

10 Click and drag to paint with white in the dark areas of the image to lighten, or digitally dodge them.

Use a Layer in the Overlay Blend Mode

DIFFICULTY LEVEL

1 Click the Default Colors icon to reset the foreground and background colors to black and white.

2 Press Option (Alt) and click the New Layer button to create a new empty layer.

The New Layer dialog box appears.

3 Click the Mode drop-down menu and select Overlay.

4 Click Fill with Overlay-Neutral Color (50% Gray) (☐ changes to ☑).

5 Type a name for the layer such as Dodge and Burn.

6 Click OK.

A The new layer appears filled with gray in the Layers panel, but the image in the main window is unchanged.

7 Repeat steps 4 to 10 described in the first part of this task.

TIPS

More Options!

You can create separate layers for dodging and burning using either method. Name one layer Burn and the other Dodge. You can then adjust the layer opacity of the dodge or burn layer individually to give you even more control and use the Layers panel's Opacity slider to adjust the effect.

Try This!

Paint over an area multiple times to increase the effect. By using the brush at a low opacity to start, you can just release the mouse button and click and paint over the same area again if the darkening or lightening is not as strong as needed with the first strokes.

Did You Know?

When you use a layer filled with 50% gray in the Overlay blend mode, the layer displays a gray thumbnail in the Layers panel, but appears as a transparent layer over the image in the main window.

Increase saturation subtly using a VIBRANCE ADJUSTMENT LAYER

When you increase the saturation in an image using a Hue Saturation adjustment, all the colors become more intense, even posterized, and some details can get lost. By applying a Vibrance adjustment layer instead, you can increase the color saturation more selectively. The Vibrance slider affects only the less saturated areas and minimizes any effect on the more saturated areas in the image, thus increasing the intensity of the colors while maintaining a more natural appearance. The Vibrance adjustment also improves skin tones more naturally than the Saturation adjustment, which affects all the colors in the image equally.

By using a Vibrance adjustment layer, rather than just a Vibrance adjustment, you can increase the intensity of the colors in an image without altering the original pixels. In addition, the Vibrance Properties panel includes a more controlled Saturation slider than the one in the Hue Saturation panel. You can use the Vibrance panel's Saturation slider to intensify overall colors without losing as much detail or posterizing colors.

The Vibrance adjustment in Photoshop offers the same color control as the Vibrance in Adobe Lightroom and Camera Raw.

1 Open an image.

2 Click the Vibrance button in the Adjustments panel.

Note: You can also click the Adjustment Layer button ( ) in the Layers panel and click Vibrance.

A A Vibrance adjustment layer and mask appear in the Layers panel.

3 Click and drag the Vibrance slider to the right to increase the intensity of the colors.

4 Click and drag the Saturation slider only slightly to the right to increase all the colors if necessary.

The colors in the image intensify.

⑤ Click and hold the View Previous State button to view the image before the slider changes were added to the adjustment.

The adjustment is temporarily hidden.

⑥ Release the mouse button to view the adjustment again.

⑦ Click and drag to adjust the sliders to increase or decrease the vibrance and saturation.

Note: You can optionally change the adjustment layer's blend mode or reduce the layer's opacity to alter the adjustment.

TIPS

Did You Know?
You can selectively increase the vibrance of an area in an image by painting with the Sponge tool (🔲), which is grouped with the Dodge and Burn tools in the toolbar. In the Sponge tool Options bar, select Saturate for the Mode and click Vibrance (🔲 changes to ☑).

More Options!
You can remove the Vibrance adjustment layer by clicking the trash can (🔲) in the adjustment layer Properties panel.
You can reset the adjustments to the default settings by clicking the Reset button (🔲) in the adjustment layer Properties panel.

Try This!
An adjustment layer affects all the layers below it in the Layers panel. You can restrict the affect of the Vibrance adjustment only to the layer immediately below it by clicking the Clip to Layer button (🔲) in the adjustment layer Properties panel. This is particularly useful if you made a selection to be adjusted and placed the selection on a separate layer.

CHANGE THE HIGHLIGHTS AND SHADOWS
nondestructively

When you have a photo in which the background is well exposed but the foreground is either too dark or washed out, you can use the Highlights and Shadows adjustment on a Smart Object layer to improve the balance in the image without permanently altering the original. The default settings in the Shadows/Highlights dialog box can be a quick fix as shown in task #51; however, the dialog box can be expanded to show more options, giving you far greater control over both the shadows and highlights, even in images with problems at both extremes of the tonal range.

Make sure that the Preview option is selected in the dialog box so the image is updated as you move each slider. The Amount slider determines how much of a correction to apply. The Tonal Width slider controls how much of the tonal range will be modified. The Radius slider controls the size of the area by increasing or decreasing the number of neighboring pixels to be included in the adjustment. Color Correction increases or decreases the saturation of the shadows or highlights being adjusted in a color photo. If the photo is grayscale, a Brightness slider darkens or lightens the areas. The Midtone Contrast slider increases or decreases the contrast in the overall the image.

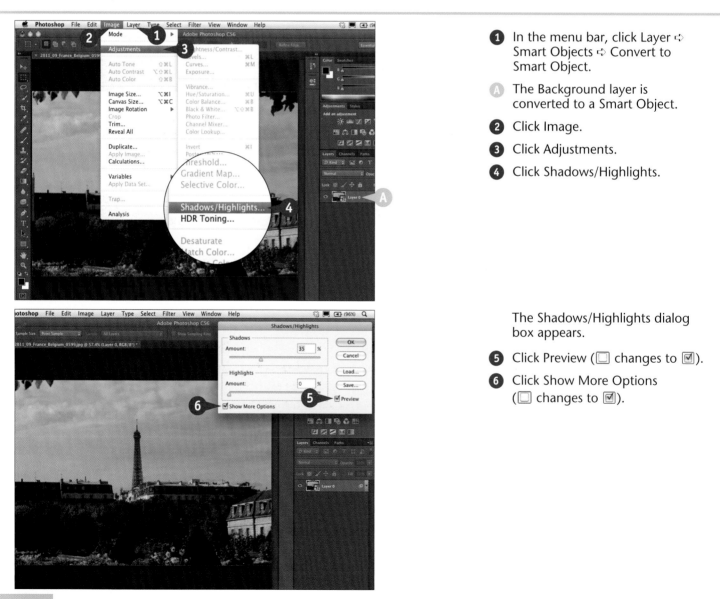

① In the menu bar, click Layer ⇨ Smart Objects ⇨ Convert to Smart Object.

Ⓐ The Background layer is converted to a Smart Object.

② Click Image.

③ Click Adjustments.

④ Click Shadows/Highlights.

The Shadows/Highlights dialog box appears.

⑤ Click Preview (☐ changes to ☑).

⑥ Click Show More Options (☐ changes to ☑).

The dialog box expands.

7 Click and drag the Shadows Tonal Width slider to the left.

8 Click and drag the Shadows Amount slider to the right to lighten the shadows

9 Click and drag the Radius slider to adjust the areas affected.

10 Repeat steps 8 to 10 for the Highlights.

11 Click and drag the Color Correction slider slightly to the right to add back a small amount of saturation.

12 Continue to adjust the sliders as needed to balance the photo.

13 Click OK.

B The Smart Filter is added to the Smart Object layer.

C You can Double-click the Shadows/Highlights Filter name in the Layers panel to reopen the filter and make changes.

TIPS

Did You Know?

For a photo with a backlit subject, you will move the Shadows slider and may not need to work with the Highlights slider at all. If the subject only is washed out because of proximity to the flash but the background is well exposed, you can focus on the Highlights slider and move the Shadows slider to 0%

Try This!

Make small adjustments. When the Shadows Tonal Width is set to 50%, the darkest half of the image is being treated as a shadow. Move it to around 30% and increase the Amount slider so only the darkest shadows are affected. Set the Highlights Tonal Width to around 80% so only the brightest tones are reduced when you decrease the Amount slider.

Did You Know?

When you adjust the Shadows and Highlights sliders, the colors can appear washed out. Use the Color Correction to increase the saturation.

SHARPEN THE PHOTO to correct digital softening

Whether your photos are scanned in or come from a digital camera, most images can benefit from some sharpening.

Image softness is inherent to digital capture. The sensor technology in digital cameras and scanners automatically introduce softness when recording images. Digital cameras require a blurring filter in front of the light-capturing sensor to average the details into pixels. Most digital cameras then apply some automatic sharpening during in-camera processing to counteract the softness. However,

because images are most pleasing when sharp, you often need to sharpen photos as the final editing step.

Photoshop includes multiple sharpening filters. However, the Smart Sharpen and Unsharp Mask filters offer more control than the others. The Unsharp Mask filter can require more experimentation when printing because it often displays a stronger sharpening effect on-screen than when the image is printed at a high resolution. Because the Smart Sharpen filter has a larger preview box and lets you control the amount of sharpening in shadow and highlight areas, it is often the best filter to use for digital sharpening.

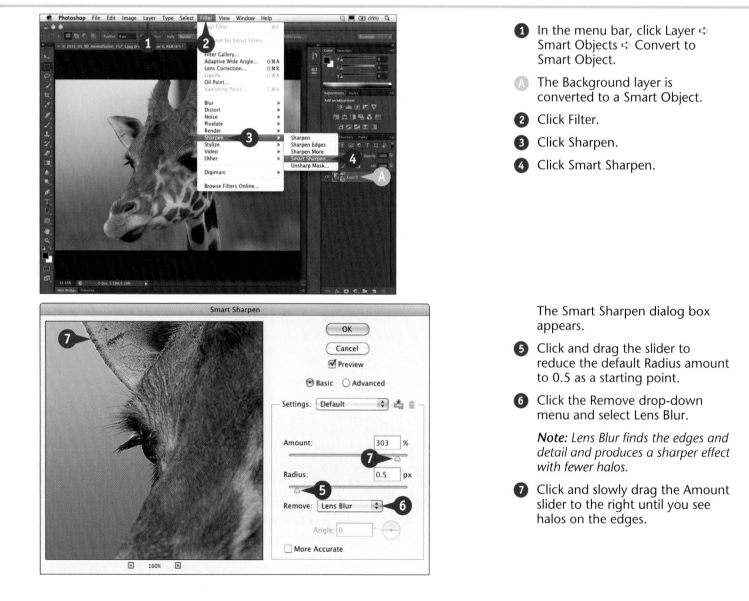

1 In the menu bar, click Layer ➪ Smart Objects ➪ Convert to Smart Object.

A The Background layer is converted to a Smart Object.

2 Click Filter.

3 Click Sharpen.

4 Click Smart Sharpen.

The Smart Sharpen dialog box appears.

5 Click and drag the slider to reduce the default Radius amount to 0.5 as a starting point.

6 Click the Remove drop-down menu and select Lens Blur.

Note: Lens Blur finds the edges and detail and produces a sharper effect with fewer halos.

7 Click and slowly drag the Amount slider to the right until you see halos on the edges.

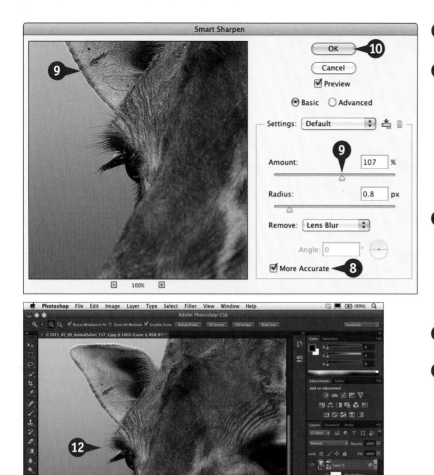

8 Click More Accurate (☐ changes to ☑).

9 Click and drag the Amount slider slowly to the left just until the halos are no longer visible.

Note: You can click and drag the Radius slider to increase the edges affected.

10 Click OK.

The image appears sharper.

11 Double-click the Zoom tool to view the image at 100%.

12 Press and hold the spacebar and click and drag in the image to view different areas and check the sharpening.

TIPS

Did You Know?

Digital sharpening is actually an illusion. It does not actually sharpen anything but rather exaggerates edges by increasing the contrast of adjacent pixels. Sharpening cannot correct an image blurred from camera shake or a moving subject.

More Options!

You can also paint on the Smart Filter's layer mask to remove the sharpening from different regions in the image. You can also use the Sharpen tool (▲) to paint directly over specific areas to sharpen them. You can even sharpen individual color channels, such as the red and green channels, to avoid exaggerating the noise in the third channel.

Important!

The amount of sharpening to apply is often a matter of personal choice. Oversharpening creates a halo effect around the edges. To sharpen images for viewing on-screen, sharpen until the image looks pleasing on your calibrated monitor. To sharpen images for print, add just enough sharpening so the image looks slightly oversharpened on the monitor.

You can sharpen the overall image and particularly the edges using a combination of the Unsharp Mask filter and the High Pass filter. With this technique, you first apply sharpening to a duplicated layer, and then duplicate the sharpened layer and apply the High Pass filter. This filter has the opposite effect of the Gaussian Blur filter. Instead of blurring edges, the High Pass filter removes any details or pixels without strong edges and retains the details where the sharpest color transitions occur.

You should generally sharpen your image in small amounts and at different times in the editing process. You first sharpen to correct the capturing blur caused by scanning or the digital camera. After resizing and color-correcting the image, you can sharpen a copy of the image for your intended type of output, that is, for viewing on a monitor or for printing.

If you sharpen your image on a separate layer, you can apply a different type of sharpening when you want to use the photo for a different type of output.

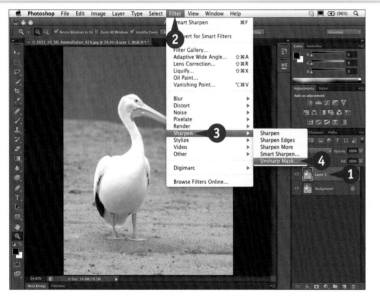

1 Press ⌘+J (Ctrl+J) to duplicate the Background layer.

2 Click Filter.

3 Click Sharpen.

4 Click Unsharp Mask.

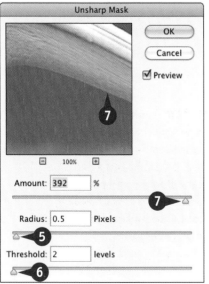

The Unsharp Mask dialog box appears.

5 Click and drag the Radius slider to reduce the default radius amount to 0.5 as a starting point.

6 Click and drag the Threshold amount to 2.

Note: Threshold determines how much contrast pixels must have from adjacent pixels before they have sharpening applied as edge pixels. The default Threshold value (0) sharpens all pixels in the image. Try Threshold values between 2 and 20 to avoid introducing noise or posterization.

7 Click and slowly drag the Amount slider to the right until you see halos on the edges.

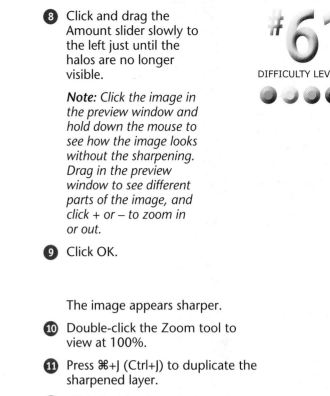

8 Click and drag the Amount slider slowly to the left just until the halos are no longer visible.

Note: Click the image in the preview window and hold down the mouse to see how the image looks without the sharpening. Drag in the preview window to see different parts of the image, and click + or – to zoom in or out.

9 Click OK.

The image appears sharper.

10 Double-click the Zoom tool to view at 100%.

11 Press ⌘+J (Ctrl+J) to duplicate the sharpened layer.

12 Click the blend mode drop-down menu and click Overlay.

13 Click Filter.

14 Click Other.

15 Click High Pass.

The High Pass filter dialog box appears.

16 Click and drag the Radius slider to 2 as a starting point and increase as necessary.

17 Click OK.

TIPS

Important!
If the image contains noise, sharpening can make the noise more pronounced. You can reduce the image noise before applying any form of sharpening.

More Options!
After applying the High Pass filter, you can use the Eraser tool ( ) and set the brush opacity in the Options bar to 50%. Then brush over edges that seem too sharp in the image to reduce or soften the effect.

Did You Know?
Sharpening sometimes shifts the colors along the edges in the image. When you use a duplicate layer to sharpen your image, you can change the layer's blending mode to Luminosity and avoid the changed edge colors.

Photoshop CS6 introduces a new set of blurring filters that can digitally create a shallow depth of field or a tilt-shift lens effect. The new tool includes a Field Blur tool, an Iris Blur tool, and a Tilt-Shift Blur tool to create the effect on an in-focus image. The Tilt-Shift Blur tool simulates the lens blur a photographer would get when using a view camera or a tilt-shift lens. The Iris Blur tool mimics a camera lens blur while allowing you to control the shape and size. The Field Blur tool allows you to apply an overall blur to the photograph or to a selection with one pin setting. You can add multiple pins, each with an increasing amount, to create a gradient blur. You can even apply different blur filters together for creative effects.

Because the new blur filters cannot be applied to a Smart Object, you can protect the original file by working on a duplicate Background layer. You can then toggle the eye icon on the blurred layer to view the before and after versions of your image.

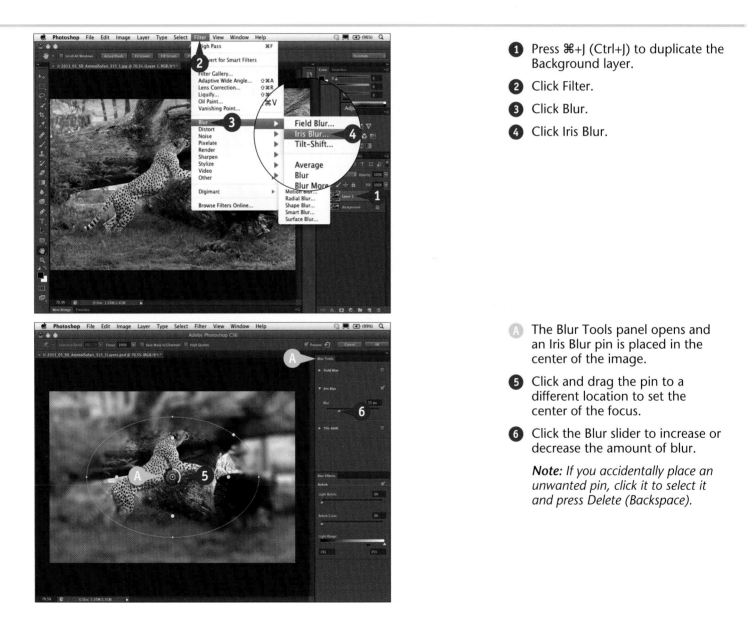

① Press ⌘+J (Ctrl+J) to duplicate the Background layer.

② Click Filter.

③ Click Blur.

④ Click Iris Blur.

Ⓐ The Blur Tools panel opens and an Iris Blur pin is placed in the center of the image.

⑤ Click and drag the pin to a different location to set the center of the focus.

⑥ Click the Blur slider to increase or decrease the amount of blur.

Note: If you accidentally place an unwanted pin, click it to select it and press Delete (Backspace).

The blurred area and amount change.

7 Click and drag any of the four corner anchors to alter the size.

8 Click and drag any of the four interior dots to increase or decrease the feather of the blur.

9 Click and drag the square anchor to change the Iris shape more into a rounded rectangle.

10 Click High Quality to create a more accurate Bokeh highlight (changes to).

11 Click OK.

The Blur tool is applied to the image.

Note: You can optionally repeat steps 2 to 10 using another blur filter for a creative effect.

TIPS

Did You Know?
Clicking Save Mask to Channels (changes to) in the Options bar adds a mask showing the blur in the Channels panel. You can then click the mask channel and paint with white or black to customize the mask shape.

More Options!
Create a selection in the photo before applying one of the blur tools. You can then apply the Selection Bleed control in the Options bar to adjust how the selected area blends or bleeds into the unselected areas.

Did You Know?
Use the Blur Effects tab to control the Bokeh. *Bokeh* is a term used to describe the quality of the out-of-focus points of light in a photo. The Light Bokeh slider controls the amount of the change. The Bokeh Color slider acts like a saturation slider for the out-of-focus areas. The Light Range sliders determine which brightness values the Light Bokeh affects.

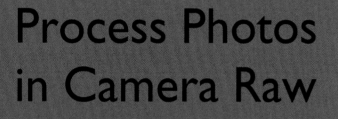

Chapter 6

Process Photos in Camera Raw

Camera Raw is a plug-in automatically included with Photoshop. RAW is a file format, such as CR2 on advanced Canon cameras or NEF or Nikon's advanced cameras.

All digital cameras first record the raw data on the sensor, and then the camera's internal processor converts the data into the file you see on the camera's LCD screen. If you select the JPEG file format in your camera, the camera's built-in processor applies the manufacturer's predetermined settings, and it decides what capture data to keep and what data to throw away to create a pleasing image. It also automatically compresses the file. When you make any changes to a JPEG or even a TIFF file, with Photoshop, you change pixels

that have already been processed and compressed inside the camera.

If instead you select the RAW format on your camera, the RAW file includes all the original uncompressed captured data. You can then process the file with Camera Raw in your computer, so you can control the desired tonal rendition, color balance, saturation, and other characteristics of the final image.

You can still adjust JPEG and TIFF files in addition to RAW files with Camera Raw and benefit from nondestructive edits. Then all the image data in the file, whether it is a JPEG, TIFF, or RAW file, is preserved and the adjustments are simply stored as metadata, in a separate small file, called a sidecar XMP data file.

DIFFICULTY LEVEL

Set the preferences to OPEN ANY IMAGE IN CAMERA RAW

#63

DIFFICULTY LEVEL

Most digital cameras can create JPEGs and sometimes TIFF files. Advanced digital cameras can also write a manufacturer's proprietary camera RAW format, such as NEF or CR2. The DNG file format, an open format created by Adobe, is also a RAW file format.

The RAW file is the most direct representation of what the camera sensor captured because the data is not processed or compressed in the camera. Such proprietary RAW files require specific software to convert the file so you can see and use it with the computer. Photoshop includes the Camera Raw plug-in to convert RAW images. However, Camera

Raw is also a powerful image editor on its own.

Camera Raw automatically launches whenever you open a manufacturer's proprietary RAW file. However, you can set the Camera Raw preferences to automatically open both JPEGs and TIFFs as well and take advantage of the Camera Raw editing tools.

You can then open any photo using Camera Raw and make specific adjustments. The edits are visible on your monitor; however, they are actually saved as data. You have not altered any of the pixels in the file.

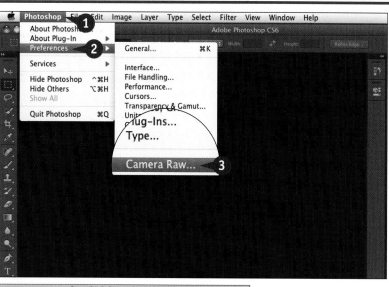

① Click Photoshop (Edit).

② Click Preferences.

③ Click Camera Raw.

The Camera Raw Preferences dialog box appears.

④ Click the JPEG drop-down menu and select Automatically Open All Supported JPEGs.

⑤ Click the TIFF drop-down menu and select Automatically Open All Supported TIFFs.

⑥ Click OK to save the Camera Raw preferences.

Although you cannot directly edit pixels on a Smart Object layer, as you can when using the Brush tool on a regular layer, working on files as Smart Objects has many benefits. You can make edits to Smart Objects without permanently changing the original file's data, so you can scale, rotate, or transform the layer and still go back to the original if you do not like the changes. When you apply filters to Smart Objects, the filters become Smart Filters, and Smart Filters can be re-edited even after they are applied to the Smart Object layer. You can duplicate a Smart Object layer multiple times, and when you edit any

one of the duplicates or the original, all the other copies are updated at the same time.

You can create Smart Objects by opening a file as a Smart Object with the menu, by using the Place command, or by converting an already open file to a Smart Object. However, if you set the Camera Raw preferences to open all JPEGs and TIFFs as in the previous task, you can also have Camera Raw automatically send the file to Photoshop as a Smart Object. This setting is not obvious; however, once you set it, the option continues to work until you deselect the option.

1 Open an image in Camera Raw.

2 Make any adjustments.

3 Click the blue underlined photo description.

> *Note: This description is also a link to the Workflow Options dialog box.*

The Workflow Options dialog box appears showing the settings of the image.

4 Click Open in Photoshop as Smart Objects (☐ changes to ☑).

5 Click OK.

A Open Image changes to Open Object in the Camera Raw dialog box.

6 Click Open Object to open the file as a Smart Object.

> *Note: All Camera Raw files will open as Smart Objects until you deselect this option.*

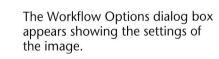

Clipped or blown highlights print as completely white areas because the image has no pixel information in these areas. Clipped highlights can ruin an otherwise good photograph and are often difficult to control with other tools. With an image open in Camera Raw, you can see the blown-out highlights by clicking the Highlight Clipping warning triangle in the histogram. The highlights without any colored pixels appear in red. Conversely, clicking the Shadow Clipping warning triangle in the histogram makes the overly dark shadow areas or completely black areas with no tonal range appear in blue.

In Photoshop CS6, the highlight recovery in Camera Raw is always enabled and linked to the Exposure slider. You can adjust the image by working with the sliders in the order they are listed in the Basic pane. First normalize the image brightness using the Exposure slider. Partially clipped highlights can be recovered by applying a negative Exposure compensation of up to −1 stop. You can then recover any leftover clipped highlights by slowly moving the Highlights slider to the left, which leaves the overall brightness of the image unchanged.

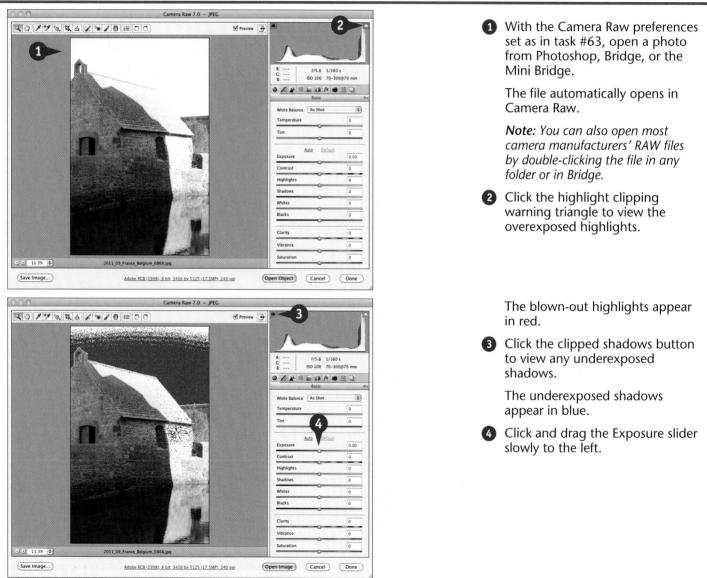

1 With the Camera Raw preferences set as in task #63, open a photo from Photoshop, Bridge, or the Mini Bridge.

The file automatically opens in Camera Raw.

Note: You can also open most camera manufacturers' RAW files by double-clicking the file in any folder or in Bridge.

2 Click the highlight clipping warning triangle to view the overexposed highlights.

The blown-out highlights appear in red.

3 Click the clipped shadows button to view any underexposed shadows.

The underexposed shadows appear in blue.

4 Click and drag the Exposure slider slowly to the left.

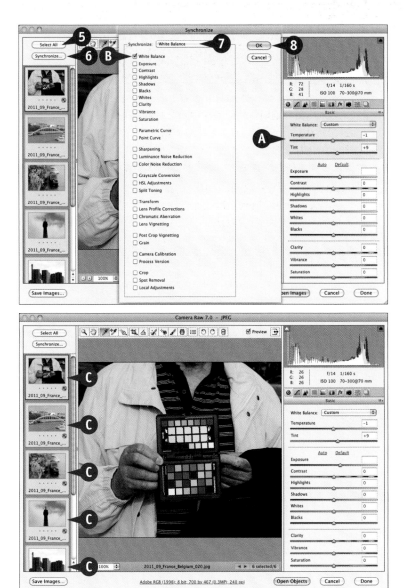

A The white balance changes and the Temperature and Tint sliders adjust accordingly.

5 Click Select All or Shift+click the other images in the Camera Raw dialog box.

6 Click Synchronize.

The Synchronize dialog box appears.

7 Click the Synchronize drop-drop menu and select White Balance.

B Only the White Balance check box remains checked.

8 Click OK.

C The white balance changes in all the other selected images and the photos appear with the Edit icon.

TIPS

More Options!

You can convert most RAW files from the various camera manufacturers into DNG files using the Adobe DNG converter, available on Adobe.com. You will then be able to open them in the future even if the manufacturer no longer supports the older file formats. Also, DNG files do not require a separate XMP, or *sidecar*, file to be linked with the original file for viewing edited photos.

Important!

The Temperature and Tint sliders adjust to make the selected color as neutral as possible. When you select and click a neutral gray area in a photo, avoid clicking a highlight area that contains a specular highlight. You can always double-click the White Balance tool (🖊) to reset White Balance to As Shot and try a different area.

Did You Know?

After you process and edit a camera RAW file using the Camera Raw plug-in, an Edit icon (📷) appears on the image thumbnail in Bridge. If the image has been cropped, the Crop tool icon (🔳) appears.

Think of a camera RAW file as your photo negative. When you process the photo in Camera Raw, you can reprocess the file at any time because although changes are viewable, you have not altered any pixels, so you can continue to make changes to render the image as you want it to appear.

Once you have made adjustments in the Basic tab, you can fine-tune the image using the other tabs in the Camera Raw dialog box. You can click the Tone Curve tab to make adjustments to the values in

specific tonal ranges in the image. Using the Point tab of the Tone Curve pane, you can add points and click and drag the line into an S-curve. You can also adjust the curve and the tones in the image using the Targeted Adjustment tool. When you select the tool and drag directly up or down on different areas in the image, the tones and the curve adjust accordingly. Using this visual method of adjusting the Tone Curve is intuitive and natural.

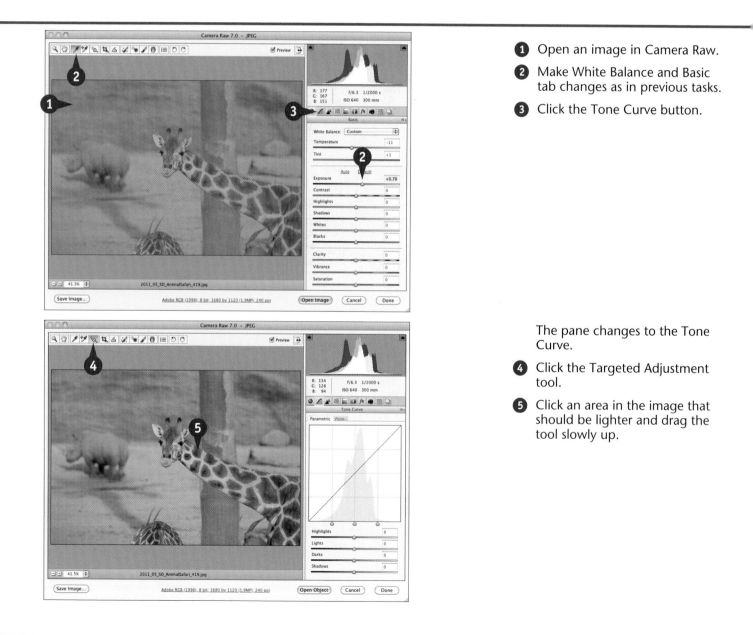

1 Open an image in Camera Raw.

2 Make White Balance and Basic tab changes as in previous tasks.

3 Click the Tone Curve button.

The pane changes to the Tone Curve.

4 Click the Targeted Adjustment tool.

5 Click an area in the image that should be lighter and drag the tool slowly up.

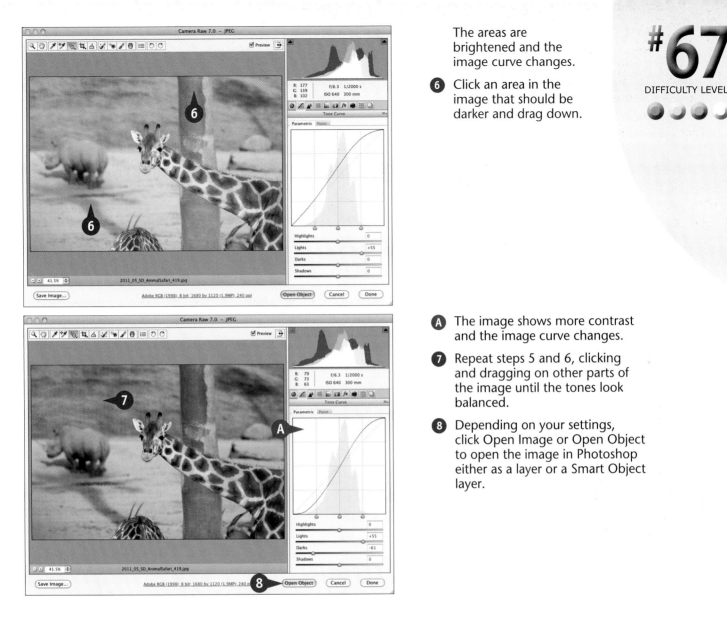

The areas are brightened and the image curve changes.

6 Click an area in the image that should be darker and drag down.

A The image shows more contrast and the image curve changes.

7 Repeat steps 5 and 6, clicking and dragging on other parts of the image until the tones look balanced.

8 Depending on your settings, click Open Image or Open Object to open the image in Photoshop either as a layer or a Smart Object layer.

TIPS

Important!

If your camera displays a histogram on the LCD, this is the histogram of the file after it has been processed in-camera using the camera's default settings. It is a histogram of the conversion to JPEG, and not the histogram of the original RAW file.

Attention!

Most cameras apply a fairly strong S-curve to the raw data so that the JPEGs you see on the camera's LCD, as well as any images you captured as JPEGs, appear more like traditional film. The on-camera histogram reflects this strong S-curve and may show blown highlights when, in fact, the highlights may be within the tonal range.

When you first open an image in Camera Raw, the tools in the Basic tab help you adjust the overall brightness, white balance, and saturation of the image. On other tabs, you can adjust different tones and colors individually, make lens corrections, alter colors in the image, sharpen and reduce noise, and even save some or all of your settings as presets so that you can reapply them to similar images.

The Graduated Filter tool in the Camera Raw dialog box enables you to apply tonal changes similar to

using a photographic graduated filter on a camera lens, but with more flexibility. For example, you can easily dramatize an open sky in a landscape photo by changing the exposure, saturation, clarity, and color of the sky or a large area and completely change the mood of the image.

You can open any file from Camera Raw as a Smart Object in Photoshop. Then you can easily reopen the Camera Raw dialog box and change the settings as you work before you save the file in Photoshop.

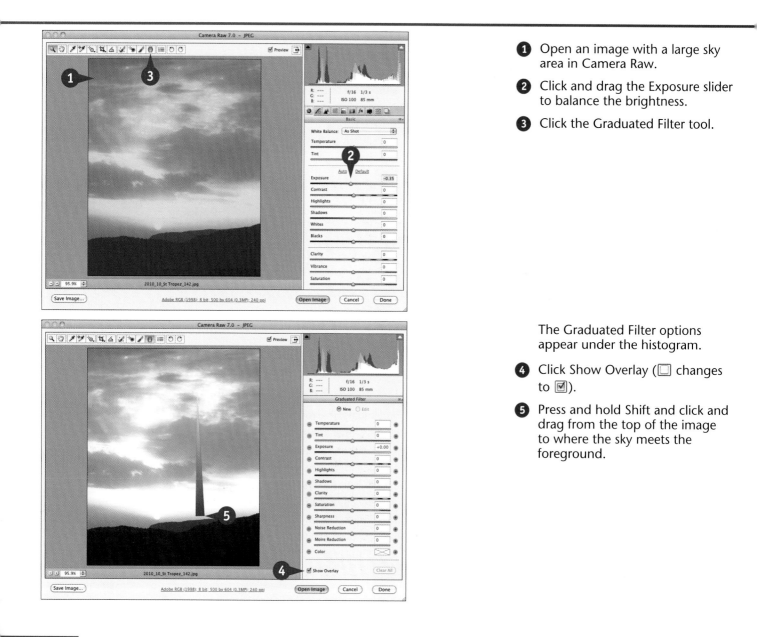

1 Open an image with a large sky area in Camera Raw.

2 Click and drag the Exposure slider to balance the brightness.

3 Click the Graduated Filter tool.

The Graduated Filter options appear under the histogram.

4 Click Show Overlay (☐ changes to ☑).

5 Press and hold Shift and click and drag from the top of the image to where the sky meets the foreground.

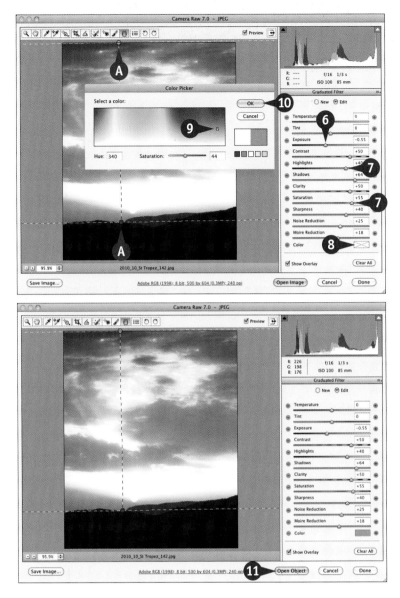

A The Graduated Filter overlay appears with two adjustment pins on the image.

6 Click and drag the Exposure slider to the left to darken the sky.

7 Click and drag the other sliders on the Graduated Filter panel to increase the intensity of the sky.

8 Click the Color box.

The Color Picker appears.

9 Click a color to apply to the sky.

10 Click OK.

The sky in the photo changes.

11 Shift+click the Open Image button.

The button changes to Open Object and the image opens as a Smart Object in Photoshop.

Note: You can optionally click Save Image to convert and save the image with the Graduated Filter adjustment, or click Done to apply the changes and close the dialog box without opening the image in Photoshop.

TIPS

More Options!

Once you have applied the Graduated Filter settings, you can continue to adjust the image in Camera Raw. Click the Zoom tool (🔍) to return to the Basic panel. The adjustments you applied with the Graduated Filter remain on the image.

Try This!

You can apply multiple Graduated Filter adjustments to an image by applying one and then selecting New (⬜ changes to ◉) to start another one. You can always go back and edit any adjustment. Make sure that Show Overlay is selected and click the Graduated Filter pin on the image.

Important!

With Camera Raw, you control the colors in the image by what you see on the screen, so it is essential to work with a properly calibrated and profiled monitor as discussed in task #14.

Creating split tone effects in the traditional darkroom was difficult and labor-intensive. With Camera Raw, you can easily create a split tone look, in which a different color is applied to the shadows and highlights. You can also visually add or remove tones while previewing the image.

This feature of Camera Raw lets you associate hue and saturation with the lightest colors separately from the hue and saturation values associated with the darkest colors in the image. You can then adjust the

Balance slider to emphasize the tone of the highlights or the tone of the shadow areas.

Because you create the split tone in Camera Raw, the alteration to the image is completely nondestructive. The original image always remains intact. You can reopen Camera Raw to change the color or saturation amounts at any time to adjust the effect.

You can apply a split tone to either a grayscale or a color image; however, the toning is often most effective on a grayscale photo with high contrasts.

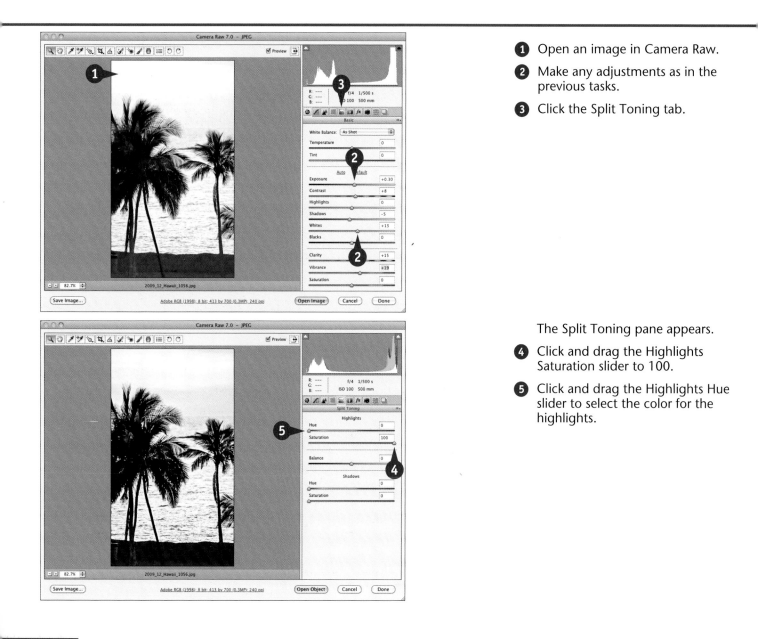

1 Open an image in Camera Raw.

2 Make any adjustments as in the previous tasks.

3 Click the Split Toning tab.

The Split Toning pane appears.

4 Click and drag the Highlights Saturation slider to 100.

5 Click and drag the Highlights Hue slider to select the color for the highlights.

The highlights in the image appear in a fully saturated color tone.

⑥ Click and drag the Shadows Saturation slider to 100.

⑦ Click and drag the Shadows Hue slider to select the color for the shadows.

The shadow areas in the image appear in a fully saturated color tone.

⑧ Click and drag the Balance slider to the right to shift the toning more into the highlights or to the left to emphasize the tones in the shadows.

⑨ Click and drag both the Highlights and the Shadows sliders to adjust the split tone effect.

⑩ Repeat steps 8 and 9 to adjust the split tone image.

The grayscale image appears as a split tone image with tinted shadows and highlights.

TIPS

Did You Know?

You can open any image into Camera Raw from the Open dialog box in Photoshop. Click File ➪ Open. Click the Format drop-down menu at the bottom of the Open dialog box and select Camera Raw from the list.

More Options!

If you add a split tone to a color image, you can still convert it to grayscale after applying split toning by clicking the HSB/Grayscale button in Camera Raw (▦).

Try This!

You can use a more gradual approach by leaving the Saturation slider set to 0 and pressing Option (Alt) as you drag the Hue sliders. The preview shows a 100% saturation of that hue. After you select the hue, you can move the Saturation sliders to the amount that you want.

Camera Raw is intended for processing the uncompressed captured data of RAW image files. In addition, you can use Camera Raw to open JPEGs and TIFFs. The Camera Raw tools can help you improve tones, color balance, and other characteristics of your photos. However, you can also use Camera Raw creatively when interpreting your images. You can simplify the details and boost the colors of a photograph in preparation for turning it into a painting with the tools and techniques shown in Chapter 9. You can also use Camera Raw to soften skin tones on snapshots when you do not want to spend a lot of time retouching the photo. If you have a JPEG file with a lot of artifacts because it was taken with a cell phone or other low-resolution point-and-shoot-type camera, you can use Camera Raw to rescue that photo by reinterpreting it in a more artistic fashion.

By exaggerating the use of the Clarity, Vibrance, and Saturation sliders, you can change an image's look from photographic to artistic. And by dramatically pushing the noise reduction sliders, you can reduce artifacts and soften the photographic details.

1 From the Bridge or Mini Bridge, Control+click (right-click) a photo.

2 Click Open in Camera Raw.

The Camera Raw dialog box appears.

3 Click and drag the Exposure slider if necessary to balance the brightness.

4 Click and drag the Clarity slider to the right.

5 Click and drag the Vibrance slider to the right.

6 Click and drag the Saturation slider to the right.

7 Continue adjusting the sliders until the colors appear more intense.

8 Click the Detail button.

The Detail panel opens.

9 Make sure the Sharpening Amount slider is set to 0.

10 Click and drag the Luminance Noise Reduction slider all the way to the right.

11 Click and drag the Luminance Detail slider to the left.

12 Click and drag the Color Noise Reduction slider to the right.

13 Click and drag the Color Detail slider to the left.

14 Continue adjusting the sliders until the image appears soft and painterly.

15 Click Open Image to open the image in Photoshop.

TIPS

Try This!

You can use this technique on photographs with people when you want to quickly soften the skin without doing major portrait retouching work. Move the Luminance slider to the right and the Luminance Detail slider to the left, keeping an eye on the image at 100% to make sure the person still looks natural.

Did You Know?

You can use this technique on a photo you plan to turn into a painting. Simplifying the details and boosting the colors help prepare the photo before using it as a base for a painting. If you are going to use the photo as a base for a sketch, reduce the saturation instead of increasing it, and increase the clarity. Then reduce the luminance noise and detail as much as possible.

More Options!

If you open the image as a Smart Object, you can make changes in Photoshop and go back to the Camera Raw window to refine the adjustments.

Chapter 7

Make Magic with Digital Special Effects

Since Photoshop's inception, photographers and graphic designers alike have been using the application for digital imaging and photo manipulation. Photoshop can transform an average shot into a good photograph, a good photograph into a great one, and a great image into creative fine art. Graphic designers can start with photographs or a blank document and create logos, magazine covers, billboards, and more without using markers or X-ACTO knives.

Just as with the previous versions, Photoshop CS6 offers many powerful tools for creating designs or enhancing photographs. Some have been improved and others are totally new to this version. Some tools and techniques simply improve the image or photograph, and others

magically transform the subject or the entire image.

You can simulate the effect of using traditional photographic filters to enhance the colors or change the areas in focus in an image. You can draw attention to one part of the image using a vignette or change the point of focus digitally after the shot has been captured. Using the Merge to HDR feature, you can combine multiple exposures to realize a photo with a wider range of tones than the camera can capture in one shot. You can change the point of focus and even the depth of field in a photo after the shot. You can digitally alter structures and maintain perspective. And you can make unwanted elements magically disappear from a photograph.

APPLY A PHOTO FILTER for dynamic adjustments

Different lighting conditions produce different color temperatures on photographic images. Although you can neutralize the white balance, you can also visually enhance an image in a traditional or creative way. The Photo Filter adjustment in Photoshop enables you to change the color balance and color temperature of an image whether it is digital or scanned from film, just as a film photographer would use colored filters in front of the lens. Because Photoshop considers the Photo Filter an adjustment rather than a filter, you find the Photo Filter adjustment under both the Image ⇨ Adjustments and Layer ⇨ New Adjustment

Layer menus. Applying the Photo Filter as an adjustment layer using the button in the Adjustments panel is the quickest way to access this adjustment and gives you the option of applying the filter selectively by painting on the layer mask.

Using a Photo Filter adjustment layer can visually change the time of day in the photo, turning midday into sunset. You can turn a bland photo into a dramatic one by applying a blue or violet filter across the entire image, or warm a cool photo by applying a warming filter.

① Open a photo.

② Arrange the panels to have more image viewing space.

③ Click the Photo Filter adjustment layer button.

Note: You can also click the New Adjustment Layer button ( ) at the bottom of the Layers panel.

The Photo Filter options appear in the Properties panel.

Ⓐ Make sure that Preserve Luminosity is selected (changes to).

④ Click the color box and select the color for the filter.

⑤ Click and drag the Density slider to the right to increase the effect if necessary.

The Photo Filter adjustment is applied to the entire image.

Note: You can duplicate the layer to increase the effect or change the layer blend mode to Hue to soften the effect.

Lens Vignetting, or the light falling off in the corners of the image, can appear in images with a large area of similarly toned background, such as a sky in a landscape image or a studio photo with the subject against a light background.

You can reduce a vignette or create one for effect, either lighter or darker, using one of the three styles in the Effects panel in Camera Raw.

The Paint Overlay style applies a soft-contrast type of vignette by blending either black or white into the edges of the image.

Highlight Priority and Color Priority both vary the exposure at the edges of the image and include a Highlights slider you can use to brighten any highlights that fall under the vignetted areas. Highlight Priority intensifies colors in the darkened areas, creating a stronger effect, but can sometimes shift colors in those vignetted areas. Color Priority creates softer transitions, particularly in the shadows, thereby preserving more of the natural colors in vignetted areas.

With any of the vignette options, you can increase or decrease the amount of vignette applied, change the midpoint and roundness, and increase or decrease the amount of feathering.

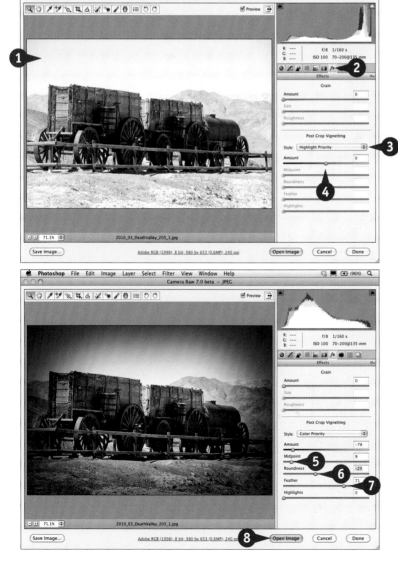

① Open an image in Camera Raw.

② Click the Effects button.

③ Click the Style drop-down menu to select a vignette style.

④ Click and drag the Amount slider to adjust the effect.

⑤ Click and drag the Midpoint slider to control how far the darkened areas extend into the photograph.

⑥ Click and drag the Roundness slider to make the vignette more square or circular.

⑦ Click and drag the Feather slider to the left for a harsher transition or right for more feathering.

⑧ Click Open Image or Open Object to open the file in Photoshop.

Remove unwanted elements with a CONTENT-AWARE BRUSH STROKE

Removing unwanted elements in a photograph has always been one of Photoshop's most magical achievements. The Clone Stamp tool made such tasks so much easier. You could also blend multiple photographs and use masks or other techniques to remove unwanted image elements. As Photoshop improved, you were able to use the Healing Brushes and Patch tool to selectively remove objects from a photograph. Photoshop's Content-Aware options for the Healing Brush tools now make it even easier to remove an element and replace it with pixels that match the lighting, tone, and even the noise of the adjacent areas so the replacement appears more natural.

With the Spot Healing Brush, you can paint directly over an area to be removed. However, you can also use the tool to stroke a path, which makes removing such things as power lines from a photograph much easier. You set the Content-Aware option and brush size, and then use the Pen tool to create the path. When you stroke the path with the brush, the line is replaced with elements that blend into the surrounding areas.

1 With an image open, click the New Layer button to add a new blank layer.

2 Click the Spot Healing Brush tool (🖌).

3 Click the Brush Preset drop-down menu and select a hard-edged brush slightly larger than the lines to be removed.

4 Click Content-Aware (⬤ changes to ⬤).

5 Click Sample All Layers (☐ changes to ☑).

6 Click the Pen tool.

7 Click the drop-down menu and select Path.

8 Click the blank layer in the Layers panel to target it.

9 With the Pen tool selected, click one end of the line to be removed.

10 Click the other end of the line.

Note: If the line is curved, you can click in the center or anywhere along the line of the path you just drew and adjust it to cover the line in the photo.

11 Click the Paths tab in the Layers panel group.

A A work path appears in the panel.

12 Click the panel menu button.

13 Click Stroke Path in the panel menu.

The Stroke Path dialog box appears.

14 Click the Tool drop-down menu and select Spot Healing Brush.

15 Click OK.

Photoshop strokes the line with a content-aware fill.

16 Click and drag the Work Path over the trash to delete it.

Note: *You may need to undo the stroke and try a different brush size to completely erase the line.*

The unwanted line is removed and the area is filled with content from adjacent areas.

17 Repeat steps 9 to 16 for any other lines in the photo.

18 Click the panel menu button and select Flatten Image to complete the edit.

TIPS

Did You Know?
By adding a new empty layer and making the edits on that layer, you do not alter the original file until you flatten the layers.

Important!
When removing multiple lines in a photo, work on one line at a time. The Content-Aware tools all work best when you make multiple smaller selections rather than one large one.

More Options!
Work on separate empty layers for each item you want to remove. That way if the Content-Aware stroke does not completely remove the line, you can easily delete the layer and redo the edit. Because the Content-Aware option randomly selects areas around the area to be removed, the results can be slightly different each time it is applied.

Use the Patch Tool to CLONE CONTENTS TO A NEW AREA

You can use a Content-Aware fill to remove and replace larger unwanted elements from photos. The Content-Aware option selects pixels from the surrounding areas and blends them into the selected section. In Photoshop CS6, you can now use a Content-Aware mode with the Patch tool to give you added control over the content that will fill larger patched areas. You can more easily remove even structured areas in a photo, and replace the pixels with pixels that blend realistically into the image. The new Content-Aware mode of the Patch tool can adapt

the cloned contents, moving lines and patterns to fit the surrounding areas. You can select the extent of the adaptation from Strict to Loose, and experiment with the different options to view how each affects the fill contents.

In addition, by using a layer mask to temporarily hide any elements you definitely do not want sampled for the patch, and by working on an empty layer above the Background layer, you can protect your main subject and the original pixels.

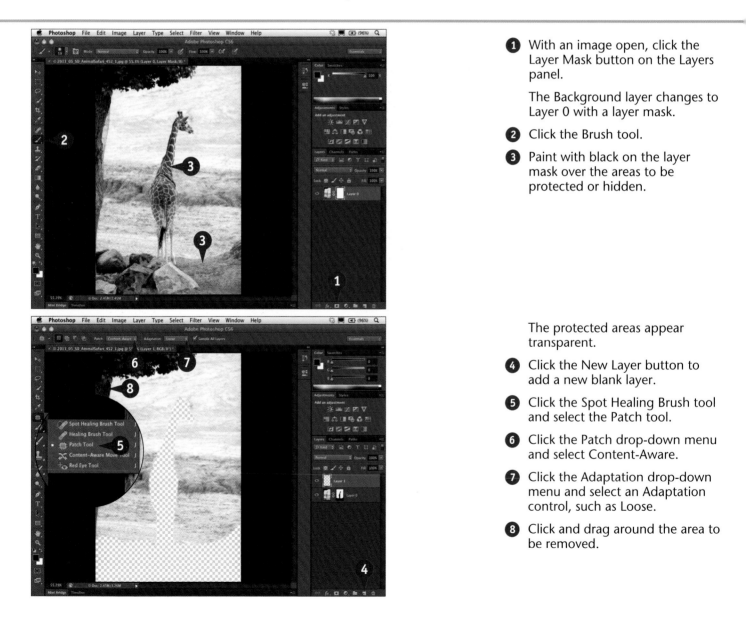

① With an image open, click the Layer Mask button on the Layers panel.

The Background layer changes to Layer 0 with a layer mask.

② Click the Brush tool.

③ Paint with black on the layer mask over the areas to be protected or hidden.

The protected areas appear transparent.

④ Click the New Layer button to add a new blank layer.

⑤ Click the Spot Healing Brush tool and select the Patch tool.

⑥ Click the Patch drop-down menu and select Content-Aware.

⑦ Click the Adaptation drop-down menu and select an Adaptation control, such as Loose.

⑧ Click and drag around the area to be removed.

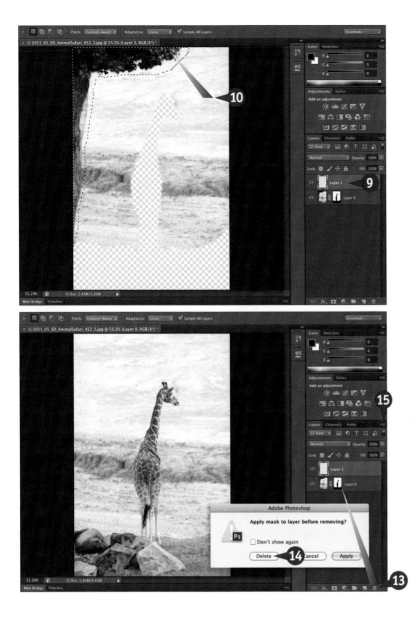

A selection marquee appears around the area.

⑨ Click the empty layer to target it.

⑩ Click inside the selected area on the photo and drag to another area in the photo.

⑪ Release the mouse.

The patched area fills with pixels blended from the surrounding areas.

Note: You can optionally click the Adaptation drop-down menu and select a different control to see if it blends better.

⑫ Press ⌘+D (Ctrl+D) to deselect the patched area.

⑬ Click and drag the layer mask thumbnail to the trash.

⑭ Click Delete in the dialog box that appears.

Important: Do not apply the layer mask.

⑮ Click the panel menu button and select Flatten Image to complete the change.

TIPS

More Options!

You can also use this masking technique when selecting an area to remove with the Lasso tool. Add a layer mask to the Background layer and paint with black over the areas to be protected. Use the Lasso or another selection tool to select the areas to be removed. Click Edit ⇨ Fill and select Content-Aware in the Fill dialog box. The masked areas are thus automatically excluded from the fill. Delete the layer mask without applying it.

Important!

Sample All Layers must be selected when you use an empty layer above the photo layer to apply the changes.

Did You Know?

The Very Strict adaptation control changes the contents of the cloned patch only slightly. The Very Loose adaptation control can introduce major changes to the cloned patch.

RECOMPOSE A PHOTO with the Content-Aware Move tool

Photoshop CS6 adds a new Content-Aware Move tool which can be used like the other Content-Aware tools to remove and replace pixels from one area of a photo to another while matching the lighting, tone, and even the noise of the adjacent areas so the replacement appears realistic. You can use the Content-Aware Move tool in the Extend mode to extend or add onto a building or other subject. The tool attempts to realign lines, structures, and patterns to appear natural in the resulting image.

You can also use the tool in the Move mode, to recompose an image and place some elements closer to others. As with the Healing Brushes and Patch tool, you can make the edits with the Content-Aware Move tool on an empty layer to avoid altering the original photo.

You make a loose selection of the item to be moved, and click and drag from inside the selection to another location. Photoshop moves the item and blends it into the new location, while filling the original area to match the surrounding pixels.

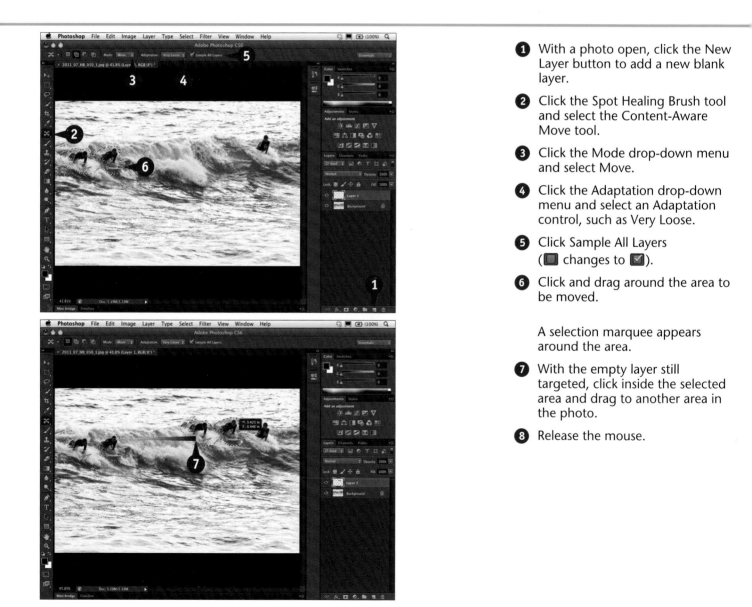

① With a photo open, click the New Layer button to add a new blank layer.

② Click the Spot Healing Brush tool and select the Content-Aware Move tool.

③ Click the Mode drop-down menu and select Move.

④ Click the Adaptation drop-down menu and select an Adaptation control, such as Very Loose.

⑤ Click Sample All Layers (▢ changes to ☑).

⑥ Click and drag around the area to be moved.

A selection marquee appears around the area.

⑦ With the empty layer still targeted, click inside the selected area and drag to another area in the photo.

⑧ Release the mouse.

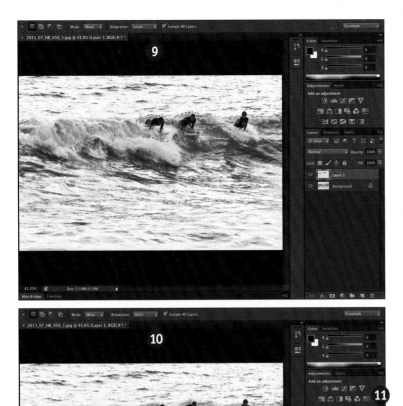

The items are moved to the new location and the old location fills with pixels blended from the surrounding areas.

9 Click the Adaptation drop-down menu and click a different control to see if the blend improves.

The moved area and the previous location area recompose with a different selection of pixels.

10 Repeat step 9 to find the most natural-looking adaptation.

11 Click the panel menu button and select Flatten Image to complete the change.

TIPS

Did You Know?
Using the Content-Aware Move tool in the Move mode can help unite group shots and bring subjects closer together.

Important!
The Content-Aware Move tool in the Move mode works best when the background in the original location and the destination are similar and the move distance is relatively short.

More Options!
You can use the Content-Aware Move tool in the Extend mode on an image with groups of birds or plants to make the photo look more densely filled with the subjects.

When you scale an image to make it fit a different aspect ratio, all the pixels in the image are affected and stretched uniformly. Although distorting a sky or a grassy field when adjusting an image to improve composition or fit a layout may not be noticeable, you cannot easily scale images with people or recognizable objects.

Photoshop includes the Content-Aware scaling feature so you can more easily upscale or downscale an image, or even change its orientation, without distorting the main subject.

You can stretch a sky, increase the length of a wall, and expand the area around the main visual content

and keep a natural aspect ratio to some areas while adapting the image to a new aspect ratio. For example, you can expand the sky in a photograph to extend upward for a magazine cover layout to allow room for the title text, without distorting the items or people in the foreground. You can also reduce the width or height of an image while maintaining the proportions of the main subject.

Depending on the image, Content-Aware scaling may require creating a selection or repositioning reference points around which to stretch the image.

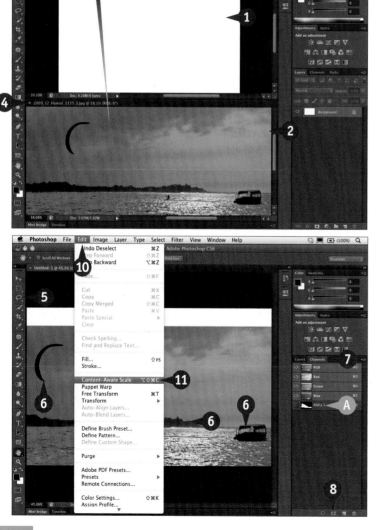

① Create a new blank document with the desired final dimensions.

Note: The amount the photo can stretch or shrink depends on the content in the photo. In this example the photo is 7.7 × 4 inches and the new document is 6.5 × 4.

② Open an image.

③ Click and drag the image over the tab for the blank document.

The image appears as a layer on the blank document.

④ Close the moved image.

⑤ Click the Lasso tool.

⑥ Click and drag around the content to protect.

⑦ Click the Channels tab.

⑧ Click the Layer Mask button to save the selection as a channel.

Ⓐ The selection is saved as Alpha 1.

⑨ Press ⌘+D (Ctrl+D) to deselect.

⑩ Click Edit.

⑪ Click Content-Aware Scale.

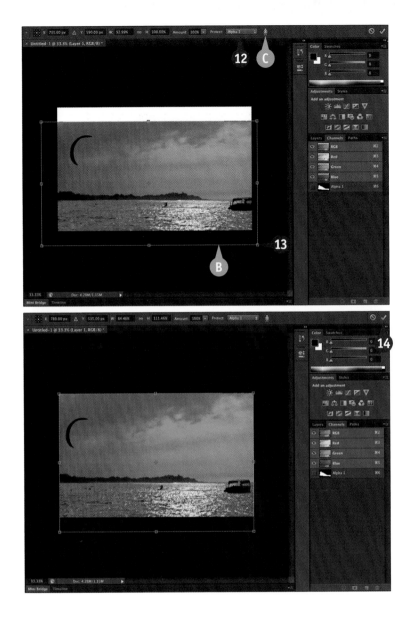

B A bounding border surrounds the image.

Note: Press ⌘+minus sign (Ctrl+ minus sign) to zoom out if necessary.

12 Click the Protect drop-down menu and select Alpha 1.

C You can optionally click the Protect Skin Tones button to protect people in the image.

13 Click and drag a handle on the bounding border to scale the image, as far as needed or until the main content starts to stretch unnaturally.

The image scales, leaving the main content at its original proportions.

14 Click the Commit button to apply the scaling.

Note: Content-Aware scaling works best when scaling in moderate amounts.

Note: You can optionally repeat steps 9 to 13 to scale the image more.

TIPS

Did You Know?
Although Content-Aware scaling can be applied to individual layers or selections, you cannot use it on adjustment layers, layer masks, individual channels, Smart Object layers, layer groups, or multiple layers at one time. To scale the Background layer, you must first click Select ➪ All.

More Options!
You can maintain the original aspect ratio of image when using the Content-Aware Scaling feature by clicking the Maintain Aspect Ratio button (⊟) in the Options bar.

More Options!
The default scaling reference point is the center of the image. You can set reference points or specify the fixed point around which the image is scaled by clicking a square on the reference point locator.

BLEND SEPARATE PHOTOS for the best group shot

Photoshop includes an Auto-Align Layers command to help you combine separate photos for panoramas or for composites. Auto-Align Layers analyzes edges and common elements in each image and brings them into alignment with each other. This tool also works well when combining multiple photos of a group so that everyone looks his or her best in the final photo.

You can drag all the separate images onto one of the images, making multiple layers. When you run the Auto-Align Layers command, Photoshop matches each layer with the others so that the similar shapes and forms match as much as possible. You can then add a layer mask to the layers to blend the images, erasing the unwanted parts of each layer. For group shots, you erase the closed eyes or grimaces to reveal the best expressions of everyone in the group.

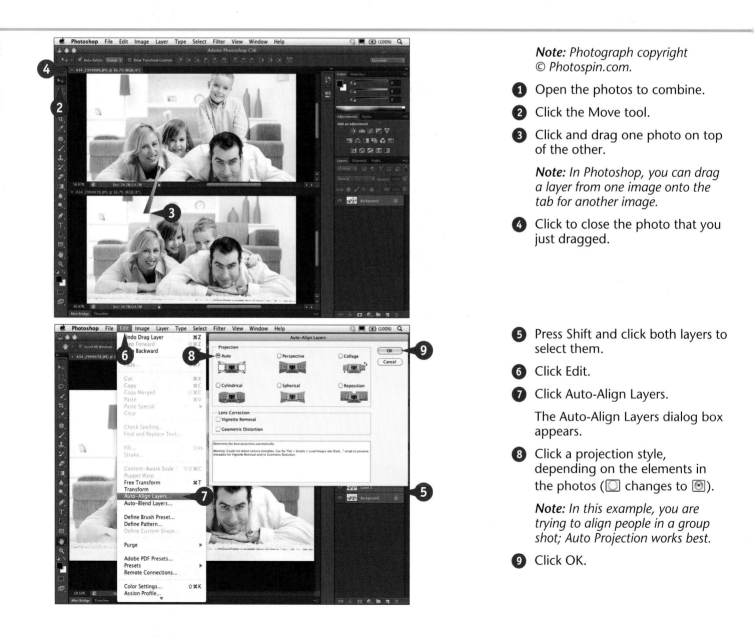

Note: Photograph copyright © Photospin.com.

1 Open the photos to combine.

2 Click the Move tool.

3 Click and drag one photo on top of the other.

Note: In Photoshop, you can drag a layer from one image onto the tab for another image.

4 Click to close the photo that you just dragged.

5 Press Shift and click both layers to select them.

6 Click Edit.

7 Click Auto-Align Layers.

The Auto-Align Layers dialog box appears.

8 Click a projection style, depending on the elements in the photos (⬜ changes to ◉).

Note: In this example, you are trying to align people in a group shot; Auto Projection works best.

9 Click OK.

A Photoshop aligns the photos by the content and renames the layers Layer 0 and Layer 1.

⑩ Click the top layer to select it.

⑪ Click Opacity and drag to the left to 60% to see the shapes below.

⑫ Click the Brush tool.

⑬ Click the Brush Preset drop-down menu and select a soft-edged brush.

⑭ Click the Layer Mask button to add a layer mask to the top layer.

⑮ Click the Switch Colors icon to set the foreground color to black.

Note: The top layer's mask should still be selected.

⑯ Paint with black on the top layer to reveal the best faces in the underlying layer for the best group shot.

B The mask displays the painted areas in black.

⑰ Click Opacity and drag to the right, back to 100%.

The final image blends the preferred subjects from both images.

⑱ If necessary, click the Crop tool and crop the image to the final size.

TIPS

Caution!
Make sure that the top layer's mask is still selected and that the foreground color is set to black when you paint on the photo to reveal the parts of the image on the layer below.

Did You Know?
Photoshop automatically selects one alignment projection option (step 8) based on the contents of the images you are combining. You can try it and then press ⌘+Z (Ctrl+Z) to undo the auto-alignment and try a different option.

More Options!
The Auto-Blend Layers command blends separate layers and tries to reduce or eliminate the perspective differences as well as the differences in colors or luminance without leaving a seam. This command works well for scenic photos.

MERGE MULTIPLE PHOTOS into an image with high dynamic range

Dynamic range in a photo refers to the ratio between the dark and bright areas. The human eye can adapt to different brightness levels, but the camera cannot. You can merge multiple photos of the same scene but with different exposures into a *high dynamic range* (HDR) image, displaying luminosity levels beyond what the human eye can see, and with more shades of color than any camera can capture in a single photo. Photoshop's Merge to HDR Pro command enables the still photographer to create a detailed photo with a wide dynamic range, and customize the settings for a realistic or more stylized final image.

The Merge to HDR Pro command works best on a series of photos taken with a tripod so that only the lighting of the image differs and nothing is moving. The aperture and ISO of the images should be the same in each photo. The shutter speed should vary from one to two f-stops in each direction. You can merge to HDR with at least three photos; however, you can include more photos with varying shutter speeds so your photos have a large variation in the image tones.

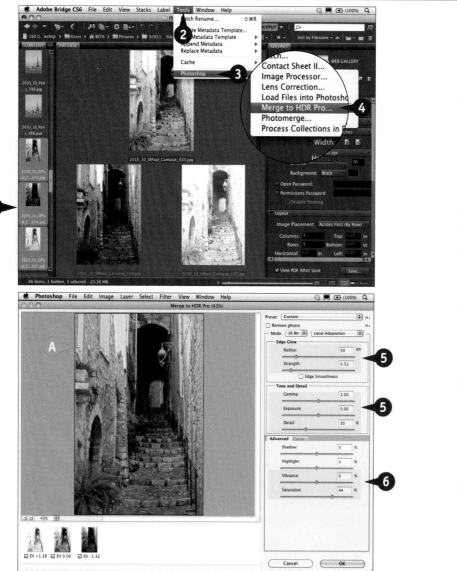

Note: *You can start from Bridge as in this task or from Photoshop by clicking Photoshop ➪ Merge to HDR Pro, and selecting the images to use.*

① In Bridge, ⌘+click (Ctrl+click) to select the images to merge.

Note: *Photos taken specifically to use with the Merge to HDR Pro command would normally appear in sequential order.*

② Click Tools.

③ Click Photoshop.

④ Click Merge to HDR Pro.

Ⓐ Photoshop opens, analyzes, aligns, and combines the images into one multilayered file, and the Merge to HDR Pro dialog box appears.

⑤ For 16-bit images, click and drag the sliders to customize the edge glow, tones, and detail.

Note: *For 32-bit images, click and drag the slider to adjust the white point of the preview image.*

⑥ Click and drag the Vibrance and Saturation sliders.

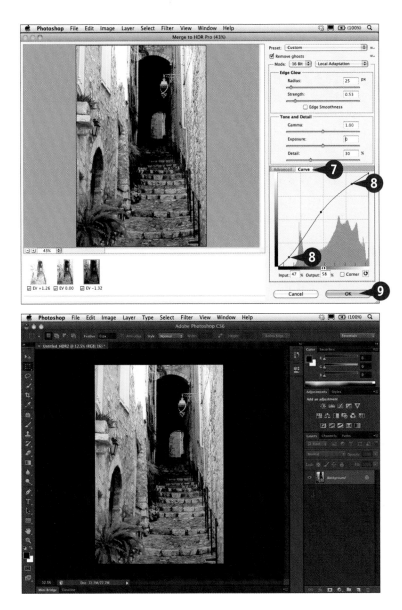

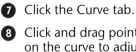

7 Click the Curve tab.

8 Click and drag points on the curve to adjust the contrast.

9 Click OK.

 # 78

DIFFICULTY LEVEL

Photoshop opens a new file named Untitled_HDR2.

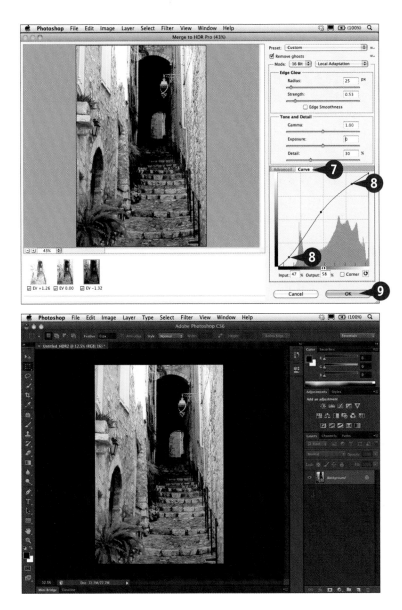

TIPS

More Options!

If your images have items in slightly different positions from one image to the next, such as moving foliage, you can click Remove Ghosts (☐ changes to ☑) in the Merge to HDR Pro dialog box. Photoshop selects the items with the best tones and hides the overlapping areas on the other images.

Important!

You can output the merged image as a 32-, 16-, or 8-bit image; however, only the 32-bit image can store all the high dynamic range data. You can convert from 32 bit to 16 or 8 bit after the image has been merged by clicking Image ➪ Mode ➪ 16 or 8 Bits/Channel and adjusting the exposure and contrast for the resulting HDR image.

Did You Know?

For the best results, use original photo files shot in the RAW format. When you merge files that have already been converted from the original RAW file format, the resulting merge may not have as much dynamic range.

Photoshop's Puppet Warp tool can be used to reposition one item in a photograph or manipulate a graphic element in a design. You can make simple adjustments to better position a distracting strand of hair or completely alter an item to give it a new position or shape, such as moving a person's hand or distorting a flower into a design. Unlike the Liquify filter, which transforms areas by moving pixels around, or the Transform command, which globally transforms the whole image, the Puppet Warp tool applies a visual mesh to your image. You can click specific areas, creating drop pins that act as anchor points, and then move specific areas to warp an area or element separately from the background.

You can also use the Puppet Warp tool to correct the perspective in a photograph. By dropping pins in each corner of items in the photo to act as anchors, you can add more pins and click and drag the edges of walls to straighten and reposition them; Photoshop adjusts the image to fit.

You can apply the Puppet Warp to a Smart Object so all your distortions are nondestructive and no pixels are permanently altered.

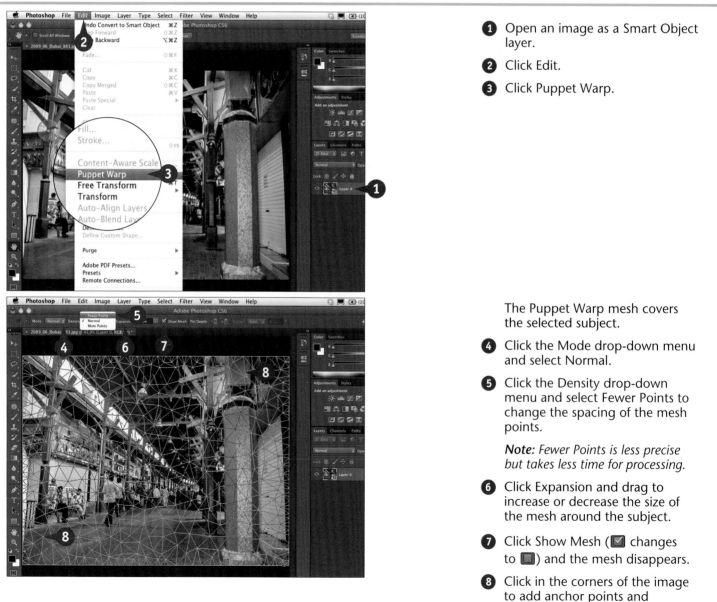

① Open an image as a Smart Object layer.

② Click Edit.

③ Click Puppet Warp.

The Puppet Warp mesh covers the selected subject.

④ Click the Mode drop-down menu and select Normal.

⑤ Click the Density drop-down menu and select Fewer Points to change the spacing of the mesh points.

Note: Fewer Points is less precise but takes less time for processing.

⑥ Click Expansion and drag to increase or decrease the size of the mesh around the subject.

⑦ Click Show Mesh (☑ changes to ▢) and the mesh disappears.

⑧ Click in the corners of the image to add anchor points and transformation pins.

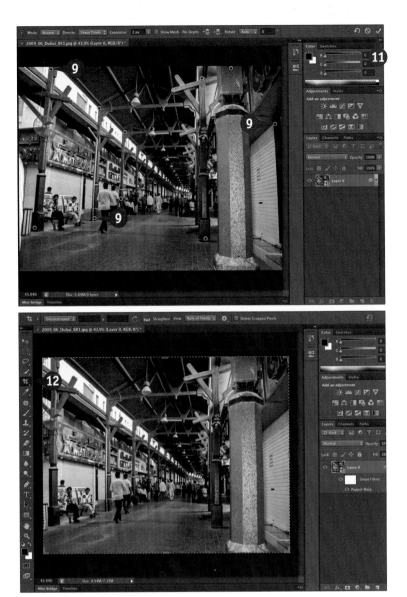

9 Click on structures or lines that should be vertical or horizontal and click and drag to realign the areas.

10 Repeat step 9 as necessary.

Note: Shift+click multiple pins and press Shift as you drag to move the selected pins at one time.

Note: To delete the pin, press Option (Alt) as you position the cursor over a pin and click when the scissors icon appears.

11 Click the Commit button to apply the Puppet Warp.

12 Click the Crop tool.

13 Crop the image as necessary.

14 Press Return (Enter) to apply the crop.

The structures in the image appear straightened and the perspective more natural.

TIPS

Did You Know?

The Options bar includes two buttons to move overlapped items, one for setting the Pin Depth forward (　) and one for setting it backward (　). Click the Remove All Pins button (　) to delete all the pins at once.

More Options!

The Distort mode setting in the Options bar enables you to distort the item with a more fluid movement. The Rigid mode gives you precise or more geometric bending around a drop pin.

Important!

You can apply the Puppet Warp tool to items on individual image layers, text layers, and shape layers, as well as to layer masks and vector masks.

APPLY HDR TONING to just one photograph

The dynamic range of a camera's sensor is more limited than the human eye. You can combine multiple photos shot at different exposures to produce a high dynamic range image that more closely resembles what the eye can see. The HDR tools in Photoshop are also often used at extreme settings to combine multiple exposures and create surrealistic effects.

With Photoshop, you can use the HDR Toning adjustment on just one image and produce a realistic photo with more detail. You can also push the sliders in reverse to intensify the shadows, highlights, and details and create an image with hyper-contrast for surrealistic effects, or diminish the intensity to soften the details to create an image with a more ethereal look, or anything in between. The default settings are for producing photorealistic images. You can select any of the other presets and also customize any settings by moving the sliders and adjusting the curve.

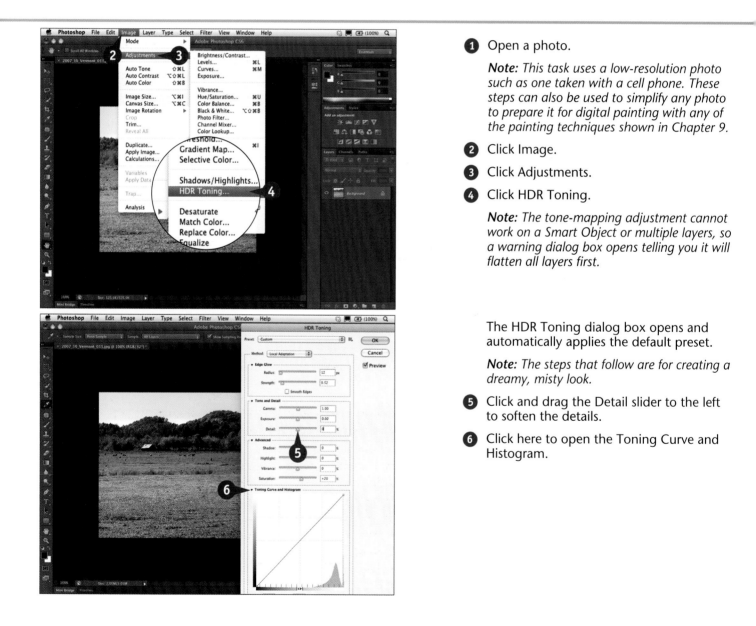

① Open a photo.

Note: This task uses a low-resolution photo such as one taken with a cell phone. These steps can also be used to simplify any photo to prepare it for digital painting with any of the painting techniques shown in Chapter 9.

② Click Image.

③ Click Adjustments.

④ Click HDR Toning.

Note: The tone-mapping adjustment cannot work on a Smart Object or multiple layers, so a warning dialog box opens telling you it will flatten all layers first.

The HDR Toning dialog box opens and automatically applies the default preset.

Note: The steps that follow are for creating a dreamy, misty look.

⑤ Click and drag the Detail slider to the left to soften the details.

⑥ Click here to open the Toning Curve and Histogram.

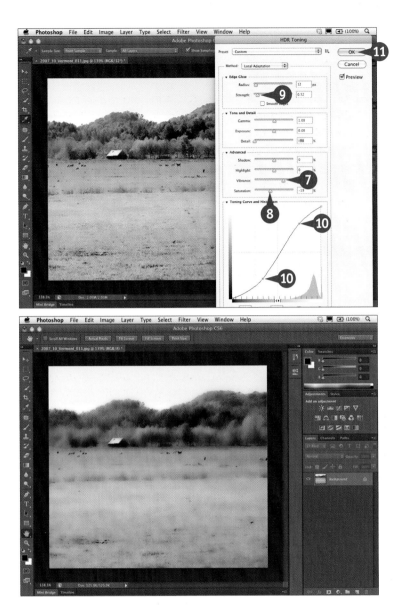

7 Click and drag the Vibrance slider to the right to increase the muted tones.

8 Click and drag the Saturation slider to the left to give a more misty or foggy look.

9 Click and drag the Strength slider to soften the image more.

10 Click two points in the Toning Curve to create a soft S-curve if necessary to increase contrast, similar to the curve shown in task #52.

11 Click OK.

The HDR tone mapping is applied to the Background layer.

#80

DIFFICULTY LEVEL

TIPS

Did You Know?

HDR toning cannot recover completely blown highlights or black shadows. Start with an image that has sufficient tonal range, with detail in both the highlights and shadows.

Try This!

You can create an extreme grayscale image using HDR Toning. Click the Preset drop-down menu in the HDR Toning dialog box and select one of the monochromatic presets. Optionally, you can use the HDR tone mapping to create a strong-contrast color image, and then add a Black & White adjustment layer, moving the sliders in the Properties panel to adjust the look.

Caution!

Watch the preview image as you work. Halos are a sign of an incorrectly tone-mapped image, so move the Edge Glow sliders carefully. And beware of grayed-out highlights when moving the Gamma slider. Small adjustments can make large changes.

INCREASE DEPTH OF FIELD with the Auto Blend tool

The depth of field you can capture depends on the type of camera, the aperture, and the focusing distance. Larger apertures, or smaller f-stop numbers, and closer focal distance produce images with a shallower depth of field, or less of the image in focus. Using smaller apertures, or larger f-stop numbers, produces photos with greater depth of field or more of the overall image in focus.

Sometimes you cannot use as small an aperture as you would need to create a photo with a very large depth of field because of the distance involved, or because of the lighting conditions. You can combine multiple shots and blend them together using the capabilities in Photoshop to create a larger depth of field.

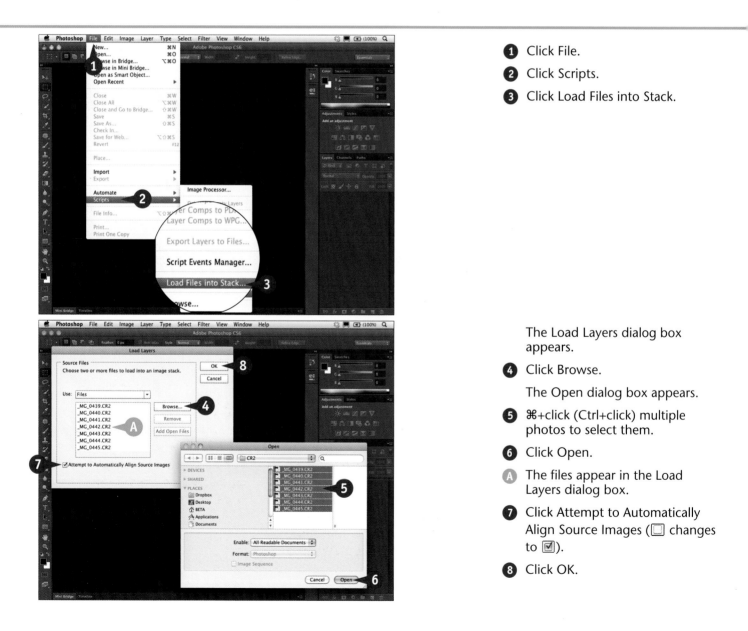

① Click File.

② Click Scripts.

③ Click Load Files into Stack.

The Load Layers dialog box appears.

④ Click Browse.

The Open dialog box appears.

⑤ ⌘+click (Ctrl+click) multiple photos to select them.

⑥ Click Open.

Ⓐ The files appear in the Load Layers dialog box.

⑦ Click Attempt to Automatically Align Source Images (☐ changes to ☑).

⑧ Click OK.

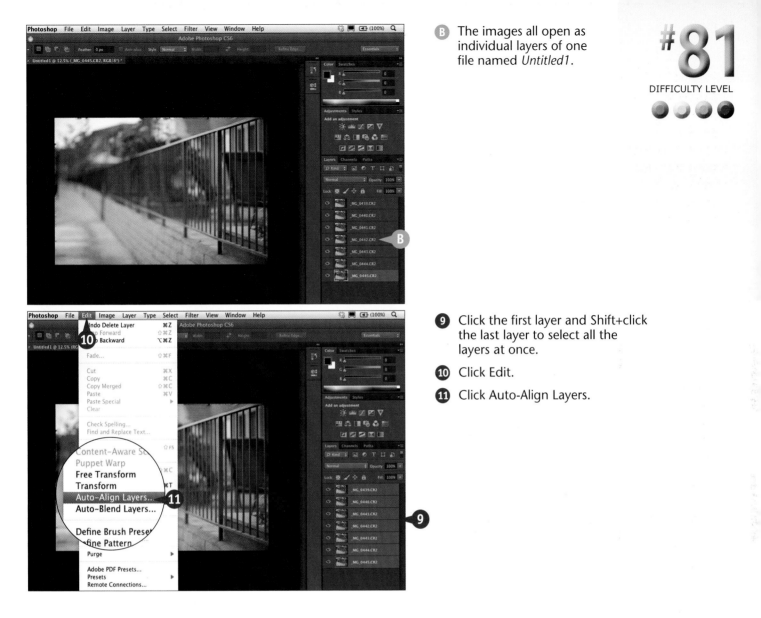

B The images all open as individual layers of one file named *Untitled1*.

#81

DIFFICULTY LEVEL

9 Click the first layer and Shift+click the last layer to select all the layers at once.

10 Click Edit.

11 Click Auto-Align Layers.

TIPS

Did You Know?
Depth of field occurs as a gradual transition, with everything in front of and behind the focusing distance of the camera lens losing sharpness.

Try This!
You can also start by selecting the files and opening them all as separate files. Then click File ➪ Scripts ➪ Load Files into Stack. In the Load Layers dialog box, click Add Open Files to select all the currently open files and click OK, and then continue with step 9.

Did You Know?
The Auto-Align Layers command aligns the layers based on similar content, such as corners and edges, in each of the different layers.

To create the best blend for extending the depth of field of the final image, you should use a tripod and use the manual focus of the camera. With the full image in the viewfinder or on the camera's LCD, manually focus on the area closest to the camera and take the first shot. Then change only the focus point to see the next area over in sharp focus. Continue taking photos until all the areas are in focus in at least one shot.

The Auto-Blend Layers command works only with RGB or Grayscale images and does not work with Smart Object layers or Background layers. And although the Auto-Blend dialog box does have an option for blending multiple images into a panorama, the Photomerge command generally produces better photo blends for panoramas.

You can use as many photos as required to capture each area of the scene in sharp focus.

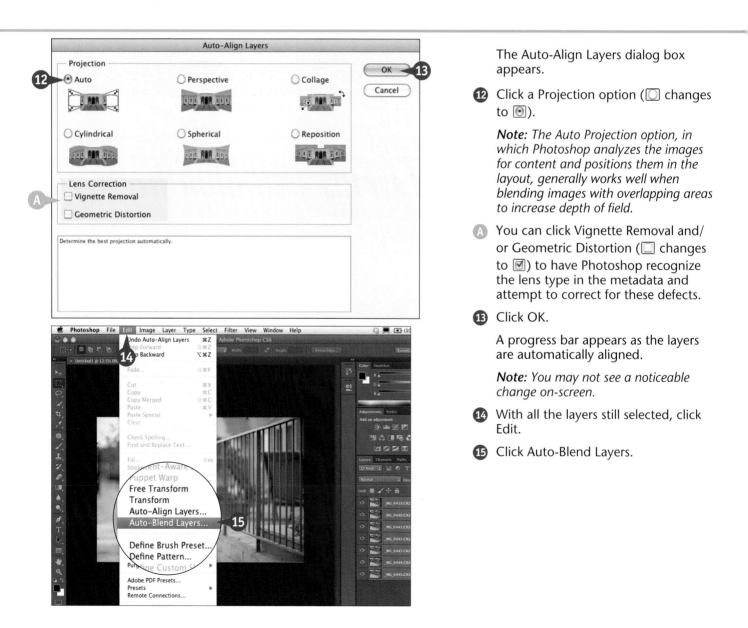

The Auto-Align Layers dialog box appears.

⑫ Click a Projection option (◉ changes to ◉).

Note: The Auto Projection option, in which Photoshop analyzes the images for content and positions them in the layout, generally works well when blending images with overlapping areas to increase depth of field.

Ⓐ You can click Vignette Removal and/ or Geometric Distortion (☐ changes to ☑) to have Photoshop recognize the lens type in the metadata and attempt to correct for these defects.

⑬ Click OK.

A progress bar appears as the layers are automatically aligned.

Note: You may not see a noticeable change on-screen.

⑭ With all the layers still selected, click Edit.

⑮ Click Auto-Blend Layers.

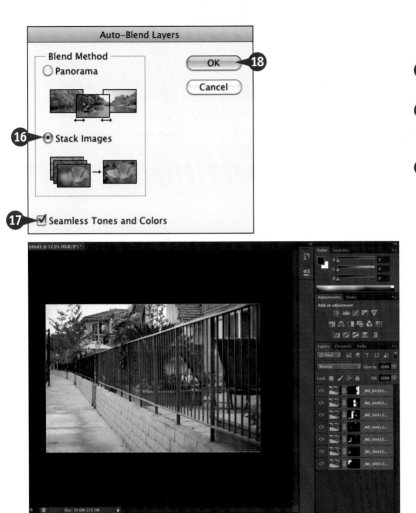

The Auto-Blend Layers dialog box appears.

⑯ Click Stack Images (☐ changes to ◉).

⑰ Click Seamless Tones and Colors (☐ changes to ☑).

⑱ Click OK.

A progress bar appears as the layers are blended based on the content, and layer masks are created.

The layers are blended using the layer masks, and the depth of field is increased, reflecting all the points in sharpest focus from each layer.

TIPS

More Options!
The Auto-Blend Layers command can also be used to create a correctly illuminated composite from multiple images of a scene with different over- or underexposed areas.

Attention!
Although you selected Attempt to Automatically Align Source Images in the Load Layers dialog box (step 7), the Auto-Blend Layers command generally works best if you apply the Auto-Align Layers command before attempting to auto-blend the layers.

More Options!
You can also convert video frames shot against a static background into layers and then use the Auto-Align Layers command to combine these frames and add or delete specific areas from the frames.

The Vanishing Point filter helps Photoshop recognize the third dimension of objects so that you can manipulate items in perspective. Using the Grid tool, you create a grid over an area, making sure to align the anchor points of the grid precisely with the corners of a rectangular area in the photo. With the first grid area set, you can extend the grid by pulling on the anchor points to cover a larger area with a blue grid in the same perspective.

Once the grid is in place, you can change the look of the image by erasing items, copying objects from one area of the image to another, or adding items from other images, all while keeping the perspective in the original photo.

And by creating a separate layer in Photoshop before applying the Vanishing Point filter, you can more easily adjust areas after you are back in the main Photoshop window.

Using the Vanishing Point filter, you can change the words on street signs and license plates, or add doors and windows to buildings. Just be sure to copy the item to be added to the clipboard *before* you choose the Vanishing Point filter on the main image.

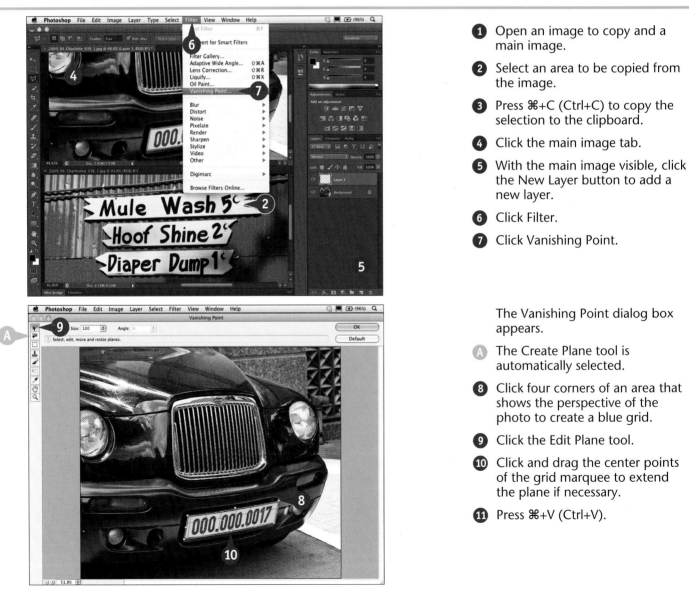

1 Open an image to copy and a main image.

2 Select an area to be copied from the image.

3 Press ⌘+C (Ctrl+C) to copy the selection to the clipboard.

4 Click the main image tab.

5 With the main image visible, click the New Layer button to add a new layer.

6 Click Filter.

7 Click Vanishing Point.

The Vanishing Point dialog box appears.

A The Create Plane tool is automatically selected.

8 Click four corners of an area that shows the perspective of the photo to create a blue grid.

9 Click the Edit Plane tool.

10 Click and drag the center points of the grid marquee to extend the plane if necessary.

11 Press ⌘+V (Ctrl+V).

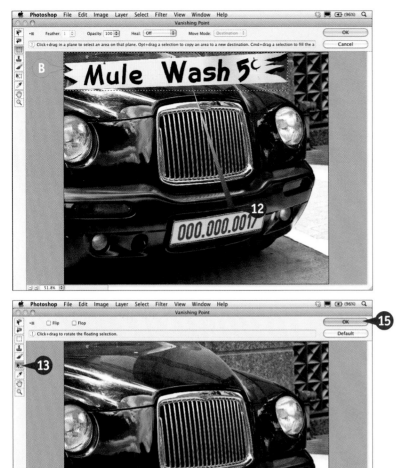

B The pasted selection appears in a corner of the Vanishing Point dialog box.

12 Click and drag the selection over the perspective plane.

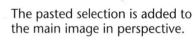

C The selection snaps into perspective on the plane.

13 Click the Transform tool.

14 Shift+click and drag the corners of the selection to adjust it into position.

Note: Depending on the size, you may need to move the selection to see the transformation anchors.

15 Click OK.

The pasted selection is added to the main image in perspective.

TIPS

More Options!

You can pull a secondary plane around a 90-degree corner and add items in perspective to different sides of a structure. You can even rotate a secondary plane by any amount to fit an angled area of a structure such as a roof.

Did You Know?

You can use the Zoom tool in the Vanishing Point dialog box (🔍) and click and drag to enlarge the area where you plan to apply the anchor points of the plane. You can also zoom-in temporarily as you place or adjust the anchor points by pressing ⌘+spacebar (Ctrl+spacebar) and clicking and dragging over the area.

Important!

You can use the Vanishing Point filter to increase the size of the building beyond the boundaries of the existing photo. Increase the canvas size first by clicking Image ⇨ Canvas Size, and then add width or height to one side of the existing image.

You can also use the Vanishing Point filter in Photoshop to help you remove items in an image while maintaining perspective.

You can edit the image in Photoshop before and after using the Vanishing Point filter. When you save the edited image as a PSD, TIFF, or JPEG, the perspective planes are saved with the file. You can then reopen the file, reapply the Vanishing Point filter, and continue to erase or edit in perspective at a later date.

Using the Vanishing Point grids takes a little practice. The first grid is the most important and must be accurate. The grid appears blue if it is showing a correct perspective plane. If the grid appears red or yellow, the grid must be adjusted using the anchor points until the grid turns blue. After extending the blue grid, you may still need to zoom in and readjust the main anchor points to better fit the perspective of the building or the subject.

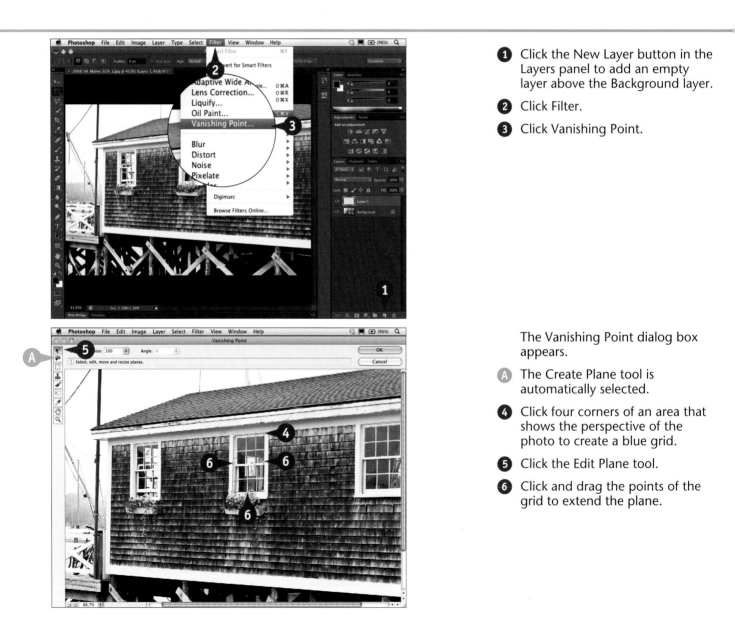

1 Click the New Layer button in the Layers panel to add an empty layer above the Background layer.

2 Click Filter.

3 Click Vanishing Point.

The Vanishing Point dialog box appears.

A The Create Plane tool is automatically selected.

4 Click four corners of an area that shows the perspective of the photo to create a blue grid.

5 Click the Edit Plane tool.

6 Click and drag the points of the grid to extend the plane.

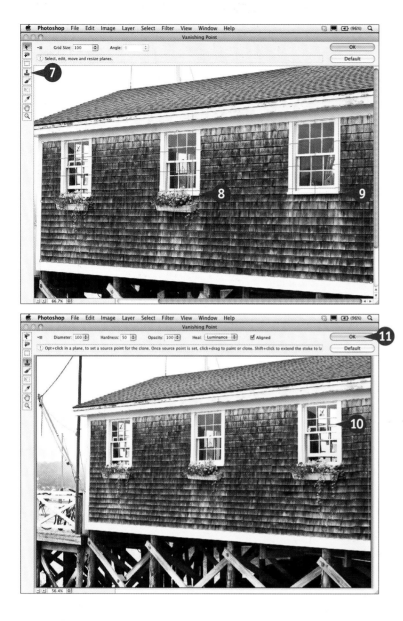

#83

DIFFICULTY LEVEL

The grid expands to fit the area.

7 Click the Stamp tool.

8 Option+click (Alt+click) in an area in the perspective plane to establish the sampling point.

9 Click and drag carefully in the area of the photo to be erased or altered.

10 Repeat steps 8 and 9, resampling if necessary to keep the look natural.

11 Click OK.

The edits are applied to the top layer.

TIPS

Important!

When erasing with the Vanishing Point Stamp tool (⬚), Option+click (Alt+click) a straight line in the area to be sampled. Then click along the same line in the area to be removed to help align the parts you will be cloning.

More Options!

Set the Heal mode in the Stamp tool options to On to blend the cloned strokes with the texture of the sampled image. Setting the Heal mode to Luminance, as in the example, blends the cloned strokes with the lighting of the surrounding pixels.

Try This!

You can save Vanishing Point grids on a separate layer in the Photoshop document. Add a new layer before using the Vanishing Point filter and create the grids. Click the Settings and Commands for Vanishing Point button (▼) in the Vanishing Point dialog box. Click Render Grids to Photoshop. Click OK, and the grids appear on the top layer of the file.

Use the Clone Stamp tool to SIMULATE A REFLECTION

You can create a reflection or a mirror image of the subject in a photo using a variety of techniques and different tools in Photoshop. You can select objects, duplicate and transform layers, adjust opacity, and more. However, you can quickly create a simulated mirror image of the subject in a photo using the Clone Stamp tool and the Clone Source feature of Photoshop.

The Clone Source tabbed panel enables you to see the reflection as a guide before you paint it; however, this panel must be moved away from the main image window to function correctly as a preview of what you are painting. You create the reflection on a separate layer so you can adjust the look using the layer opacity or a blended layer mask, or both.

Depending on the subject matter, angle of the subject, and intended use of the photo, your mirrored image can be convincingly realistic.

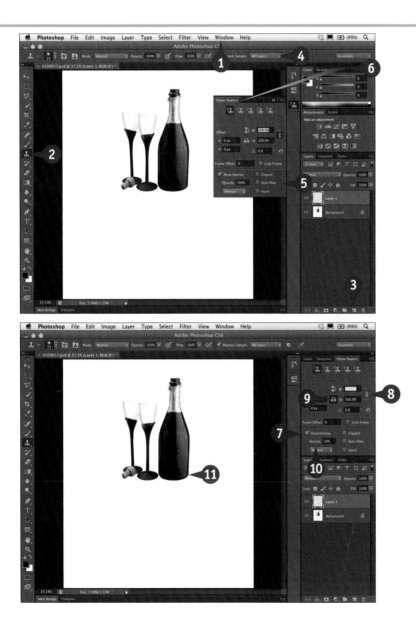

Note: Photograph copyright © Photospin.com.

1 Click Window ⇨ Clone Source to open the Clone Source panel.

2 Click the Clone Stamp tool.

3 Click the New Layer button on the Layers panel to create a new layer.

4 Click the Sample drop-down menu and select All Layers.

5 In the Clone Source panel, clear Clipped, Auto Hide, and Invert (☑ changes to ☐).

6 Click and drag the Clone Source panel away from the image window.

7 Click Show Overlay (☐ changes to ☑).

8 Make sure the Maintain Aspect Ratio link is not selected.

9 Click the Flip Vertically button.

10 Click Opacity and drag to the left to reduce the preview opacity to 50% or lower so you can see both the reflection and the original subject as you work.

11 Press Option (Alt) and click at the bottom of the subject to be mirrored to sample it.

12 Move the cursor away from the image window.

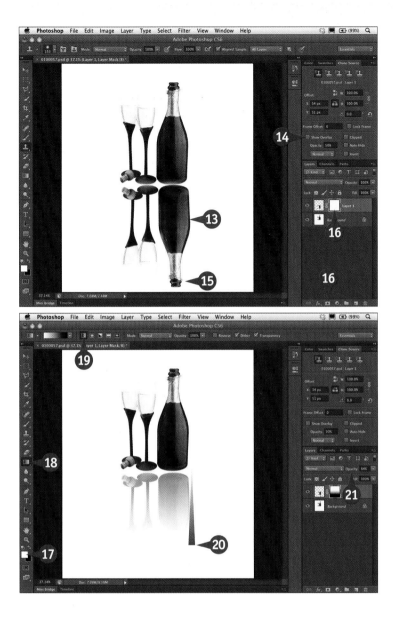

The reflection appears as an overlay on the image.

⑬ Click and drag using the Clone Stamp tool and a large brush to paint-in the reflection.

Note: Start painting close to the spot you originally sampled in step 11.

⑭ Click Show Overlay (☑ changes to ▣).

⑮ Click and drag with the Clone Stamp tool to finish painting the reflection.

⑯ Click the Layer Mask button to add a layer mask.

⑰ Press D to reset the foreground and background colors to white and black.

Note: The foreground color should be white.

⑱ Click the Gradient tool.

⑲ Click the Linear gradient.

⑳ Click and drag from near the bottom of the subject down to the bottom of the reflection using a white-to-black gradient.

The reflection appears to fade away from the subject.

㉑ Click the layer's Opacity slider and drag to make the reflection appear realistic.

TIPS

Did You Know?
The Clone Stamp reflection technique works well on product shots and can also be used as a creative tool for special effects with rasterized type.

More Options!
The Clone Source feature works with the Healing Brush tool (▨) as well as with the Clone Stamp tool.

Try This!
You can change the Offset values in the Clone Source panel to change the distance of the reflection from the subject. You can also vary the angle of the reflection by clicking and dragging the angle icon (◺) or typing a set number of degrees in the Clone Source panel.

Apply a shape to a wrinkled surface with a
DISPLACEMENT MAP

You can create, place, or paste one image onto another and blend the pasted image into the Background layer by changing the blend mode. The layer blending modes control how the colors in the top image combine with the pixels in the underlying image. They do not affect the texture of either image. To make the top layer blend into the texture of the base image and make the final image appear more realistic, you can use the Distort filter and a special file called a *displacement map*.

A displacement map is a grayscale version of an image saved as a Photoshop file. The Displace filter then uses the displacement map essentially as an applied texture. The black areas are the low points and the light areas are the high points of the contours of the original image.

You can copy one image onto another, such as a logo design onto any background, and can make the logo appear to be a part of the background image. You can also add a design or text directly on another layer and make the design blend into the folds of fabric, or whatever texture is in the background image.

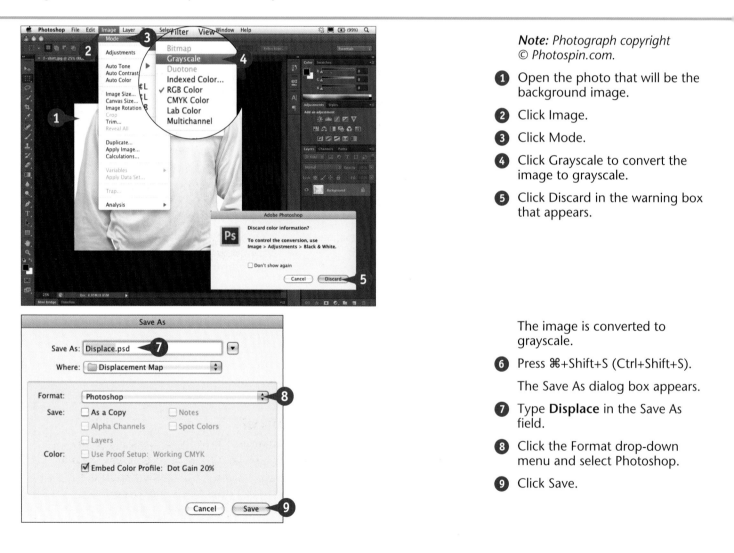

Note: Photograph copyright © Photospin.com.

1. Open the photo that will be the background image.

2. Click Image.

3. Click Mode.

4. Click Grayscale to convert the image to grayscale.

5. Click Discard in the warning box that appears.

The image is converted to grayscale.

6. Press ⌘+Shift+S (Ctrl+Shift+S).

   The Save As dialog box appears.

7. Type **Displace** in the Save As field.

8. Click the Format drop-down menu and select Photoshop.

9. Click Save.

10 Open the original image again.

11 Click the Custom Shape tool.

12 Click a custom shape and fill color from the Options bar.

13 Click and drag out a shape onto the image.

14 Press ⌘+T (Ctrl+T) to transform and position the vector shape.

15 Click and drag the Transform anchors to reposition the shape.

16 Click the Commit button.

17 Click the Type tool and type some text on the image to go with the vector shape.

18 Repeats steps 14 to 16 to adjust and commit the text.

TIPS

Did You Know?

If your grayscale image has very strong contrasts, you can reduce the amount of texture in the displacement map image by somewhat blurring the image after changing it to grayscale. Click Filter ➪ Blur ➪ Gaussian Blur. Increase the Radius slightly and click OK. Then save the image as the displacement image in the Photoshop (.psd) format.

More Options!

If the subject appears in the background image and the text or design layer needs to go on a wall or cloth behind the subject, you can add a layer mask and paint with black to hide the effect on certain areas, bringing the subject back in front.

The Displace filter applies the displacement map to wrap one image precisely over the other, forcing the top layer to reflect the contours of the base layer. Other Photoshop filters such as Conté Crayon, Glass, Lighting Effects, and Texturizer also load other images or textures to produce their effects. However, not all of these filters load the second image in the same way. The Displace filter specifically distorts an image based on the different values of gray in the displacement map image. The greater the contrast in

the gray values, the more texture appears in the blended image.

This technique works best if both original images are the same size and resolution. If you are using two separate images, start by resizing both photos to match. If the images are not the same size, the Displace filter either resizes or tiles the map, depending on the settings you select in the Displace dialog box. Stretch To Fit resizes the map, whereas the Tile option repeats the map, creating a pattern.

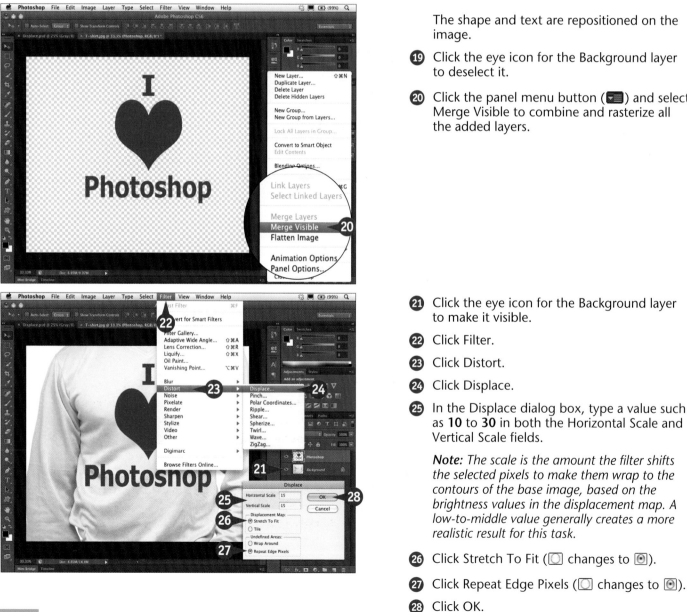

The shape and text are repositioned on the image.

19 Click the eye icon for the Background layer to deselect it.

20 Click the panel menu button (⊞) and select Merge Visible to combine and rasterize all the added layers.

21 Click the eye icon for the Background layer to make it visible.

22 Click Filter.

23 Click Distort.

24 Click Displace.

25 In the Displace dialog box, type a value such as **10** to **30** in both the Horizontal Scale and Vertical Scale fields.

Note: The scale is the amount the filter shifts the selected pixels to make them wrap to the contours of the base image, based on the brightness values in the displacement map. A low-to-middle value generally creates a more realistic result for this task.

26 Click Stretch To Fit (◯ changes to ◉).

27 Click Repeat Edge Pixels (◯ changes to ◉).

28 Click OK.

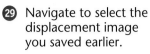

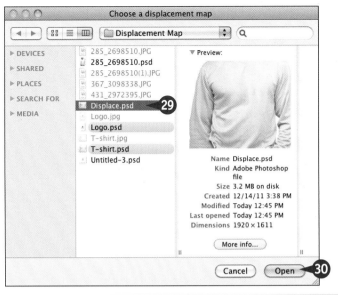

The Choose a Displacement Map dialog box appears.

㉙ Navigate to select the displacement image you saved earlier.

㉚ Click Open.

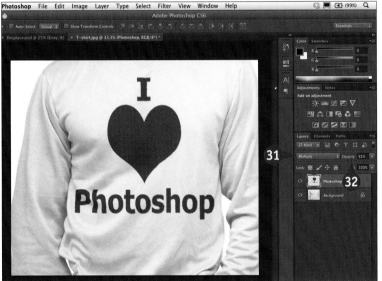

The shape is distorted and blends into the Background layer, wrapping around the contours in the background image.

㉛ Click the blend mode drop-down menu and select Multiply.

㉜ Click Opacity and drag to the left to reduce the layer opacity to fit your image.

TIPS

Important!

Photoshop cannot recognize a displacement map image with layers. Be sure to flatten any image you plan to use as the displacement map before saving it as a Photoshop (.psd) file.

Try This!

You can convert the photo to a black-and-white image using the Adjustments panel. Use the sliders to control the amount of dark and light areas for the contours of the displacement map. Flatten the image before saving it as the displacement Photoshop file.

More Options!

You can place any vector art or another image onto the background image. However, when you use the File ⇨ Place command, the artwork automatically converts into a Smart Object. Make sure you have placed the file in the proper location before applying the Distort filter, which rasterizes the vector layer.

Chapter 8

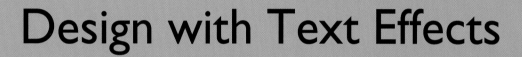

Design with Text Effects

Although Photoshop is not a page-layout application, the new character styles and paragraph styles panels in CS6 add more page design and text options than previous versions. You can add text to photographs for impact or to create an original design. You can also create special text effects to give personality to the words or even use the words alone to create the design. And you can save styles you set up so you can reapply them quickly.

With Photoshop, you can add effects to text in more creative ways and more quickly than is possible using traditional tools. Not only can you see the end result instantly, but you also have complete creative freedom to make changes without wasting any paper or ink. By combining layer styles, patterns, colors, and fonts, you can create type with just the right look for your project. You can use text on

images and make the words appear as part of the photograph and, conversely, make the photo appear as part of the text.

When you type in Photoshop, the text is placed on a type layer as *vectors*, or mathematically defined shapes that describe the letters, numbers, and symbols of a typeface. You can warp, scale, or resize the words, edit the text, and apply many layer effects to the text while preserving the crisp edges. Some commands, such as the filter effects, painting tools, and the perspective and distort commands and tools, however, require the type to be *rasterized*, or converted to a normal layer filled with pixels. Be sure to edit the text before rasterizing because, once the type layer has been converted, the letters are essentially pixels on a layer and are no longer editable as text.

DIFFICULTY LEVEL

If you upload your proofs to a website for client approval, or if you sell your digital artwork online, you want people to see the images but not to use the files without your permission. You can add a custom watermark with a transparent look to any image to protect it and still keep the image visible.

A custom watermark can be as simple as your name and the copyright symbol, and you can use the copyright symbol as a text character or as a separate shape as in this task. After writing, using a Wacom stylus, or typing your name on a type layer and

adding a large copyright symbol as a shape layer, you can add any kind of bevel or embossed style to your personalized watermark. You can even copy the two layers to another photo to apply the same custom watermark. To give a transparent look to each layer, you can lower the Fill opacity, which affects only the fill pixels, leaving the beveled areas appearing like a glass overlay. You can use this same technique for other text or shape layers on any image to give them a transparent look.

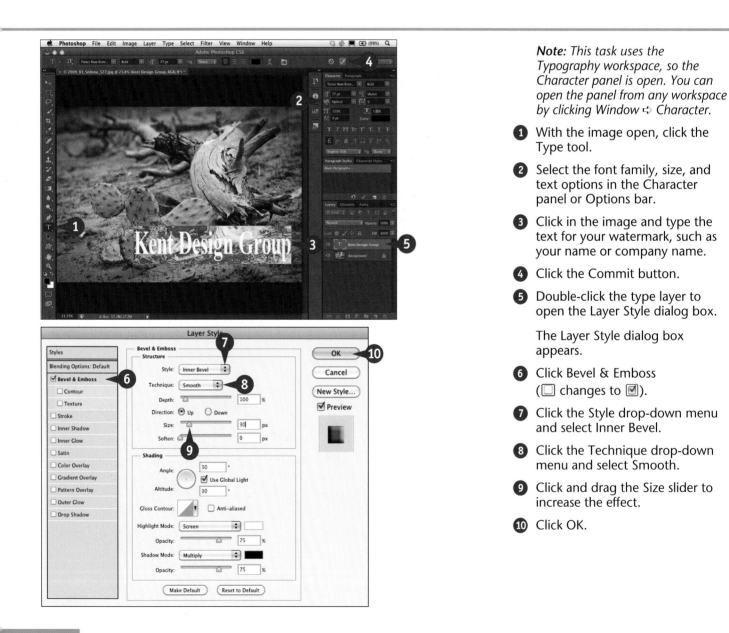

Note: This task uses the Typography workspace, so the Character panel is open. You can open the panel from any workspace by clicking Window ➪ Character.

① With the image open, click the Type tool.

② Select the font family, size, and text options in the Character panel or Options bar.

③ Click in the image and type the text for your watermark, such as your name or company name.

④ Click the Commit button.

⑤ Double-click the type layer to open the Layer Style dialog box.

The Layer Style dialog box appears.

⑥ Click Bevel & Emboss (☐ changes to ☑).

⑦ Click the Style drop-down menu and select Inner Bevel.

⑧ Click the Technique drop-down menu and select Smooth.

⑨ Click and drag the Size slider to increase the effect.

⑩ Click OK.

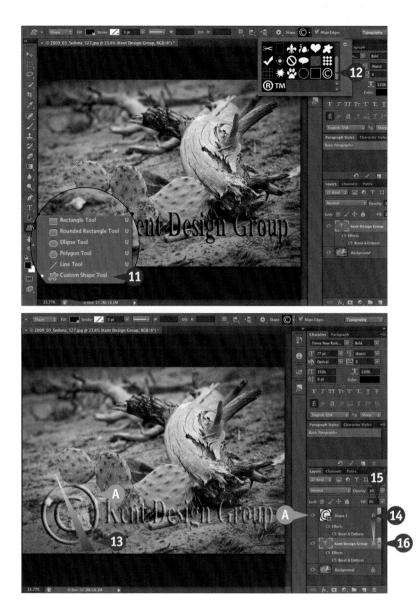

11 Click and hold the Rectangle tool and select the Custom Shape tool.

12 Click the Shape drop-down menu and select the copyright symbol.

13 Press Shift and click and drag in the photo to create a copyright symbol.

A The copyright symbol appears on the image and as a shape layer in the Layers panel.

14 Press Option (Alt) and click and drag the Layer Style button from the type layer to the shape layer to copy the effect.

The same emboss style is applied to the copyright symbol.

15 Double-click in the Fill field and type **0**.

16 Click the type layer to select it and repeat step 15.

The name and copyright symbol appear embossed on the image.

TIPS

Caution!
The Custom Shape tool has three options on the Options bar. When you select the Shape tool for the copyright symbol, make sure that Shape appears on the Options bar rather than Paths or Pixels.

Did You Know?
The Layers panel includes two types of sliders. The Opacity slider affects the visibility of both the filled pixels and the layer style. The Fill slider affects only the transparency of the filled pixels without changing any style that is applied.

Important!
Double-clicking the Type thumbnail in the Layers panel selects and highlights all the type on that layer. Double-clicking the blank space next to the name of a layer opens the Layer Style dialog box.

MAKE TEXT WRAP **around a subject**

In Photoshop, you can add text in several ways. When you type, the text is placed on a type layer and the words remain editable until you rasterize the type, convert the type to a shape layer, or flatten the layer. You can scale, skew, or rotate the text to fit a design. You can control the flow of the characters you type within a bounding box by typing text as a paragraph, either horizontally or vertically. For text in a rectangular shape, you can use the Type tool to drag diagonally and define a bounding area and then click and type the text. Typing text as a paragraph is

useful for creating brochures, scrapbooks, or various design projects.

You can make paragraph text wrap around an object by using custom shapes as text bounding boxes or by creating a shape to use as a container for text. You can drag out any solid shape selected from the Custom Shape picker using the Custom Shape tool and type into the shape as a bounding box. You can also use the Pen tool to create an original path to use as the bounding box. You can then fill the shape with paragraph text to create unique visual effects.

Note: *Photograph copyright © Photospin.com.*

1. With the image open, click the Pen tool or the Freeform Pen tool depending on the intended design.

2. Select Path in the Options bar.

3. Click and drag with the Freeform Pen tool to draw a container for the text.

   Note: *If you chose the Pen tool in step 1, click along an area with the Pen tool to create the container.*

4. Click the starting point to close the shape.

5. Click the Type tool.

6. Select the font style, size, color, and alignment in the Options bar.

7. Move the cursor inside the shape.

   The cursor appears as an insertion cursor in a circle (ⓘ).

8. Click inside the shape.

   Note: *If you click the shape line instead of inside the shape, the cursor appears as an insertion cursor with a line across it (⟊) and the text then follows the line instead of staying inside the shape.*

A bounding box surrounds the shape.

9 Type the text until the shape is full.

10 Click the Commit button.

The shape and bounding box disappear.

11 Click the Move tool.

12 Click and drag in the shape to reposition it on the page if necessary.

TIPS

More Options!

You can also use a Custom Shape to fill with text. Be sure to select the Path option for the shape in the Options bar.

Did You Know?

Click the Custom Shape picker in the Options bar, and then click the gear menu button (⚙) to load more shapes. Select one of the shape sets listed, or select All from the choices in the menu and click Append to add the shapes to the current set.

Try This!

You can copy text from another document, an e-mail, or even a website and paste it into the shape. Select the text in the other document, and press ⌘+C (Ctrl+C) to copy. Click the Photoshop document. Use the Type tool (T) to click in the shape. Press ⌘+V (Ctrl+V) to paste the text.

WARP TEXT for a fun effect

You can create many different effects with type by warping the letters into various shapes. Although you can warp text on a rasterized layer, the letters lose their sharp edges and appear fuzzy. Using Photoshop's Warp Text feature gives text a completely new look and keeps the text sharp-edged and editable.

Type the text and then use the Warp Text dialog box to transform it. You can select from a variety of warp styles and use the sliders to alter the look. You can control the direction of the warp as well as the size of the letters. Because the warp style is an attribute of the type layer, you can change the style at any time by reselecting the layer with the Type tool and opening the Warp Text dialog box. As long as the text is on an editable type layer, you can change the letters and color them individually. With the text on a separate layer, you can also apply any layer styles before or after warping the text.

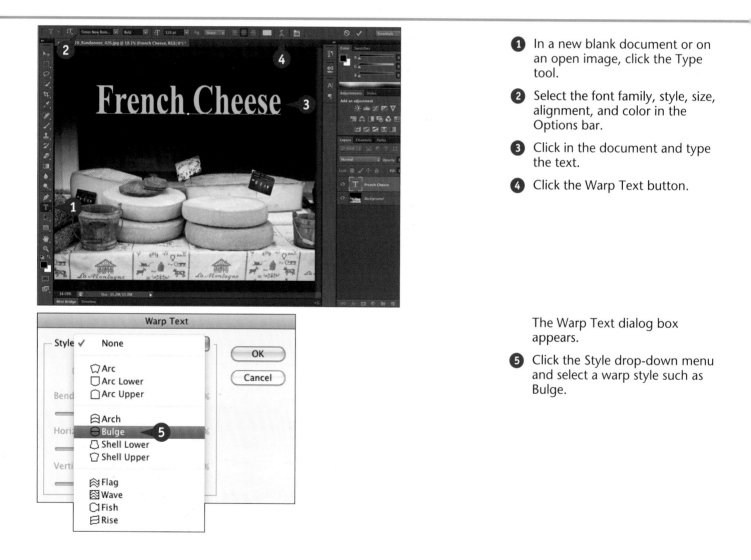

① In a new blank document or on an open image, click the Type tool.

② Select the font family, style, size, alignment, and color in the Options bar.

③ Click in the document and type the text.

④ Click the Warp Text button.

The Warp Text dialog box appears.

⑤ Click the Style drop-down menu and select a warp style such as Bulge.

The text in the image changes to match the style selected.

⑥ Click and drag the Bend slider to change the amount of warp.

⑦ Click and drag the Horizontal Distortion slider to adjust the direction of the effect.

⑧ Click and drag the Vertical Distortion slider to change the effect.

⑨ Click OK to commit the warp.

⑩ Click the Commit button.

The text is warped on the Type layer, but still editable.

You can change the text color and style; see the tip section for more information.

TIPS

Try This!
You can click the Add a Layer Style button (*fx*) at the bottom of the Layers panel to add effects such as a drop shadow.

Did You Know?
You can change the color of the text after you warp it. Select the Type tool (T) and click and drag across the text to highlight it. Change the color by clicking the color box in the Options bar or by clicking the foreground color in the toolbar. Select another color from the Color Picker, and click OK to close the dialog box. Click the Commit button (✓) in the Options bar.

More Options!
To see the color of the type as you change it, highlight the type. Then press ⌘+H (Ctrl+H), to Hide Extras. The type remains selected but the highlighting is not visible. When you select another foreground color in the Color Picker, you instantly see the color on your text.

When you warp a type layer, the letters always bend the shape to some degree, even if you set the Bend slider to 0 in the Warp Text dialog box. You can use the Edit menu's Transform submenu to scale, rotate, skew, or flip the text; however, the Perspective function is unavailable for a type layer. If you rasterize the layer, turning the letters into pixels, and then use the Perspective function to create the illusion of text disappearing into the distance, the characters blur as you change the angles. You can,

however, add realistic perspective to type and preserve the crisp edges by converting the type layer to a shape layer.

Converting type to shapes changes the type layer into a vector layer. The text appears outlined. The outline is actually a temporary path which appears in the Paths panel as well. The text is no longer editable, but you can add layer styles and use all the transformation tools to change the look.

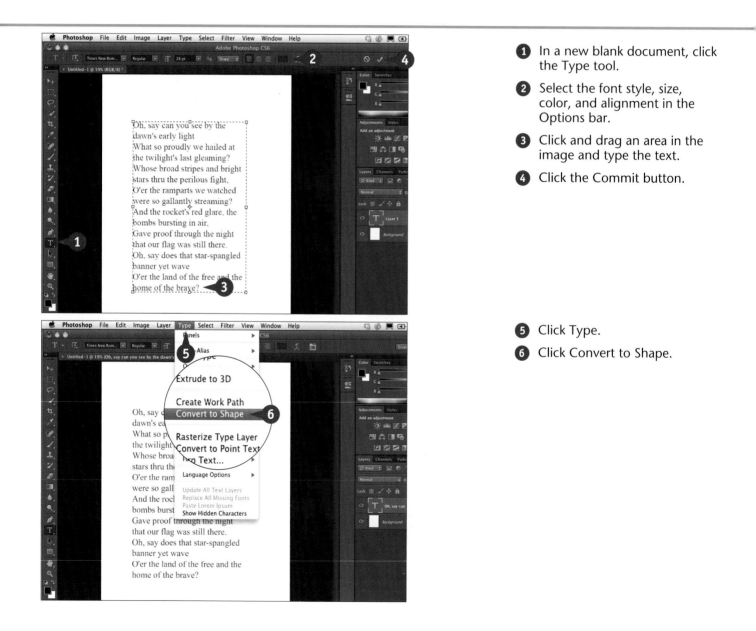

① In a new blank document, click the Type tool.

② Select the font style, size, color, and alignment in the Options bar.

③ Click and drag an area in the image and type the text.

④ Click the Commit button.

⑤ Click Type.

⑥ Click Convert to Shape.

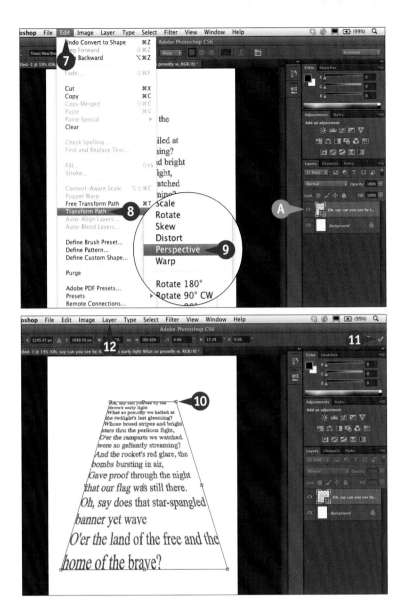

#89

DIFFICULTY LEVEL

Ⓐ The type layer in the Layers panel changes to a shape layer.

⑦ Click Edit.

⑧ Click Transform Path.

⑨ Click Perspective.

The text has a bounding box with anchor points.

⑩ Click any of the corner anchors and drag to change the shape of the text.

⑪ Click the Commit button.

⑫ To finish the transformation, click Layer ➪ Rasterize ➪ Shape.

The layer is rasterized and the text retains its sharp edges even as it appears in a perspective plane.

TIPS

Change It!

You can change the look of the type, add a drop shadow or a glow, bevel and emboss, or even add a gradient. Click the Layer Style button (⬛) at the bottom of the Layers panel and select any of the options.

Important!

You should always select a typeface variant in the Options bar or the Character panel. You cannot convert a type layer into a shape if the type has a faux bold applied. Make sure to check the type attributes in the Character panel and deselect the Faux Bold option if necessary (⬛).

More Options!

You can change all the type attributes using the Character panel. Click Type ➪ Panels ➪ Character Panel. You can also open the Character Styles panel and save a style with specific character attributes.

Create a PHOTO-FILLED TITLE

You can easily create mood-inspiring or memory-evoking titles for a photo or album page by making a photograph fill the letters. Photoshop includes four different Type tools: the Horizontal and Vertical Type tools and the Horizontal and Vertical Type Mask tools. When you use the Type Mask tools, Photoshop automatically creates a selection in the shape of the letters. However, using the regular Type tools to create photo-filled titles gives you more control over the design and makes it easier to see the area of the photo that the letters will cut out.

Filling text or any other object with a photograph or other image is one of the many collage and masking techniques in Photoshop. You type text and use a *clipping mask* to *clip* the photograph so that it shows only through the letters and *masks* the rest of the photo. Because the letters are on an editable Type layer, you can change the text even after the letters are filled with the image. You can also add a drop shadow or emboss the type layer to make the letters stand out.

① Open a photograph to use as the base photo.

② Click the Type tool.

③ Select the font style, size, color, and alignment in the Options bar. The size will be readjusted when you transform the text in step 5.

Note: Thick sans serif fonts work best for this effect.

④ Click in the image and type the text.

⑤ Press ⌘ (Ctrl) and click and drag the transformation anchors to stretch the type.

⑥ Click the Commit button.

⑦ Click and drag the Background layer over the New Layer button to duplicate it.

⑧ Click and drag the Background copy layer above the type layer.

⑨ Click Layer.

⑩ Click Create Clipping Mask.

200

A The Background copy layer is indented with an arrow in the Layers panel, but the image does not change.

⓫ Click the type layer to select it.

⓬ ⌘+click (Ctrl+click) the New Layer button to create a new empty layer named Layer 1 below the type layer.

Note: Clicking the New Layer button ( ) places a new layer above the selected layer. ⌘+clicking (Ctrl+clicking) places it below.

⓭ Press D to reset the foreground and background colors.

⓮ Press Option+Delete (Alt+Backspace) to fill the layer with black.

The photo appears to fill the letters on a black background.

⓯ Click the Move tool.

⓰ Click the Background copy layer.

⓱ Click and drag in the image to move the photo into position inside the letters.

⓲ Click the type layer to select it.

⓳ Click the Layer Style button to add a Bevel & Emboss layer effect.

TIPS

More Options!

You can change the background color for the text. Press ⌘+Delete (Alt+Backspace) in step 14 to fill the layer with white rather than black. Or click in the color box in the toolbar to open the Color Picker and select a different foreground color. Close the Color Picker and then press Option+Delete (Alt+Backspace).

Important!

Be sure to highlight the Background copy layer, which must be above the type layer, when you create the clipping mask. Changing the stacking order of the layers after a clipping mask has been applied can remove the clipping mask.

More Options!

You can create a clipping mask using two different keyboard shortcuts. Press Option (Alt) and click between the two layers in the Layers panel, or select the layer and press ⌘+Option+G (Ctrl+Alt+G) to clip it to the layer below.

Create a realistic COLORED SHADOW

When you apply a drop shadow to text using a Layer Style drop shadow, the shadow is gray. Actual shadows of text or other objects are not gray and do not always have the same opacity. Shadows reflect the colors of the objects they cover. If you select another color for the shadow in the Layer Style dialog box, the shadow appears unnatural and uniform in color.

You can add type to a photo and have the shadow appear with the same colors that occur in the real world. Create a selection and add a Brightness/Contrast adjustment layer. Then, link the shadow

layer to the text layer, and reposition the text in the image. The shadow follows the moved text, automatically adjusting itself to the colors in the image below.

You can use the same technique to add a realistic shadow to text or to any object in an image. Add depth to natural-light shadows under a tree or increase the shadow of a person in a sunlit photo. The greater the number of colors and textures the shadow affects, the more natural your colored shadow appears.

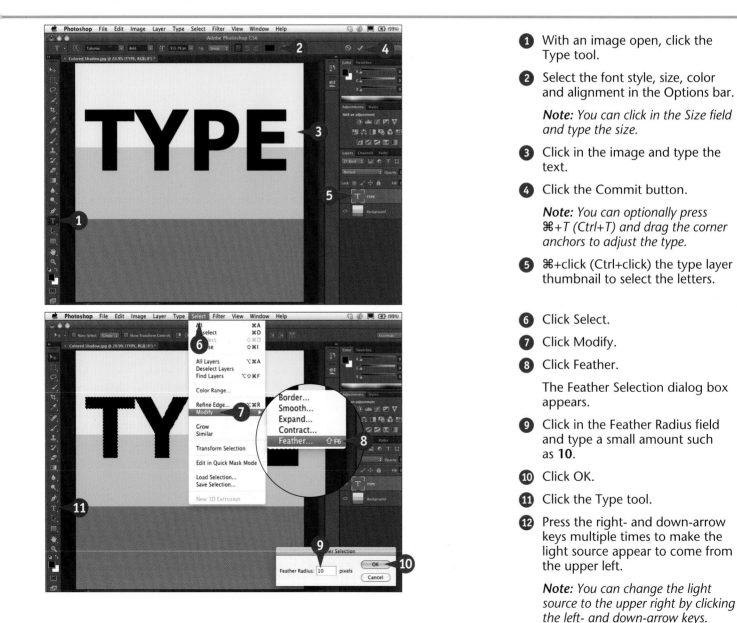

1 With an image open, click the Type tool.

2 Select the font style, size, color and alignment in the Options bar.

Note: You can click in the Size field and type the size.

3 Click in the image and type the text.

4 Click the Commit button.

Note: You can optionally press ⌘+T (Ctrl+T) and drag the corner anchors to adjust the type.

5 ⌘+click (Ctrl+click) the type layer thumbnail to select the letters.

6 Click Select.

7 Click Modify.

8 Click Feather.

The Feather Selection dialog box appears.

9 Click in the Feather Radius field and type a small amount such as **10**.

10 Click OK.

11 Click the Type tool.

12 Press the right- and down-arrow keys multiple times to make the light source appear to come from the upper left.

Note: You can change the light source to the upper right by clicking the left- and down-arrow keys.

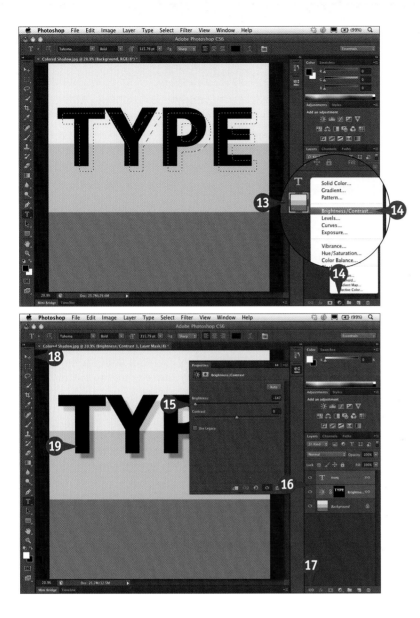

The selection marquee moves down and to the right.

⑬ Click the Background layer thumbnail to select it.

⑭ Click the Adjustment Layer button in the Layers panel, and click Brightness/Contrast.

The Brightness/Contrast sliders appear in the properties panel, and the selection marquee is hidden.

⑮ Click and drag the Brightness slider to the left to create the drop shadow.

⑯ ⌘+click (Ctrl+click) both the adjustment layer and the type layer in the Layers panel to select them.

⑰ Click the Link Layers button.

The type and its shadow are now linked.

⑱ Click the Move tool.

⑲ Click and drag the text around in the photo.

The shadow follows the text, and the shadow's colors automatically adjust to the colors in the area of the photo below.

TIPS

More Options!

You can also keep the type and its shadow separate by not linking them as in steps 16 and 17. You can then move the type and its shadow independently to view the shadow in a new position for a different effect.

Did You Know?

You can quickly change the alignment of type using keyboard shortcuts. Click in the type and press ⌘+Shift+L (Ctrl+Shift+L) to align left; press ⌘+Shift+R (Ctrl+Shift+R) to align right; and press ⌘+Shift+C (Ctrl+Shift+C) to align center.

Did You Know?

The size of the feather radius (see step 9) sets the width of the feathered edge of the selection and ranges from 0 to 250 pixels. A small feather radius in a very large image may not be visible, and a large feather radius in a smaller image can spread too far away from the selection.

You can create a design using type as the central element by changing the letter styles and size, adding layer effects, warping the text, or adding perspective. You can also make the individual letters interweave and interact with each other to add more interest to any project. By converting type layers to shapes and overlapping them, you can make some of the areas transparent to the background, creating new design elements. Add a shape to the text, make the letters intertwine with the shape, and you can create eye-catching logos or page titles.

When you convert a type layer to a shape, the text is no longer editable. However, you can still move individual letters. You can transform, warp, and resize one letter at a time or a group of letters. You can also add layer styles to the grouped design elements and change the look completely. Because the letters and shapes are all on one layer, the color and any layer styles that you use are applied to all the elements on the layer. Flatten the layers as a final step in creating the design.

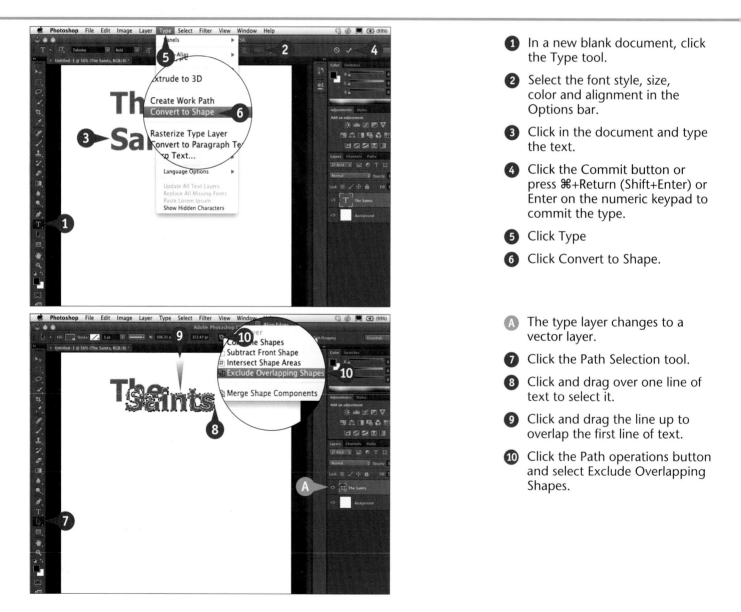

① In a new blank document, click the Type tool.

② Select the font style, size, color and alignment in the Options bar.

③ Click in the document and type the text.

④ Click the Commit button or press ⌘+Return (Shift+Enter) or Enter on the numeric keypad to commit the type.

⑤ Click Type

⑥ Click Convert to Shape.

Ⓐ The type layer changes to a vector layer.

⑦ Click the Path Selection tool.

⑧ Click and drag over one line of text to select it.

⑨ Click and drag the line up to overlap the first line of text.

⑩ Click the Path operations button and select Exclude Overlapping Shapes.

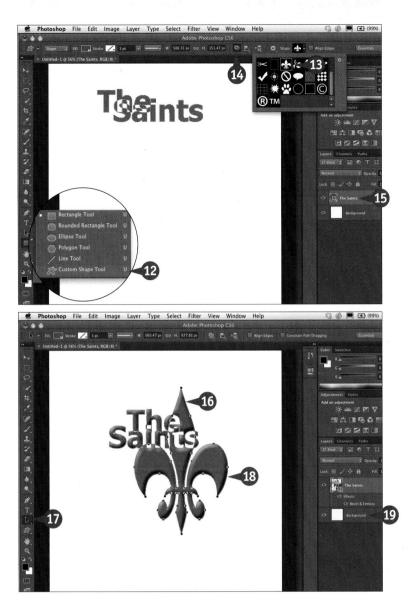

The areas of text that overlap are reversed out.

⑪ Repeat steps 8 to 10 for any other lines of text.

⑫ Click and hold the Rectangle tool and click the Custom Shape tool.

⑬ Click the Shape drop-down menu and click a shape to select it.

⑭ Click the Path operations button and select Exclude Overlapping Shapes.

⑮ Make sure that the vector layer thumbnail in the Layers panel is selected.

⑯ Click and drag to draw a shape over the letters.

The areas of the shape and text that overlap are reversed out.

⑰ Click the Path Selection tool.

⑱ Click the shape and drag it to reposition it in the design if necessary.

The shape interacts differently with the type as it overlaps different areas.

⑲ Click the Background layer to view the design.

TIPS

More Options!

You can apply a layer style to the shapes and letters. Click the shape or the letters with the Path Selection tool (🔲) and try adding an Inner Shadow or a Bevel and Emboss layer style. Click Texture and select a pattern for the Texture Elements. The pattern is applied to all the colored areas.

Important!

The vector layer thumbnail in the Layers panel must be selected before adding the shape in step 16, and all the type and the shapes must be on the same layer for the Exclude Overlapping Shapes button (🔲) to function.

Did You Know?

The Path Selection tool (🔲) is quite different from the Move tool (🔲). You can use the Path Selection tool to move individual letters or the shape separately. Click one letter and move it to create a different look. To undo the move, click the previous state in the History panel.

Format text with YOUR OWN PARAGRAPH STYLE

Photoshop CS6 now includes paragraph and character styles so you can quickly style a section of text and save the style to use on other documents.

Paragraph styles control all the type elements of type. Character styles control the font face, size, color, kerning, leading — all the elements found in the Character panel. If you apply a paragraph style and then apply a new character style to a selection, the character style overrides the original paragraph style. The individual settings in the Character panel, Paragraph panel, and Options bar continue to function as in previous versions and override any applied style on a one-time basis.

You can type a section of text into a document. Select a portion of the text and set the options for both character and paragraph styling using the Character and Paragraph panels. You then create a new style using the newly formatted text as an example. You can select any other text and apply the new style with one click. If you make a change to a character or paragraph style, all instances of the style, even on different layers, are automatically updated.

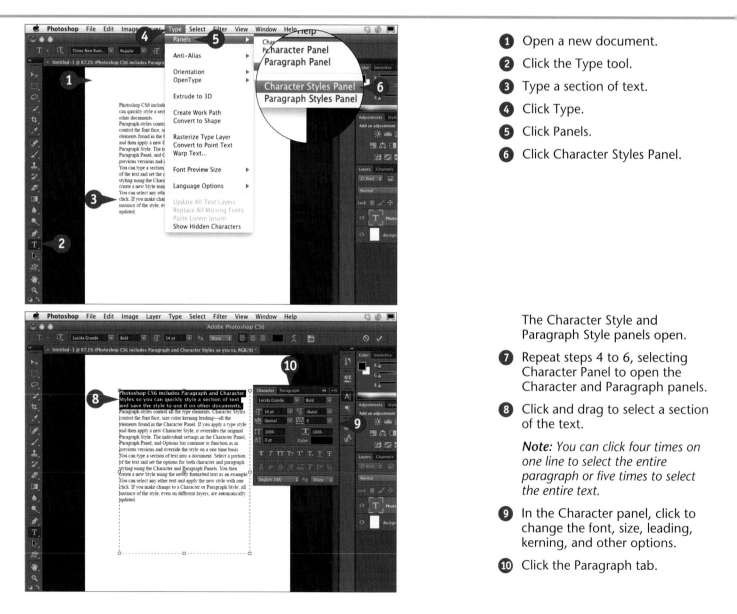

1 Open a new document.

2 Click the Type tool.

3 Type a section of text.

4 Click Type.

5 Click Panels.

6 Click Character Styles Panel.

The Character Style and Paragraph Style panels open.

7 Repeat steps 4 to 6, selecting Character Panel to open the Character and Paragraph panels.

8 Click and drag to select a section of the text.

Note: You can click four times on one line to select the entire paragraph or five times to select the entire text.

9 In the Character panel, click to change the font, size, leading, kerning, and other options.

10 Click the Paragraph tab.

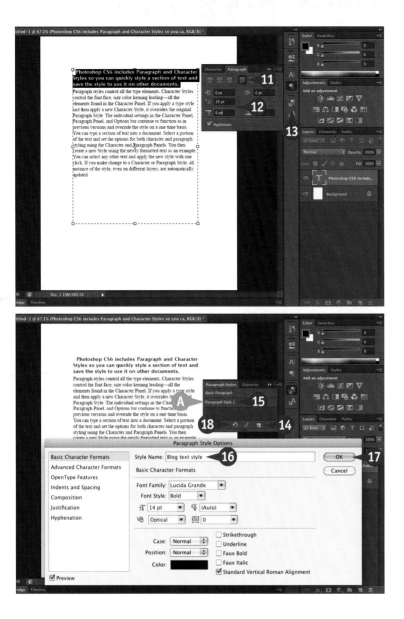

11 Click a paragraph alignment option.

12 Type the paragraph indent and space before a paragraph.

13 Click the Paragraph Style button to open the panel.

Note: *The Basic Paragraph style temporarily shows a plus sign.*

14 Click the New Paragraph Style button.

A A new style named Paragraph Style 1 appears in the list.

15 Double-click Paragraph Style 1.

The Paragraph Style Options dialog box appears.

16 Type a name for your new paragraph style.

Note: *You can optionally make any other changes to the style by clicking the attributes listed and editing the settings.*

17 Click OK.

The new style appears in the Paragraph Styles panel.

18 Click the Clear Override button to convert all the text on that layer to the new style.

TIPS

More Options!

Both paragraph styles and character styles can be created in two ways: start by selecting a section of text, formatting it, and creating a new style as in this example, or start by opening either the Paragraph Styles or the Character Styles panel, clicking the panel menu button (🔳), selecting Style Options, typing a name for the style, and setting the attributes.

Try This!

A plus sign by a style name indicates changes to the text that override the style. You can clear the overrides by clicking the panel menu button (🔳) in either the Paragraph Styles or the Character Styles panel and selecting Clear Override or by clicking the Clear Override button on the panel (🔳). You can also click the Redefine button (🔳) to merge the overrides and redefine the style.

Did You Know?

If you edit a style even with a non-text layer, such as the Background layer, targeted, all the changes propagate to all layers in the document that use that style.

Chapter 9

Create Digital Artwork from Photographs

Even if you claim to have no artistic abilities, you can still produce art-like images with photographs and Photoshop tools. If you do have some artistic skills, drawing and painting with Photoshop can expand your creative horizons. Photoshop CS6 includes more natural media tools than previous versions. New Erodible tip brushes that wear down like traditional pencils, new Airbrush tips and built-in brush rotation, along with the Mixer Brush tool and Bristle tips, help you draw and paint with a variety of styles.

Although Photoshop's art tools are very powerful, no "Click Here for Art" button exists. Some of the filters, especially when applied in combinations, can produce interesting effects; however, a truly traditional painted or drawn result still requires a lot of patience, time, and multiple tools and steps.

The key to creating digital artwork is to vary the tools and techniques, combining different layers, effects filters, masks, and blend modes. You can try any of the techniques in this chapter with different art media. For example, you can use the Mixer Brush Cloning Paint Setup shown in task #104 with watercolors or pastels, as well as with oil paints.

For most art tasks, you should expand the Layers panel as much as possible and load some of the included tool presets, such as the Airbrushes, Artists Brushes, and Dry Media brushes, and also load additional brush presets. And when transforming a photograph into art, you will get better artistic results if you start by reducing the amount of photographic detail.

DIFFICULTY LEVEL

Make any photo appear SKETCHED ON THE PAPER

You can make a photo appear to be sketched on the page, giving a traditional photograph an entirely new look. You can also apply this technique with a digital drawing or painting for a hand-drawn or hand-painted look. The main image appears to be applied to the paper using charcoal, colored pencils, or a paintbrush, leaving the edges and brush marks visible.

You can start with any photograph or already drawn or painted project. Add a new layer filled with white over the Background layer. Next, use the Eraser tool to erase through the white, revealing areas of the image on the underlying layer. You can configure the Eraser tool with any of Photoshop's brush settings and change them as you continue sketching the photo onto the page. The greater the number and opacity of the brush strokes, the more of your photograph appears on the white layer. By selecting rough-edged brushes and varying the opacity and styles of the strokes you use, your photo takes on the characteristics of a sketched image.

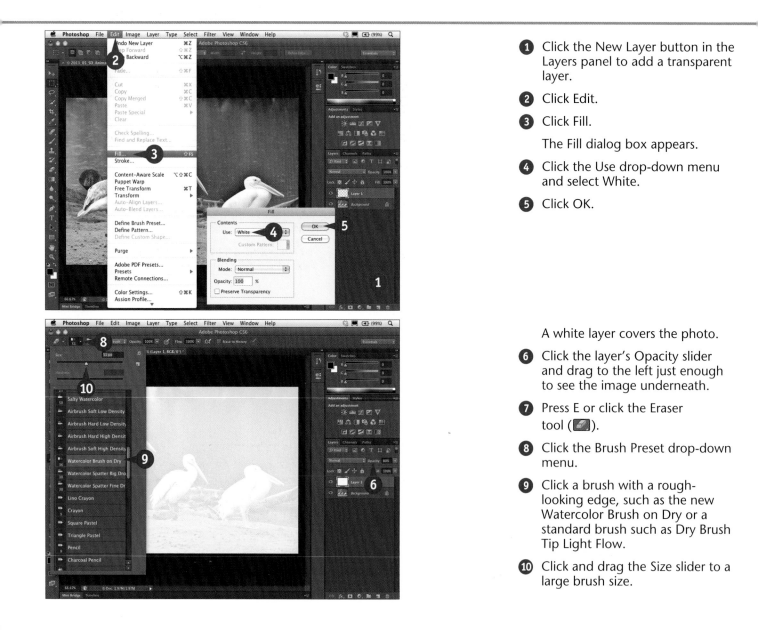

1 Click the New Layer button in the Layers panel to add a transparent layer.

2 Click Edit.

3 Click Fill.

The Fill dialog box appears.

4 Click the Use drop-down menu and select White.

5 Click OK.

A white layer covers the photo.

6 Click the layer's Opacity slider and drag to the left just enough to see the image underneath.

7 Press E or click the Eraser tool (□).

8 Click the Brush Preset drop-down menu.

9 Click a brush with a rough-looking edge, such as the new Watercolor Brush on Dry or a standard brush such as Dry Brush Tip Light Flow.

10 Click and drag the Size slider to a large brush size.

Note: *If you selected a standard brush, click Opacity in the Options bar and drag to lower the brush opacity for the first layer of strokes. If you selected a Bristle tip or Erodible tip brush you can skip this step.*

⑪ Click and drag across the image using several broad strokes.

⑫ Click and drag over some areas again to increase the opacity.

Note: *With a standard brush, click Opacity and increase the brush opacity for the next layer of strokes.*

⑬ Continue clicking and dragging to paint in the image.

⑭ Click the layer's Opacity slider and drag to the right to return the opacity to 100%.

⑮ Continue applying just enough strokes until the image looks hand-sketched.

⑯ Click the Crop tool and crop the image if necessary.

⑰ Click the Commit button to apply the crop.

The image appears to be brushed or sketched on a page.

TIPS

Customize It!

You can view brushes by name rather than stroke thumbnail. Click the Brush Preset drop-down menu in the Options bar to open the Brush picker. Click the gear menu button (⚙) on the top right to open the Brush picker menu. Click Small List or Large List. You can return to the default brush set anytime by selecting Reset Brushes from the same list.

More Options!

You can add more brushes to the Brush picker. Click the Brush Preset drop-down menu in the Options bar to open the Brush picker. Click the gear menu button (⚙) on the top right. Click a brush set from the bottom section, such as Dry Media Brushes. Click Append in the dialog box that appears to add the brushes to the existing list.

ADD YOUR OWN SIGNATURE to any artwork

You can sign your digital projects one at a time after printing them, or you can apply a digital signature from within Photoshop. You can create a large-sized custom signature brush and save it in your Brush picker. You can then quickly apply your signature digitally to all your art projects.

You can change the Size slider in the Brush picker to add a signature to your images with any size signature brush, and you can apply the signature in any color by selecting a specific color as the foreground color before applying the brush.

When you sign your project, add a new transparent layer for the signature. You can then add layer styles and easily change the color of the signature or even create a blind embossed signature effect.

Creating your own signature brush is best accomplished using a Wacom pen tablet because signing your name with a mouse, trackball, or trackpad is difficult. If you do not use a pen tablet, create a logo with the Custom Shape tool and the Type tool as in task #92, and save that as your signature brush preset.

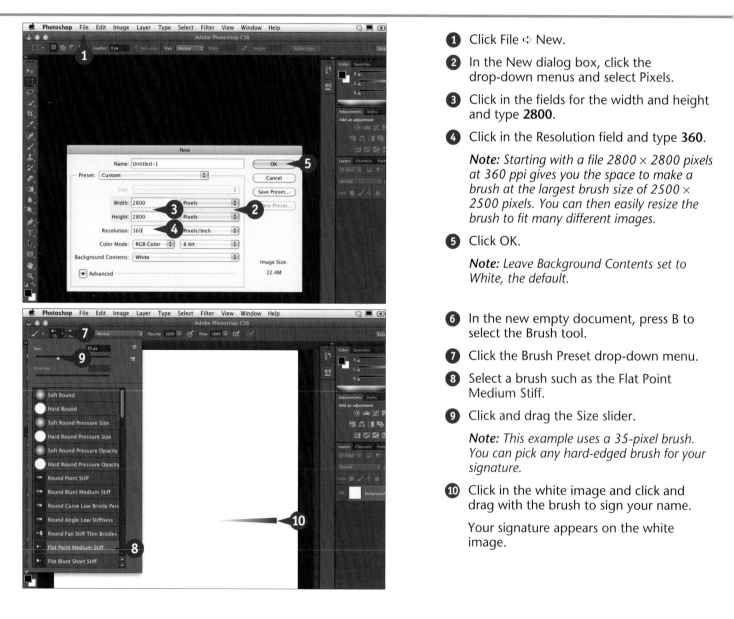

① Click File ➭ New.

② In the New dialog box, click the drop-down menus and select Pixels.

③ Click in the fields for the width and height and type **2800**.

④ Click in the Resolution field and type **360**.

Note: *Starting with a file 2800 × 2800 pixels at 360 ppi gives you the space to make a brush at the largest brush size of 2500 × 2500 pixels. You can then easily resize the brush to fit many different images.*

⑤ Click OK.

Note: *Leave Background Contents set to White, the default.*

⑥ In the new empty document, press B to select the Brush tool.

⑦ Click the Brush Preset drop-down menu.

⑧ Select a brush such as the Flat Point Medium Stiff.

⑨ Click and drag the Size slider.

Note: *This example uses a 35-pixel brush. You can pick any hard-edged brush for your signature.*

⑩ Click in the white image and click and drag with the brush to sign your name.

Your signature appears on the white image.

⓫ Click the Rectangular Marquee tool.

⓬ Click and drag just around your signature.

⓭ Click Edit.

⓮ Click Define Brush Preset.

The Brush Name dialog box appears.

⓯ Type a name for your signature, such as **My Signature Brush**.

⓰ Click OK to save the signature brush.

⓱ Open an image.

⓲ Click the New Layer button to add an empty layer.

⓳ Press B to select the Brush tool.

⓴ Click the Brush Preset drop-down menu.

㉑ Select your signature brush and click and drag the Size slider to adjust the size to fit the image.

㉒ Click once in the image.

Your signature appears.

Ⓐ You can click the Add a Layer Style button to add a drop shadow or bevel.

TIPS

Did You Know?
You can create a custom brush from any signature or any other image up to 2500 × 2500 pixels in size. Signature brushes work best when created with a brush hardness set at 100%.

Attention!
If you create your original signature in color, the custom brush is still created in grayscale. You can change the signature color by changing the foreground color before applying the signature brush or after applying it to the image on a separate layer.

Try This!
Add a drop shadow and bevel to the signature layer using the Layer Styles dialog box. Then lower the Fill opacity of the layer to 0 to give your signature a blind embossed look.

SIMULATE A PAINTED EFFECT with a filter

You can quickly create an oil painting from any photo using Photoshop CS6's new Oil Painting filter. The filter lets you visually control the brush style and lighting angle in a large preview window. You can apply the Oil Painting filter to a Smart Object, or to any pixel layer, so you can combine the effect with other layers for a completely unique look.

Artistic filters generally give a more painterly look to a "simplified" photo, that is, one with fewer details. You can remove the digital noise and add vibrance to the colors, as well as reduce the amount of detail

before applying the filter by opening the image in Camera Raw. Use the Luminance and Color sliders, as shown in task #70, for a softer look. Or apply single image HDR toning as in task #80. Most painting and drawing filters also work best on smaller files with lower resolutions than normal photographic files.

You can simply apply the oil filter to the photo layer, or you can build up layers for more creative options.

Start by adding a white background layer, run the filter on the photo layer, and then add a layer mask filled with a canvas pattern to finish the look.

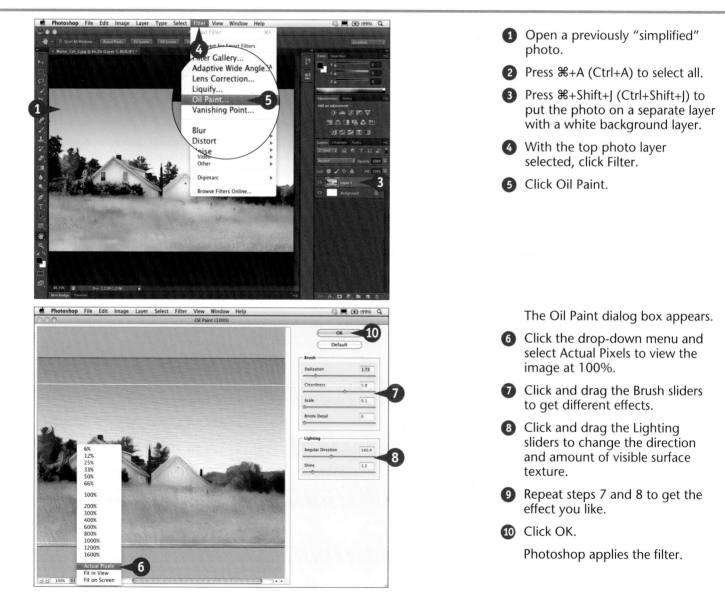

1. Open a previously "simplified" photo.

2. Press ⌘+A (Ctrl+A) to select all.

3. Press ⌘+Shift+J (Ctrl+Shift+J) to put the photo on a separate layer with a white background layer.

4. With the top photo layer selected, click Filter.

5. Click Oil Paint.

The Oil Paint dialog box appears.

6. Click the drop-down menu and select Actual Pixels to view the image at 100%.

7. Click and drag the Brush sliders to get different effects.

8. Click and drag the Lighting sliders to change the direction and amount of visible surface texture.

9. Repeat steps 7 and 8 to get the effect you like.

10. Click OK.

Photoshop applies the filter.

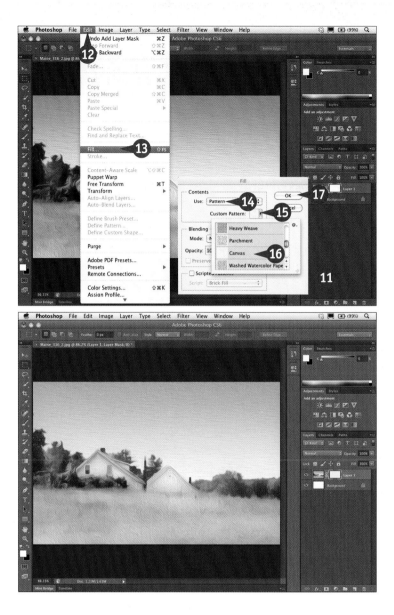

11 Click the Layer Mask button in the Layers panel to add a layer mask to the painted layer.

12 Click Edit.

13 Click Fill.

The Fill dialog box appears.

14 Click the Use drop-down menu and select Pattern.

15 Click in the Custom Pattern drop-down menu.

16 Click Canvas.

17 Click OK.

Note: To load the Artist Surfaces as patterns, click the gear menu button (⚙▾), click Artist Surfaces, and click Append in the dialog box.

The layer mask fills with the canvas pattern, making the oil painting look more traditional.

TIPS

More Options!

Once you apply a filter, the last settings of that filter are saved and the filter appears at the top of the Filter menu. You can reapply the filter with the same settings to the same or another layer by clicking Filter ➪ Oil Paint in this case, or pressing ⌘+F (Ctrl+F).

Did You Know?

Once you have applied a filter to a layer and before you do any other steps, you can fade the filter effect by clicking Edit ➪ Fade Oil Paint in this case, or by pressing ⌘+Shift+F (Ctrl+Shift+F). The fade option disappears as soon as you perform any other steps.

Important!

The Shine slider in the Oil Paint filter reacts very quickly. Instead of trying to slide it slowly to increase or decrease the effect, click in the box and press the up and down arrows to increase or decrease the amount.

You can create a unique design using a high-contrast black-and-white image and a gradient background or fill. You can easily transform any photograph into a high-contrast black-and-white image using an adjustment layer. You visually control the maximum contrast in your photo and determine the areas to turn black and the areas to change to white. You can customize the design by adding a solid color or a colored gradient and using a blend mode to combine the effects.

Start with either a color or a grayscale image and add a Threshold adjustment layer to convert the image to high-contrast black and white. By adding another adjustment layer with a color or a gradient fill and then setting the top layer to either the Lighter Color or Darker Color blend mode, you can give the design a completely different look. All the changes you make are applied using adjustment layers so the image remains completely editable, enabling you to experiment and try different colors and gradients until you find the best design for your project.

1 With an image open, click the Threshold button in the Adjustments panel.

Note: Select an image with strong contrasting areas for the best results.

The Threshold properties panel appears and the color information in the photo is changed to either black or white.

2 Click and drag the Properties panel title bar so you can see the photo.

3 Click and drag the slider to the right to make more tonal values shift to black or to the left to change more tones to white.

4 Click the New Adjustment Layer button.

5 Click Gradient.

Note: Clicking Solid Color produces a two-tone stylized effect with only one color and either white or black.

The Gradient Fill dialog box appears.

6 Click in the gradient bar to open the Gradient Editor.

The Gradient Editor appears.

7 Click a different preset.

8 Click OK to close the Gradient Editor dialog box.

9 Click OK to close the Gradient Fill dialog box.

The gradient is applied as a separate adjustment layer covering the image.

10 Click the blend mode drop-down menu and select Darker Color to make the gradient cover only the non-black areas in the image.

11 Click and drag the Opacity slider to reduce the effect.

The gradient layer blends with the high-contrast of the image.

TIPS

More Options!
You can create your own custom gradient in the Gradient Editor. Double-click in each of the lower color stops under the gradient to open the Color Picker and select a new color.

Try It!
Instead of selecting Darker Color (step 10), click the blend mode drop-down menu in the Layers panel and select Lighter Color. The image changes, applying the gradient blend to the previously black areas in the image.

Did You Know?
The Darker Color mode displays only the lowest color value from both the blend and base layer; conversely, Lighter Color shows only the highest value color. For example, with the gradient layer in Lighter Color blend mode, only the lightest color value in the image layer below — white in this case — appears through the gradient layer.

Control the colors to POSTERIZE A PHOTO

Photoshop includes a Posterize command in the Image ➪ Adjustments menu that automatically posterizes an image by mapping the Red, Green, and Blue channels to the number of tonal levels that you set. Although it requires more steps, you can control the posterization and get more creative results by using three adjustment layers in succession rather than the posterization command.

Use a Black & White adjustment layer to convert the photo to a grayscale image. Then apply a Posterize adjustment layer, specifying the levels that

correspond to the number of colors you want in the final image. A lower number of levels limits the number of colors that will be included, making the image more stylized. Finally, use a Gradient Map adjustment layer to map a color to each of the levels of gray. You can edit any of the adjustment layers to change the colors or levels until you get the look that you want. For the best result, select a photo with a main subject on a plain background, or extract the subject and place it on a black background.

① Press ⌘+J (Ctrl+J) to duplicate the Background layer.

② Click the Black & White button in the Adjustments panel.

The image turns to grayscale and the options in the Properties panel change.

③ Click and drag the Properties panel title bar so you can see the photo.

④ Click Auto or click the Preset drop-down menu and select a different preset to see if the contrast improves.

⑤ Move the color sliders to enhance the contrast.

⑥ Click the Posterize button in the Adjustments panel.

The options in the Properties panel change.

7 Type a low number such as **3** or **4** in the Levels field.

Note: *Use a low number to limit the color gradations when creating a posterized effect.*

8 Click the Gradient Map button in the Adjustments panel.

The Properties panel for the Gradient map appears.

9 Click in the gradient bar.

TIPS

Attention!

You get better results if you match the number of gray levels with the number of color stops in the gradient. To add more gray levels, double-click the Posterize thumbnail in the Layers panel and increase the number of levels. Then double-click the Gradient Map thumbnail and add more color stops.

Try This!

If you want a more realistically colored image, fill the color stops on the right in the Gradient Editor with the lightest colors that you want in the image and the color stops on the left with the darkest colors. The greater the number of color stops and the more colors you use, the wilder the image appears.

Important!

The Poster Edges filter, located in the Artistic filters in the Filter Gallery, creates a completely different look, more like an etching than a posterized print.

After posterizing the first photo by following all the steps in this task, you can duplicate the steps on four different copies of the original photo. Use different colors for each copy and place them in a new document to replicate the Andy Warhol–like layouts with four posterized and juxtaposed images.

To create the second copy, open your posterized image and click File ➪ Save As to give the copy another name. Click the Gradient Map thumbnail in the Layers panel to reopen the Gradient Map options of the Properties panel. Click in the gradient to open

the Gradient Editor again. Change the colors for each of the four color stops, always selecting the darkest colors for the leftmost color stops and the lightest colors for the rightmost color stops. Click OK to close the Gradient Editor. Click File ➪ Save, saving the second version with all the layers. Repeat this process until you have four different versions of the image.

To finish the project, you can follow the steps in task #33 to create a quadriptych, or just create a new empty document and click File ➪ Place to place each of the four images on the page.

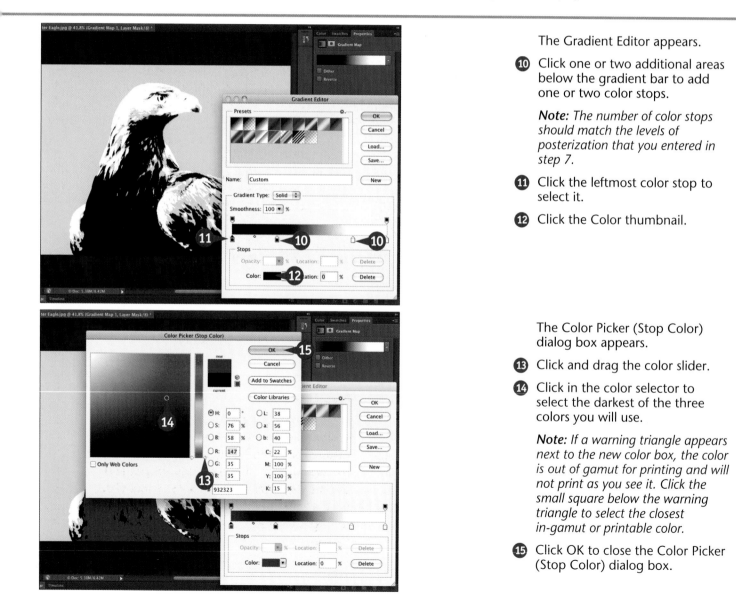

The Gradient Editor appears.

⑩ Click one or two additional areas below the gradient bar to add one or two color stops.

Note: *The number of color stops should match the levels of posterization that you entered in step 7.*

⑪ Click the leftmost color stop to select it.

⑫ Click the Color thumbnail.

The Color Picker (Stop Color) dialog box appears.

⑬ Click and drag the color slider.

⑭ Click in the color selector to select the darkest of the three colors you will use.

Note: *If a warning triangle appears next to the new color box, the color is out of gamut for printing and will not print as you see it. Click the small square below the warning triangle to select the closest in-gamut or printable color.*

⑮ Click OK to close the Color Picker (Stop Color) dialog box.

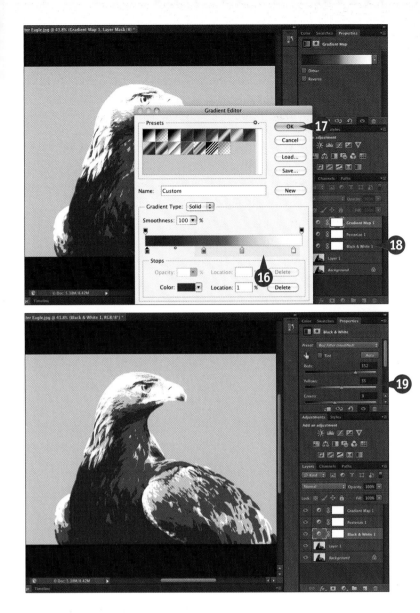

16 Click each of the other color stops and repeat steps 12 to 15 to change the color.

17 Click OK to close the Gradient Editor.

18 Double-click the Black & White adjustment layer in the Layers panel.

The Black & White options appear in the Properties panel.

19 Click and drag the color sliders to change the amount and areas of posterized colors.

20 Press ⌘+S (Ctrl+S) to save the file with all the layers so you can readjust it later.

The final image looks like a posterized and stylized print design from another era.

TIPS

Customize It!

Use the Dodge and Burn tools to change individual areas. Click Layer 1, the Background copy layer, and click the Dodge tool (🔍). Click and drag in the image to make some areas lighter. Click the Burn tool (✊) and click and drag other areas to make them darker. You can lower the Exposure setting in the Options bar to lessen the change.

More Options!

Instead of using a Gradient Map, you can merge the Background copy with the Black & White and the Posterize adjustment layers, and then add colors individually to gray areas. Select the first gray area using the Magic Wand (🪄) with a tolerance of 0. Click the foreground color and select a new color. Press Option+Delete (Alt+Backspace) to fill the selection.

Photoshop CS6 introduces new Erodible tip and Airbrush tools. You can use these tools, along with the Mixer Brush tool, Bristle tips, and Heads Up Display, for any drawing or painting project, whether starting from a reference photo or starting with a blank canvas or paper.

Erodible tips are similar to graphite or pastels in that they wear down with use over time. The Airbrush tips are like painting with an airbrush, with a preview of the spray projection available when using a stylus or by setting the Mouse Pose in the Brush panel to show the projection with a mouse.

The Mixer Brush tool lets you blend colors together directly on open documents. You can specify the wetness of the canvas and the amount of paint for the brush to pick up.

The Bristle tips show the length, thickness, density, and texture of the brushes for more natural painting.

The HUD is an on-screen color picker. Pressing ⌘+Control+Option (right-click+Alt+Shift) as you click makes the HUD appear under the cursor. Drag the cursor without lifting the keys to change the hue or lightness/saturation.

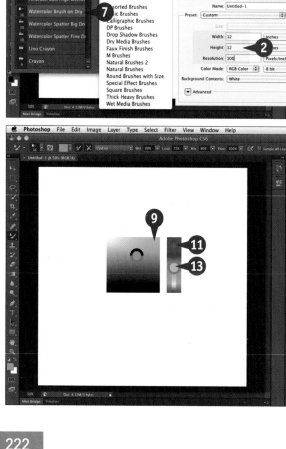

① Click File ➪ New.

② In the New dialog box, click in the fields and set the width and height to 12 inches and the resolution to 100.

③ Click OK.

④ With the new document open, click and hold the Brush tool and select the Mixer Brush tool.

⑤ Click the Brush Preset drop-down menu.

⑥ Click the gear menu button (⚙) and select Large List.

⑦ Click a brush such as Watercolor Brush on Dry.

⑧ Press ⌘+Control+Option (right-click+Alt+Shift) as you click and hold the pen or the mouse button.

⑨ When the HUD appears, release the three keys and drag the cursor around the shade box.

⑩ Still pressing and holding the pen or mouse button, press the spacebar.

⑪ Position the cursor over the Hue bar.

⑫ Release the spacebar without lifting the pen or releasing the mouse button.

⑬ Drag along the Hue bar to select a hue.

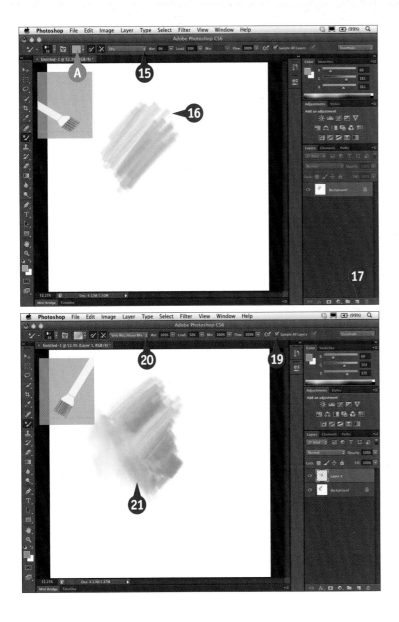

14 Lift the pen or release the mouse button to select the color.

A The Current Brush Load swatch fills with the selected hue and shade.

15 Click the drop-down menu and select Dry.

16 Click and drag to paint in the blank document.

17 Click the New Layer button to add a new transparent layer.

18 Repeat steps 8 to 14, selecting a different hue and shade, and click and drag to add more lines that touch or overlap the original painted lines.

19 Click Sample All Layers (◼ changes to ☑).

20 Click the drop-down menu and select Very Wet, Heavy Mix.

21 Click and drag over the lines to blend the painted strokes.

TIPS

Did You Know?
You can load multiple colors on a tip at one time by pressing Option (Alt) as you click an area. You can change the settings to load the brush after each stroke (☑), or to clean the brush after each stroke (☒) with the two buttons in the Options bar.

More Options!
You can set Photoshop's general preferences to view the HUD as a color wheel or a color strip. With the HUD on-screen, you can press the spacebar and release the keys to temporarily lock the HUD in place, and move over the hue selector to change the hue.

Try This!
Use the Brush tool to experiment with the Bristle tip brushes. The Mixer Brush tool causes the Bristle tip brushes to react more slowly. Change the bristle qualities in the Tool picker. You can also minimize or turn off the on-screen brush preview using the tiny arrows and X on the preview window.

SKETCH TRADITIONALLY with digital brushes

Sketching with a pencil is often the beginning step for many forms of drawing or painting. A sketch can be as simple as a line drawing of the subject or as complex as a finely shaded graphite illustration. You can create a pencil sketch on a blank document using any of the new erodible brushes such as the pencil, triangle or square pastel, or the charcoal pencil.

If you do not have any drawing experience, you can start with a reference photo and apply Photoshop's sketch filters in the Filter Gallery. However, these tend to give the sketch a uniform computerized look.

You can still create a sketched look from a reference photograph without knowing how to draw using this technique, which applies a Gaussian Blur to a duplicated and inverted layer of a grayscale photo. You can then soften the computerized look by sketching over the visible parts of the photo on a separate white layer with Photoshop's Mixer Brush tool and different brush tips. Using a Wacom tablet and stylus gives you more flexibility to create a truly realistic drawing based on a photo.

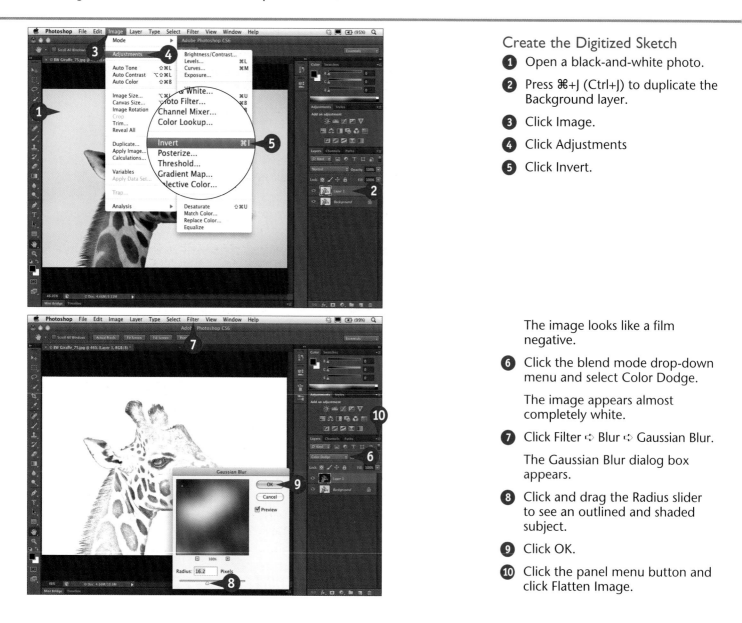

Create the Digitized Sketch

① Open a black-and-white photo.

② Press ⌘+J (Ctrl+J) to duplicate the Background layer.

③ Click Image.

④ Click Adjustments

⑤ Click Invert.

The image looks like a film negative.

⑥ Click the blend mode drop-down menu and select Color Dodge.

The image appears almost completely white.

⑦ Click Filter ➪ Blur ➪ Gaussian Blur.

The Gaussian Blur dialog box appears.

⑧ Click and drag the Radius slider to see an outlined and shaded subject.

⑨ Click OK.

⑩ Click the panel menu button and click Flatten Image.

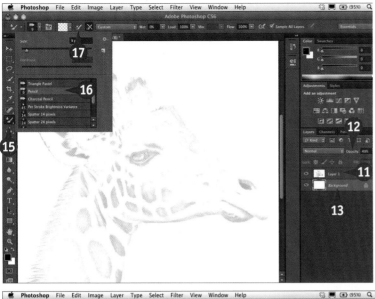

Sketch with a Hand-Drawn Look

⑪ Press ⌘+J to duplicate the new Background layer.

⑫ Click and drag the opacity for Layer 1 to 35–50%.

⑬ Click the original Background layer to select it.

⑭ Press ⌘+Delete (Ctrl+Backspace) to fill it with white.

⑮ Click the Mixer Brush tool.

⑯ Click the Brush drop-down menu and select Pencil.

⑰ Click here to deselect Load Brush After Each Stroke.

⑱ Click Wet and drag to 0%.

⑲ Click Load and drag to 100%.

⑳ Click Flow and drag to 100%.

㉑ Click Sample All Layers (■ changes to ☑).

㉒ Click and drag on the white Background layer with short strokes, following the visible lines and sketching over the darkest areas on the image.

㉓ Click the eye icon for the top layer on and off to see your sketch work.

100
DIFFICULTY LEVEL

TIPS

More Options!

You can add additional pencil lines using the regular Brush tool and the Pencil brush preset. Add a new layer above the Background layer. With the regular Brush tool selected, click the Brush Preset drop-down menu and select Pencil. Lightly draw over any lines that need to be darker, or sketch on your own over areas.

Try This!

You can blend pencil strokes on any layer, just as you could with traditional sketching. Click the Mixer Brush tool and select Stump Blender Auto Clean in the Tool picker. Leave all the options at the default settings. Click one layer and rub over the lines to blend them.

Did You Know?

Sketching from a reference photograph is easier and looks more like natural media when the subject is on a plain background.

Create a digital PEN-AND-INK DRAWING

You can create the look of a pen-and-ink drawing from a photograph using a variety of methods in Photoshop. Often the method you use depends on the subject matter of the original. Photoshop includes many filters such as Find Edges, which finds areas of contrast and outlines them; however, the filter applies the colors in the image to the edges. By changing a duplicated layer to high-contrast grayscale first and then applying the Smart Blur filter in the Edges Only mode, you get a black image with white lines. You can then invert the image to get black lines

on a white background. Depending on the look that you want, you can apply a filter such as Other ➪ Minimum using a 1-pixel radius to thicken the lines.

Often, the artistic effects do not work well on a large image. If your art project seems too photographic, click File ➪ Revert, and then click Image ➪ Image Size to reduce the image size before applying the filters. You can also reduce the amount of detail with a Median or noise reduction filter, before applying Photoshop filters to achieve artistic-looking results.

1. Click Filter ➪ Noise ➪ Median.

2. In the Median dialog box, click and drag the radius to 1 or 2, depending on the size of the image, to remove some detail.

3. Click OK.

4. Press ⌘+J (Ctrl+J) to duplicate the Background layer.

5. Click the Black & White Adjustment button.

6. In the Properties panel, click the Preset drop-down menu and select a preset such as Infrared to get a high-contrast grayscale image.

7. Press ⌘+E (Ctrl+E) to merge the adjustment layer with Layer 1.

8. Click Filter ➪ Blur ➪ Smart Blur.

9. In the Smart Blur dialog box, click the Quality drop-down menu and select High.

10. Click the Mode drop-down menu and select Edge Only.

11. Click and drag the Radius and Threshold sliders to see white outlines of the main features of your image.

12. Click OK.

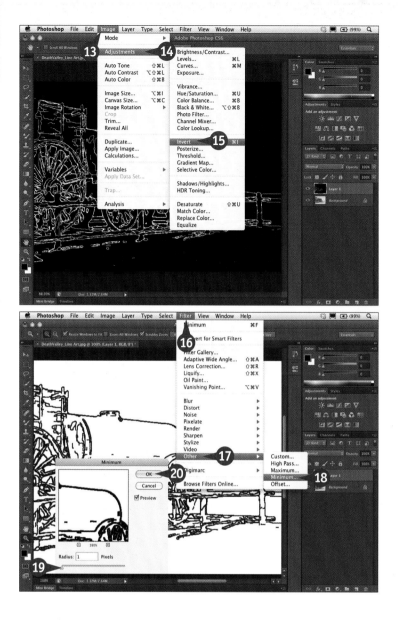

The Smart Blur filter is applied, and the image turns black with white outlines.

⑬ Click Image.

⑭ Click Adjustments.

⑮ Click Invert.

The drawing appears as black lines on a white background.

⑯ Click Filter.

⑰ Click Other.

⑱ Click Minimum.

⑲ Set the radius to 1 in the Minimum dialog box.

⑳ Click OK.

The lines get darker.

Note: *You can optionally click Edit ⇨ Fade Filter, and drag the slider to slightly thin the lines.*

TIPS

Did You Know?

You can also make the lines thicker and darker by clicking Filter ⇨ Filter Gallery. When the Filter Gallery appears, select Artistic, and then Smudge Stick. Reduce the stroke length to 0.

More Options!

You can get better results by increasing the contrast in the original image. After the grayscale conversion (steps 5 and 6), click Image ⇨ Adjustments ⇨ Levels. Move both the Highlight and the Shadow sliders slightly toward the center to increase the contrast.

More Options!

You can also create a pen and ink drawing by selecting Filter ⇨ Stylize ⇨ Find Edges. Then click the Threshold button (⊡) in the Adjustment panel. Slowly drag the slider to the right to increase the density of the lines or to the left to create more white areas.

Pastels are sticks of colors made from ground pigment and bound with resin or gum. Pastel drawings, popular since the 18th and 19th centuries, show broad painterly strokes, with rich colors blended or smudged in semi-opaque layers. Pastel papers generally have a rough surface texture to capture the pigment, and the paper texture often shows through the pastels in areas on the drawing.

You can re-create the look of a pastel drawing without knowing how to draw using Photoshop and a reference photo. This pastel drawing technique works best on a photo with one main subject and few distracting details. Start by opening the photo in Camera Raw and reducing the noise. Use the sliders in the Detail tab to reduce the luminance and color noise. You can instead apply the Noise filter in Photoshop and select Reduce Noise or Median to slightly blur the photographic detail. You can also add white around the subject with a vignette in Camera Raw or add a white border with a reverse crop as in task #32.

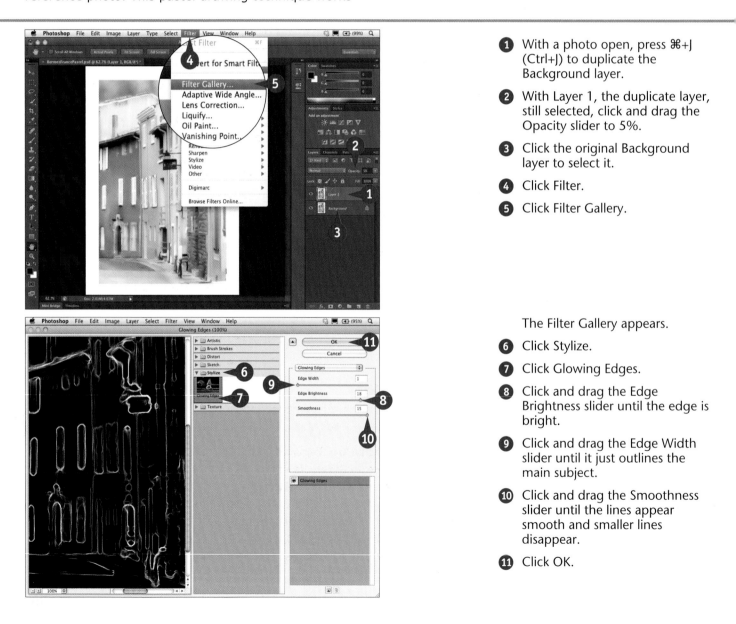

1. With a photo open, press ⌘+J (Ctrl+J) to duplicate the Background layer.

2. With Layer 1, the duplicate layer, still selected, click and drag the Opacity slider to 5%.

3. Click the original Background layer to select it.

4. Click Filter.

5. Click Filter Gallery.

The Filter Gallery appears.

6. Click Stylize.

7. Click Glowing Edges.

8. Click and drag the Edge Brightness slider until the edge is bright.

9. Click and drag the Edge Width slider until it just outlines the main subject.

10. Click and drag the Smoothness slider until the lines appear smooth and smaller lines disappear.

11. Click OK.

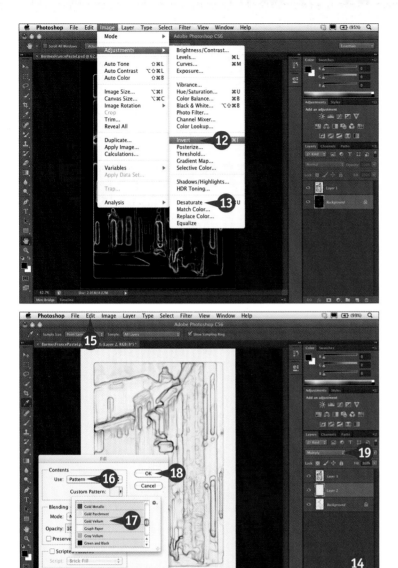

The Filter Gallery closes with the changes applied to the Background layer.

⑫ Press ⌘+I (Ctrl+I) to invert the image, or click Image ➪ Adjustments ➪ Invert.

⑬ Press ⌘+Shift+U (Ctrl+Shift+U) to desaturate the image or click Image ➪ Adjustments ➪ Desaturate.

The Background layer changes to an outline drawing on a white background.

⑭ Click the New Layer button in the Layers panel.

⑮ Click Edit ➪ Fill to open the Fill dialog box.

⑯ Click the Use drop-down menu and select Pattern.

⑰ Click the Custom Pattern drop-down menu and select a colored paper such as Gold Vellum or Gold Parchment.

⑱ Click OK.

Layer 2 fills with the colored paper.

⑲ Click the blend mode drop-down menu and select Multiply.

The drawing shows through the colored paper.

TIPS

Important!

You can view the Custom Patterns as a list to make finding the pattern you want easier. Click the Use drop-down menu and select Pattern. Then click the Custom Pattern drop-down menu. Click the gear menu button (⚙.) and select Small List. The Patterns are now listed by name. Load more pattern sets by clicking the gear menu button again and select the Colored Paper pattern set from the bottom section of the drop-down menu. Click Append in the dialog box that appears so the patterns are added to the existing list.

Try This!

To see the document in full on the screen, double-click the Hand tool (🖐) in the toolbar or click Fit Screen on the Options bar. To zoom to 100%, double-click the Zoom tool (🔍) in the toolbar.

You apply the Glowing Edges filter to delineate the subject matter and then change the colored lines to black. You can either use the lines as a guide and draw within the lines or brush over them to blend the edges in with the colors. To create a natural-looking pastel drawing, start with a larger brush size and draw-in the main color areas. Be sure to click and drag your brush strokes, following the contours of the subject.

Although this technique applies the pastels on a tinted paper, you can create the pastel drawing on a white background by skipping steps 14 to 20. You can also use the steps in this task with different Mixer Brush tool presets to create different looks. Try Pencil–Soft Opaque for a colored pencil look or Angle–Flat Opaque for a more brushed oil effect. Be sure to adjust the settings in the Options bar as in steps 26 to 29 each time you select a different tool preset.

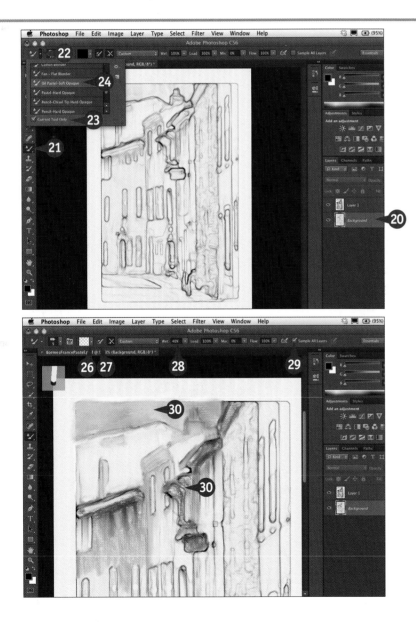

20 Press ⌘+E (Ctrl+E) to combine the colored layer with the Background layer.

21 Click the Mixer Brush tool.

22 Click the Tool Preset drop-down menu.

23 Click Current Tool Only (⬜ changes to ☑).

Only the Mixer Brush tool presets appear in the list.

24 Click Oil Pastel–Soft Opaque.

25 Press ⌘+spacebar (Ctrl+spacebar) to zoom into the image.

26 Click the drop-down menu and select Clean Brush.

27 Click here to deselect Load Brush After Each Stroke.

28 Click Wet and drag to the left to 40%.

29 Click Sample All Layers (⬜ changes to ☑).

30 Click and drag in the image to add the pastel colors.

The drawing appears on the colored paper.

31 Press the left bracket key several times to reduce the brush size.

32 Press the spacebar and click to move around the image.

33 Continue to click and drag, following the outlines, but drawing over them to blend the colors.

Note: Leave some areas empty so the paper shows through.

The pastel drawing covers most of the paper.

34 Double-click the Hand tool to zoom to fit.

35 Click the eye icon for Layer 1 to deselect it.

36 Click the panel menu button and select Flatten Image.

TIPS

Did You Know?

As a finishing touch, you can brush in some photographic details by increasing the Opacity for Layer 1, the top layer, from 5% to about 35%. Then select the Background layer, the bottom layer, and click and drag over a few corners or edges.

More Options!

For a softer pastel look, click the Enable Airbrush-Style button (image) in the Options panel before you start brushing-in the pastel colors.

Attention!

Avoid covering the image with even brush strokes. Using a Wacom tablet and stylus you can more easily vary the pressure as you draw. Be sure to leave some areas lighter and some areas without pastel colors for a more hand-drawn look.

Change a photograph into a PEN-AND-COLORED-WASH DRAWING

You can easily transform a photograph into a pen-and-colored-wash drawing by applying different filters and adjustments to multiple layers. Traditional artists sometimes use India ink and a diluted ink wash to visualize the light and shadow areas before beginning a painting. The technique is also often used in figure studies to create expressive drawings. When applied to a landscape or cityscape, the pen line and diluted ink wash produces an image with a unique look. In the 17th century, Nicholas Poussin and Rembrandt applied such techniques to create rich and varied drawings. Pen-and-ink-wash drawings are similar to and yet different from traditional watercolors, which generally do not use black lines.

Prepare an image by reducing the noise, brightening the image, and increasing the saturation. Then make multiple duplicates of the Background layer and edit each layer by applying different filters. You transform one of the duplicated layers into a layer of simplified outlines from the edges in the photograph. Then, with an added layer filled with white to act as the background, you use the Brush tool to paint the washes.

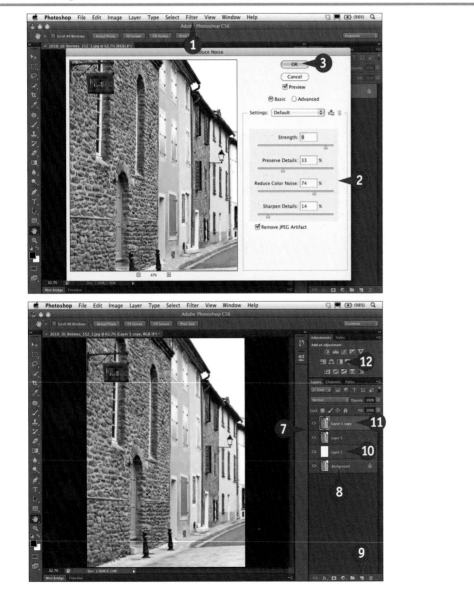

1 With an image open, click Filter ➪ Noise ➪ Reduce Noise.

2 In the Reduce Noise dialog box, click and drag the sliders to reduce the noise.

3 Click OK.

4 If necessary, increase the brightness and then the saturation using adjustment layers.

5 Press ⌘+Shift+E (Ctrl+Shift+E), multiple times if necessary, to combine any added layers.

6 Press D to reset the foreground and background colors.

7 Press ⌘+J (Ctrl+J) twice to make two duplicates of the Background layer.

8 Click the Background layer to select it.

9 Click the New Layer button to create a new empty layer.

10 Press ⌘+Delete (Ctrl+Backspace) to fill the empty layer with white.

11 Click the top layer, Layer 1 copy, to select it.

12 Click the Black & White button in the Adjustments panel.

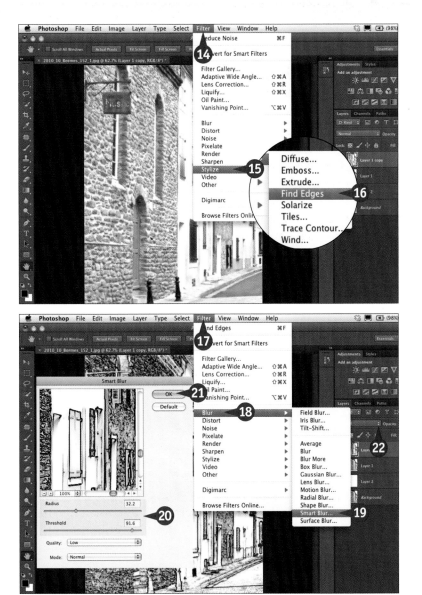

The top layer changes to a grayscale image and the Black & White options appear in the Properties panel.

Note: You can optionally click and drag the sliders or click Auto to change the style of grayscale image.

⑬ Press ⌘+E (Ctrl+E) to merge the Black & White adjustment layer with the layer below.

⑭ Click Filter.

⑮ Click Stylize.

⑯ Click Find Edges.

The image resembles a strong line-art drawing.

⑰ Click Filter.

⑱ Click Blur.

⑲ Click Smart Blur.

The Smart Blur dialog box appears.

⑳ Click and drag the Radius and Threshold sliders to soften the edges and reduce the details.

㉑ Click OK.

㉒ Click the blend mode drop-down menu for the top layer and select Multiply.

TIPS

Important!
For more artistic results, start by reducing the size of the image. Click Image ➪ Image Size. Set one of the pixel dimensions in the top section of the Image Size dialog box to about 1000 pixels. The filters are more effective on this size of image, and the brush strokes appear more like traditional brush strokes on paper.

Change It!
Change the brush or the brush tip shape as you paint with white on the black mask. With a regular brush selected, you can click the Brush Panel Toggle button (🖌) in the Options bar. Click Brush Tip Shape and change any of the attributes.

Customize It!
You can also create a dual brush to change the brush strokes even more. Click the Brush Panel Toggle button (🖌) in the Options bar. Click Dual Brush and click a different brush sample box. Click and drag the sliders to alter the brush style.

The other duplicated layer provides the base for the colors. You use the Noise filter to reduce the details in that duplicated layer even more, so that it has a less photographic appearance. Then you paint on a layer mask to make the colored washes appear. For this digital technique, as with a traditional watercolor painting, you add the washes using large, lighter opacity brushes first, increase the opacity for the next sets of washes, and finally work with smaller, more opaque brushes to define the details. You can modify the brush sizes and brush tip shapes for each

different wash to add variety and make the result appear less digitally created.

You can use any photo to create the pen-and-colored-wash drawing; however, the results look more like a traditional pen-and-ink wash when the steps are applied to a low-resolution image. As with every project in Photoshop, you can achieve a similar effect in multiple ways. Each photo also gives you a slightly different result.

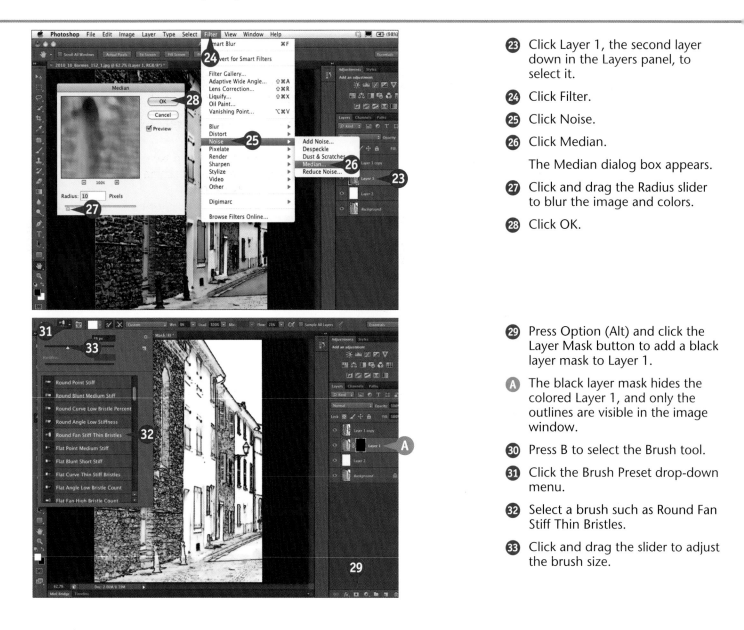

㉓ Click Layer 1, the second layer down in the Layers panel, to select it.

㉔ Click Filter.

㉕ Click Noise.

㉖ Click Median.

The Median dialog box appears.

㉗ Click and drag the Radius slider to blur the image and colors.

㉘ Click OK.

㉙ Press Option (Alt) and click the Layer Mask button to add a black layer mask to Layer 1.

Ⓐ The black layer mask hides the colored Layer 1, and only the outlines are visible in the image window.

㉚ Press B to select the Brush tool.

㉛ Click the Brush Preset drop-down menu.

㉜ Select a brush such as Round Fan Stiff Thin Bristles.

㉝ Click and drag the slider to adjust the brush size.

103

34 Click Flow and drag to the left to reduce the brush flow to about 20%.

35 Click and drag in the image, painting with white on the mask to bring in the colored wash.

Note: Use brush strokes in the direction that fits the objects in the image and increase or decrease the Flow to add more or less color per stroke.

The colors appear as large washes.

36 Press the left bracket key several times to reduce the brush size.

37 Click and drag to paint over more details.

B You can click the top layer and paint-in other colors using the regular Brush tool.

TIPS

Did You Know?

You can make the drawing appear to have multiple layers of washes by starting with a very low brush opacity in the Options bar for the first set of brush strokes, and then increasing the opacity as you brush a second and third time.

Change It!

You can change the blend mode of the top layer after you finish painting in step 37 to change the final look of the pen-and-wash drawing. Try Hard Light or Darken rather than Multiply for totally different looks.

Attention!

To make the washes appear as though they were painted by hand on white paper, be sure to leave some areas around the edges unpainted, letting the white layer show through.

Turn a photo into a HAND-PAINTED OIL PAINTING

In Photoshop CS6, the Oil Paint filter lets you quickly give an oil-painted look to any photo. The Mixer Brush tool and Bristle tip brushes give the artist a truly natural way of painting on a computer. And the Airbrush and Erodible brush tips react more like traditional than digital tools. You can create a new document and paint from scratch with any brush using the Color Picker or the Heads Up Display (HUD) to select and change colors.

With Photoshop, you can also create an original oil painting from a photograph and give it a traditionally painted look using a combination of a new action and new Mixer Brush tool presets. The action creates a white background layer, turns your photo into a reference layer with reduced opacity, and adds three layer groups, each including a transparent cloning painting layer and a hue/saturation adjustment layer. By painting on the cloning layers with the Mixer Brush tool and specific types of tool presets, you can blend the colors from the reference layer with increasing amounts of detail on each successive layer group.

1 Open an image, expand the canvas, and create a white border around the photo.

Note: To expand the canvas, use the reverse-crop technique described in task #32, selecting white as the fill color, and flattening the image.

A white border appears around the image.

2 Click Window ➪ Actions.

3 In the Actions panel, click Mixer Brush Cloning Paint Setup.

4 Click the Play button.

5 Click Continue in the dialog box that appears.

A The action builds a number of layers and places the Reference layer at 50% opacity as the top layer.

6 Click the Underpainting layer.

7 Click the Mixer Brush tool.

8 Click the Tool Preset drop-down menu.

9 Click the gear menu button (⚙).

10 Click Artists' Brushes.

11 Click OK in the dialog box that appears so the Artists' Brushes replace the existing tool presets.

236

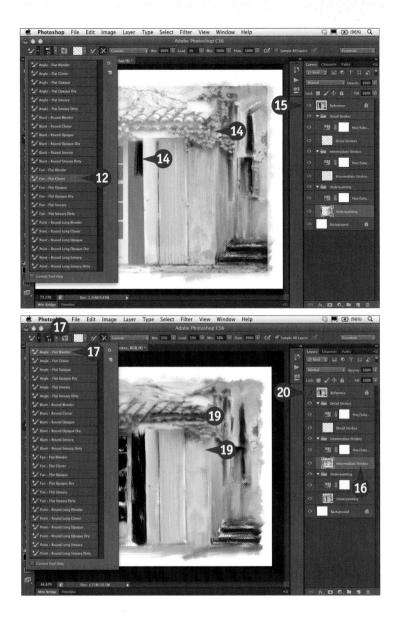

The Tool picker menu now lists only the Artists' Brushes.

12 Click a cloner brush such as Fan – Flat Cloner.

13 Press the left bracket key to reduce the brush size.

14 Click and drag following the shapes in the image to paint-in the basic colors.

Note: Paint over the edge and into the white border for a realistic effect.

15 Click the eye icon for the Reference layer on and off to check your work.

16 Click the Intermediate Strokes layer.

17 Click the Tool Preset drop-down menu and select a blender such as Angle – Flat Blender.

18 Press the left bracket key to reduce the brush size.

19 Click and drag with smaller strokes, following the lines and shapes in the image.

20 Click the eye icon for the Reference layer on and off to check your work.

#104

DIFFICULTY LEVEL

TIPS

Try This!
You can add a canvas-colored layer as a background for a realistic look. After running the action, click the white Background layer. Press ⌘+J (Ctrl+J) to duplicate it. Click Edit ➪ Fill. Click the Use drop-down menu and click Color. Select a color for the canvas in the Color Picker, such as R 248, G 242, and B 224. Click OK to close the Color Picker and again to close the Fill dialog box, and fill the layer.

Caution!
Paint following the general shapes in the reference image. Start with large brushes and make them smaller as you paint-in details on each succeeding layer.

More Options!
You can adjust the hue and saturation for any of the layer groups by double-clicking the adjustment layer for the group and moving the sliders to alter the look of your painting.

To replicate a traditionally painted image, you should start as traditional painters do, that is, with a large brush and block in basic areas of color. Then reduce the brush size and continue painting in more details. You can compare your painting and the original photo as you work by clicking the eye icon of the Reference layer off and on. You can add a canvas texture over the painted image, and add a canvas-colored layer as a background for a more realistic look.

With the Brush tool selected, you control the settings for regular brushes using the Brushes panel. With the Mixer Brush tool selected, the settings for each tool preset is stored with the preset and shown in the Options bar. Changing these options changes the way the Mixer Brush tool functions as it paints or blends colors. And if you select a Mixer Brush tool preset from the Tool picker and then select a brush preset from the Brush picker, the brush preset settings override the tool preset settings.

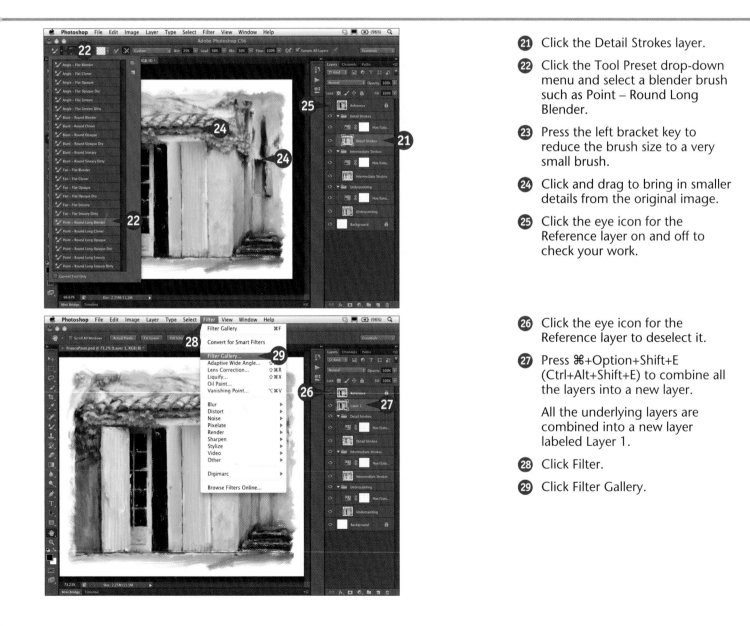

㉑ Click the Detail Strokes layer.

㉒ Click the Tool Preset drop-down menu and select a blender brush such as Point – Round Long Blender.

㉓ Press the left bracket key to reduce the brush size to a very small brush.

㉔ Click and drag to bring in smaller details from the original image.

㉕ Click the eye icon for the Reference layer on and off to check your work.

㉖ Click the eye icon for the Reference layer to deselect it.

㉗ Press ⌘+Option+Shift+E (Ctrl+Alt+Shift+E) to combine all the layers into a new layer.

All the underlying layers are combined into a new layer labeled Layer 1.

㉘ Click Filter.

㉙ Click Filter Gallery.

The Filter Gallery dialog box appears.

30 Click Texture.

31 Click Texturizer.

32 Click the Texture drop-down menu and select Canvas.

33 Click and drag the sliders to increase the scaling and relief.

Note: The preview image shows the details at 100%.

34 Click OK.

The Canvas texture is applied to the finished painting.

TIPS

Try This!

You can add more layer groups by selecting the group and pressing ⌘+J (Ctrl+J). Then you can paint on the layer in the copied group, and add different sized brush strokes to vary the effect.

Important!

The Brushes and Mixer Brush tools work quite differently. Brushes paint with color on the layer selected. Mixer Brush tools, depending on the tool preset and settings in the Options bar, mix paint from the layer. With Sample All Layers checked, the Mixer Brush tool mixes the paint from the other visible layers above and below.

Did You Know?

The Mixer Brush Cloning Paint Setup action as well as the Artists' Brushes, Airbrushes, Dry Media, and Pencil Mixer Brush, were created by John Derry. You can find many more of these special brushes on his site at www.pixlart.com.

Paint a DIGITAL WATERCOLOR

You can create a digital watercolor starting with a blank document and paint from scratch with the new watercolor brushes to add colors in progressive layers. You can also create a digital watercolor from a photograph and give it a traditionally painted look. Although Photoshop's Filter Gallery includes a Watercolor filter, this filter does not render a realistic-looking watercolor.

Traditional watercolor paintings have transparent colors, minimal transitions of color tones, and loosely defined shapes without black outlines.

The technique in this task uses the Pattern Stamp tool and the entire image as a pattern for a base image. The Pattern Stamp tool's Impressionist option mixes the photo's colors on the paper.

You start by simplifying the photo using the Camera Raw technique or by applying the Reduce Noise filter or the Median filter. Both these filters are in the Filter menu under Noise. Then add white space around the photo using a reverse crop or by creating a white vignette. You paint on multiple layers with the Pattern Stamp tool and the Impressionist setting, and change the brush style and size according to the image.

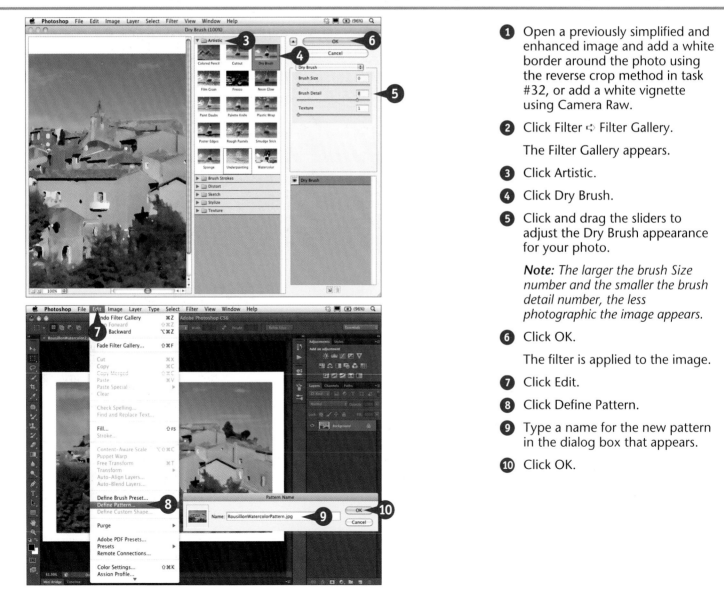

① Open a previously simplified and enhanced image and add a white border around the photo using the reverse crop method in task #32, or add a white vignette using Camera Raw.

② Click Filter ➪ Filter Gallery.

The Filter Gallery appears.

③ Click Artistic.

④ Click Dry Brush.

⑤ Click and drag the sliders to adjust the Dry Brush appearance for your photo.

Note: The larger the brush Size number and the smaller the brush detail number, the less photographic the image appears.

⑥ Click OK.

The filter is applied to the image.

⑦ Click Edit.

⑧ Click Define Pattern.

⑨ Type a name for the new pattern in the dialog box that appears.

⑩ Click OK.

11 Click the New Layer button.

12 Press ⌘+Delete (Ctrl+Backspace) to fill the layer with white.

13 Click the New Layer button again.

14 Click the Layer Mask button.

15 Click Edit ➪ Fill.

16 Click the Use drop-down menu and select Pattern.

17 Click the Custom Pattern drop-down menu and select Gouache Light on Watercolor.

18 Click OK to fill the layer mask.

19 Press ⌘+J (Ctrl+J) twice to make two more copies of this painting layer and mask.

20 Click the top painting layer's layer mask.

21 Repeat steps 15 to 18, this time selecting Washed Watercolor Paper.

22 Click the Background layer.

23 Press ⌘+J (Ctrl+J) to duplicate the Background layer.

24 Click and drag the Background layer copy to the top of the layer stack.

25 Click and drag the Opacity for the Background copy layer to about 30%.

TIPS

Important!
Load the Wet Media Brushes from the gear menu button (⬚) in the Brush picker before you start. If you click OK rather than Append in the dialog box when asked to replace the current brushes, you will have a shorter list and more appropriate brushes for painting.

Did You Know?
A true watercolor palette includes only gray and no black paint at all. Photoshop's Watercolor filter in the Filter Gallery adds too much black to replicate a traditional watercolor and also dulls the colors.

Change It!
You can change the settings for any brush by clicking the Brush Panel Toggle button (⬚) in the Options bar to open the Brushes panel. Try clicking the word *Texture* and make changes to the scale, depth, or pattern to add texture to your brush.

The painting layers each have a layer mask filled with a watercolor paper pattern from the Artist Surfaces pattern set. You can load these patterns using the gear menu button in the Custom Pattern section of the Fill dialog box. To finish the painting, paint with the Mixer Brush tool to blend the colors on each painting layer so the image appears to be painted rather than digitally generated.

The painting will appear more natural if you click and drag in the document following the contours of the subjects, and use small brushes and strokes to paint from the photo. Avoid painting over every pixel and covering the entire painting. Traditional watercolor paintings often have rough edges and some unpainted areas allowing the white background to show through. You can optionally add more layers and change each painted layer's opacity to alter the look.

The same technique can be used to paint with other mediums such as digital pastels and oils for different looks.

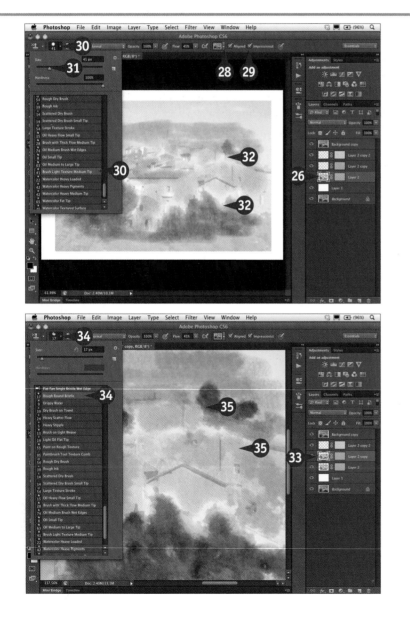

26 Click the bottom painting layer to select it.

27 Click the Pattern Stamp tool (⬛).

28 Click the drop-down menu and select the custom pattern you just created.

29 Click Impressionist (⬛ changes to ☑).

30 Click the Brush Preset drop-down menu and select Brush Light Texture Medium Tip.

31 Adjust the size to paint the large areas of color.

32 Click and drag in the image to paint, leaving some areas unpainted.

Note: Reduce the brush size as you work in smaller areas by pressing the left bracket key.

Note: Press ⌘+spacebar (Ctrl+spacebar) to zoom in as needed.

33 Click Layer 2 copy, the next layer up.

34 Click the Brush Preset drop-down menu and select the Rough Round Bristle, adjusting the brush size according to the image.

35 Click and drag in the image to paint over other more detailed sections, leaving some areas unpainted.

36 Click Layer 2 copy 2, the next layer up.

37 Click the Brush Preset drop-down menu and select Watercolor Heavy Loaded.

38 Click and drag the brush size to a small size.

39 Click Impressionist to deselect it (☑ changes to ▢).

40 Click the eye icon for the Background copy layer on and off to check your work.

41 Click and drag in the image to paint the more detailed areas, leaving some areas unpainted.

42 Click the Mixer Brush tool.

43 Click the Tool Preset drop-down menu and select the Fan – Flat Blender.

44 Click Sample All Layers in the Options bar to deselect it (☑ changes to ▢).

45 Click and drag with a small brush size in each of the painting layers to blend the paints on that layer.

TIPS

Try This!

When using the Mixer Brush tool, open the Tool Preset drop-down menu and click Current Tool Only (▢ changes to ☑). Then click the gear menu button (⚙) and click any of the sets at the bottom of the menu. Click OK to replace the existing tool presets. The drop-down menu appears more organized and displays only the new presets for the selected tool.

More Options!

You can create your own tool preset by changing the settings in the Options bar with a tool selected, and then clicking the Create New button (📄) and giving your tool a descriptive name.

Important!

Load the Artist Surfaces patterns using the gear menu button (⚙) on the Pattern menu. These pattern surfaces can be used to fill a layer mask or a group mask, or to fill another layer.

Chapter 10

Give Your Images a Professional Presentation

Most photos or designs, from family snapshots to a professional portfolio, can be improved when properly displayed or framed. For professional designers, a powerful presentation can help keep an art director happy. For photographers, an elegant display can make all the difference in securing a new client or keeping a current one. Even snapshots look more professional when you add a digital matte or a simulated frame. Photoshop makes it easy to show your images in a professional manner.

You can add mattes and frames to enhance any image with minimal effort using the frame actions included with Photoshop. You can also create your own mattes and frames or change

the matte and frame colors. Photoshop can also help you apply an artistic edge to a photo using a sequence of filters from the Filter Gallery, or you can brush an artistic edge onto any images by hand using the Brush tool. You can add space and borders to make a photo look like a gallery print. You can create a contact sheet as a visual index of all the photos in one client folder or on one CD or DVD. You can prepare a custom slide show with professional transitions, burn it to external media, or save it as a PDF document and send it to friends or clients as an e-mail attachment. You can even use Photoshop to design and upload your own photo gallery to a website. With Photoshop, you can display all your images with a professional touch.

DIFFICULTY LEVEL

You can add interest and give a finished look to your photographs by adding a digital matte or frame to your images. You can quickly apply a variety of mattes or frames using an action from the Actions panel in Photoshop. The Frame Channel - 50 pixels shown in this task puts your photo on a larger white canvas and lets you fill a 50-pixel-wide channel with any color or even a pattern. Select a color from the image itself to create a coordinating digital matte.

Photoshop includes many more frame actions; however, not all are loaded when you first open the application. To apply other frame actions, click the panel menu button on the Actions panel and click Frames to load the additional frames actions. You can then play any of these actions to frame or matte your photo. Some frame actions require a selection inside the image. Others stop so you can select a color for the frame.

Actions are stored as files with the *.atn* extension in the Photoshop Actions folder in the Presets folder.

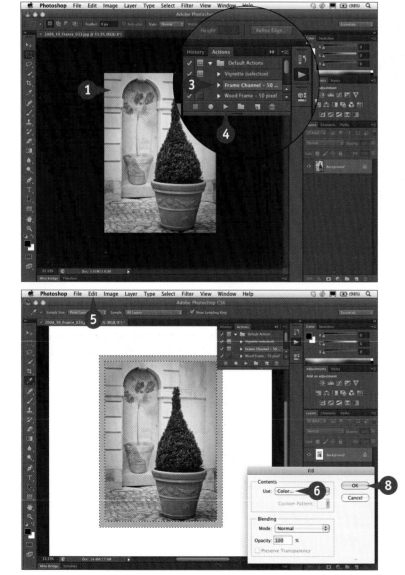

① Open an image.

② Press Option+F9 (Alt+F9) to open the Actions panel.

Note: *You can optionally click Window ➪ Actions to open the Actions panel.*

③ Click Frame Channel - 50 pixels.

④ Click the Play button.

Note: *A warning dialog box appears. If your image is over 100 pixels wide and tall, click Continue.*

Photoshop plays the action, leaving a 50-pixel channel selected around the photo.

⑤ Click Edit ➪ Fill.

The Fill dialog box appears.

⑥ Click the Use drop-down menu and select Color.

⑦ When the Color Picker appears, click a color in the image to select it and click OK.

⑧ Click OK in the Fill dialog box.

The 50-pixel channel is filled with the color.

⑨ Press ⌘+D (Ctrl+D) to deselect the channel.

You may have a photo with a large background area but not enough resolution to crop and resize it. You can instead transform the excess background into a frame to help focus the attention on the main subject. Making a line frame from the photograph itself is a quick way to give a classic and finished look to any image. You make a selection in the photo as if you were going to crop it. You then invert the selection to create the frame. You can even vary the frame shape by using the Elliptical Marquee tool to select the area with an elliptical frame. To create any style of line frame from within the photograph, place the frame area on its own layer above the Background layer and change the blend mode to Screen to lighten the area that will become the frame.

To separate the frame from the photo even more, stroke the borders of the new frame layer by applying a layer style. You can change the default stroke color to any color that fits your image. As a final touch, add a drop shadow and an inner shadow, and even a bevel-and-emboss look.

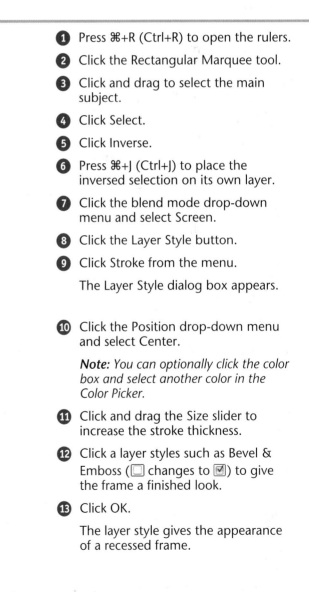

1. Press ⌘+R (Ctrl+R) to open the rulers.
2. Click the Rectangular Marquee tool.
3. Click and drag to select the main subject.
4. Click Select.
5. Click Inverse.
6. Press ⌘+J (Ctrl+J) to place the inversed selection on its own layer.
7. Click the blend mode drop-down menu and select Screen.
8. Click the Layer Style button.
9. Click Stroke from the menu.

   The Layer Style dialog box appears.

10. Click the Position drop-down menu and select Center.

    Note: You can optionally click the color box and select another color in the Color Picker.

11. Click and drag the Size slider to increase the stroke thickness.

12. Click a layer styles such as Bevel & Emboss (☐ changes to ☑) to give the frame a finished look.

13. Click OK.

    The layer style gives the appearance of a recessed frame.

Apply a filter to give a photo an ARTISTIC EDGE

You can give any photo an artistic look by adding an irregular edge using the Filter Gallery and the Brush Strokes filters. By moving the photo or artwork to its own layer and adding a white Background layer, you can quickly create a unique artistic edge. The Filter Gallery enables you to combine the filters in different ways and use the same technique to create a variety of different edges to fit each image. Make a selection on the top layer just inside the edge of the image and then add a layer mask to delineate the borders of the

image. The artistic edge starts from the selected area. Open the Filter Gallery and start adding different layers of Brush Strokes filters. The Preview window of the Filter Gallery shows the edge effect in reverse. The white areas represent the photo area, and the black areas represent what will be cut away. Every time you change the various sliders for the Brush Strokes filters, your edge effect changes in the Preview window of the Filter Gallery. And you can add multiple layers of filters all within the Filter Gallery.

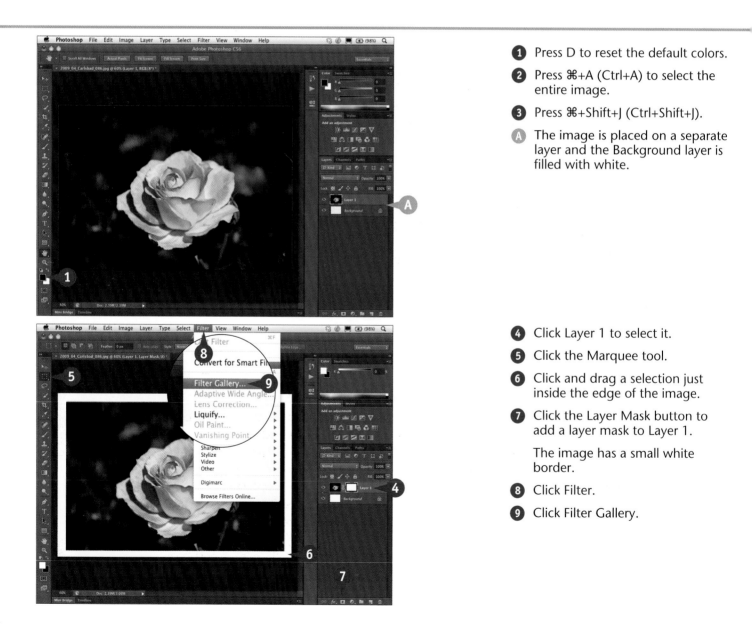

① Press D to reset the default colors.

② Press ⌘+A (Ctrl+A) to select the entire image.

③ Press ⌘+Shift+J (Ctrl+Shift+J).

Ⓐ The image is placed on a separate layer and the Background layer is filled with white.

④ Click Layer 1 to select it.

⑤ Click the Marquee tool.

⑥ Click and drag a selection just inside the edge of the image.

⑦ Click the Layer Mask button to add a layer mask to Layer 1.

The image has a small white border.

⑧ Click Filter.

⑨ Click Filter Gallery.

The Filter Gallery opens.

⑩ Click the Brush Strokes tab.

⑪ Click Sprayed Strokes.

⑫ Click and drag the Stroke Length and Spray Radius to increase or decrease the strokes.

⑬ Click the New Effect Layer button.

A new Sprayed Strokes layer is added and the effect changes.

⑭ Repeat step 13 to create additional Sprayed Stroke layers.

⑮ Click OK.

The custom edge is applied to the photo.

TIPS

Did You Know?
Add as many Filter Effects layers as your computer's memory allows. Each one you add changes the look of the custom photo edge. Change the order of the layers in the Filter Gallery dialog box, and the overall style of the edge changes as well.

More Options!
For a light-colored image, darken the edge for a stronger effect. Click the Layer Style button (fx) in the Layers panel. Click Drop Shadow. Drag the Distance slider to 0. Drag the Spread slider up to darken the edges.

Customize it!
You can create your own custom border by painting with a natural media brush. Follow steps 1 to 3 in this task. Click the Background layer and click Image ➪ Canvas Size. Click Relative and add 1 inch to both the Width and Height fields to enlarge the background. Add a new blank layer between the Background and photo layers. Click a rough-edged brush and paint your custom edge with black on the middle layer.

When you want to display your artwork, you need to add a frame. Although you can print your image with a frame you create in Photoshop, your artwork will look more professional if you print the image and display it in a real frame. Using a matte adds an even more finished look to the artwork. You can purchase a matte to go in the frame, or you can create a realistic one using the layer styles and additional layers. You can create a matte of any size to fit your image and

your frame, and you can even add a color to the matte to match a hue in the image.

You can add the matte directly to the edges of the image, or you can add a separate layer so the image has a border. The matte appears to be placed on top of the image just as a traditional matte would look. You can then print and frame the artwork, or use the matted image in a web gallery for a professional result.

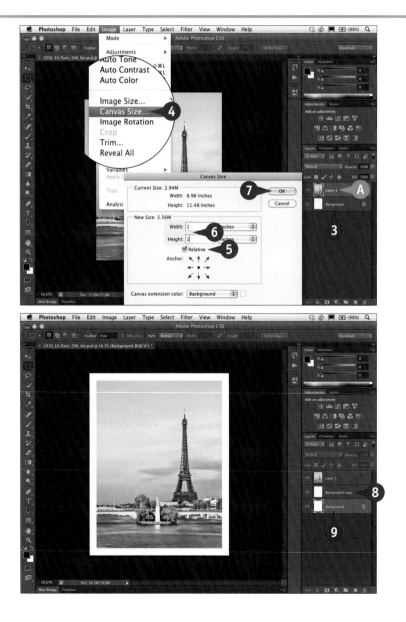

① Press ⌘+A (Ctrl+A) to select the image.

② Press ⌘+Shift+J (Ctrl+Shift+J).

Ⓐ The image is placed on a separate layer and the Background layer is filled with the current background color.

③ Click the Background layer.

④ Click Image ➪ Canvas Size.

⑤ In the Canvas Size dialog box, click Relative (☐ changes to ☑).

⑥ Type 1 inch for the width and height, depending on the image size.

⑦ Click OK.

The image appears with a white border.

⑧ With the Background layer selected, press ⌘+J (Ctrl+J) to duplicate the Background layer again.

⑨ Click the Background layer to select it.

⑩ Repeat steps 4 to 7 to create another larger Background layer, this time typing **3** inches for the width and height.

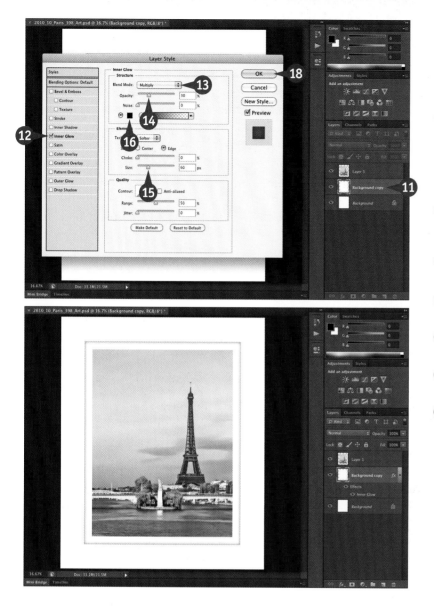

⓫ Double-click the middle layer labeled Background copy.

The Layer Style dialog box appears.

⓬ Click Inner Glow (☐ changes to ☑).

The Inner Glow options appear in the dialog box.

⓭ Click the blend mode drop-down menu and select Multiply.

⓮ Click and drag the Opacity slider to 30%.

⓯ Click and drag the Size slider to 60 px.

⓰ Click the color swatch to open the Color Picker.

⓱ Select black and click OK to close the Color Picker.

⓲ Click OK to close the Layer Style dialog box.

The image appears with a white border and a realistic white matte.

TIPS

More Options!

Change the matte color to match a color in the image. Click the Background layer. Click Edit ➪ Fill. In the Fill dialog box, click the Use drop-down menu and select Color. When the Color Picker appears, position the cursor over the image and click a color to select it. Click OK in the Color Picker and click OK in the Fill dialog box. The matte fills with the selected color.

Did You Know?

You can save the Matte style and use it again. Double-click the middle layer labeled Background copy to reopen the Layer Style dialog box. With the Inner Glow settings you selected, click New Style. Type a name for the style. Click both Include Layer Effects and Include Layer Blending Options (☐ changes to ☑). Click OK. Your custom style is now listed when you click Styles at the top left in the Layer Style dialog box.

You can give your photograph a professional finish by making it look like a gallery print. This technique is effective for both color and grayscale photographs. Gallery prints generally have wide white, black, or even gray borders depending on the tones in the image. The photo is placed in the top portion of the border or frame area, allowing the name of the gallery, artist, and artwork to fit under the image in stylized type.

After making a selection of the photo and placing it onto its own layer, you enlarge the canvas size by about 3 inches using the Relative option to add the space evenly all around the photo. You then add more space below the photograph, to extend the area for the text. You can add a stroke or even a double stroke around the outside edge of the photo to give a finished look to the gallery print. The strokes can be the same or different colors, and each stroke can have a different pixel width.

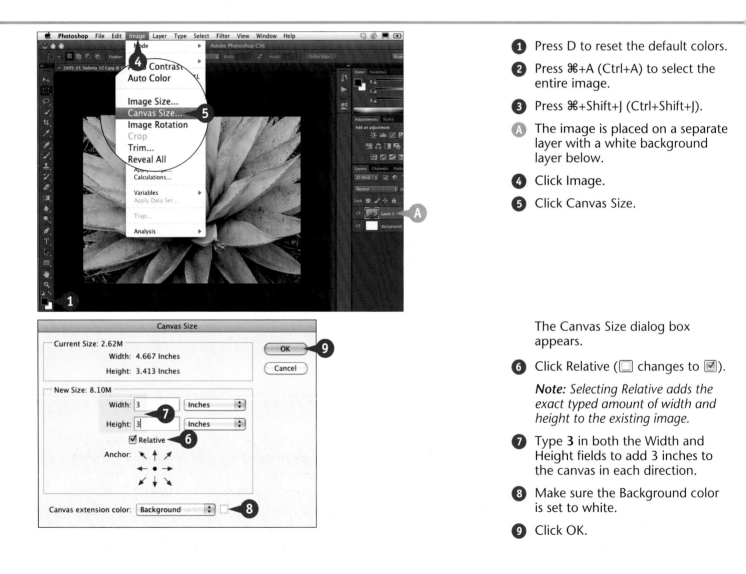

1. Press D to reset the default colors.

2. Press ⌘+A (Ctrl+A) to select the entire image.

3. Press ⌘+Shift+J (Ctrl+Shift+J).

A. The image is placed on a separate layer with a white background layer below.

4. Click Image.

5. Click Canvas Size.

The Canvas Size dialog box appears.

6. Click Relative (☐ changes to ☑).

Note: Selecting Relative adds the exact typed amount of width and height to the existing image.

7. Type **3** in both the Width and Height fields to add 3 inches to the canvas in each direction.

8. Make sure the Background color is set to white.

9. Click OK.

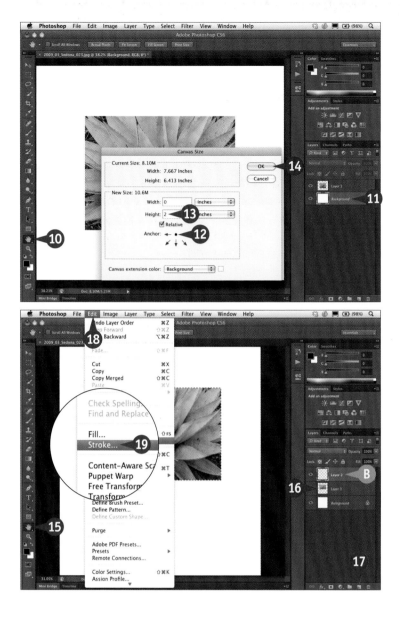

10 Double-click the Hand tool to fit the image to your screen.

The image is centered in a wide white border.

11 With the Background layer selected, repeat steps 4 and 5 to open the Canvas Size dialog box again.

Note: *Relative remains selected.*

12 Click the top center arrow of the Anchor grid so the center anchor circle appears on top.

13 Click in the Height field and type **2** to add 2 inches to the bottom of the white border.

14 Click OK.

The photo is offset in the white border.

15 Double-click the Hand tool to center the image on the screen.

16 ⌘+click (Ctrl+click) the photo thumbnail in the Layers panel to select the photo.

17 Click the New Layer button to add a new empty layer.

B The new layer is automatically selected.

18 Click Edit.

19 Click Stroke.

TIPS

Change It!

Set the canvas color to black in the Canvas Size dialog box for a dramatic effect. Use white for the inside border stroke color and gray for the outside border stroke color, and type the text using white or gray.

Try This!

For a realistic look, type a print number or the words **artist's proof** on the left side under the border using black for the color and a script-styled font. You can then make the stylized letters appear to be written in pencil by lowering the opacity of the type layer. Using the Type tool (T), click the center title under the image, and click the Horizontal Scale button ( ) in the Character panel to widen the overall spacing, or the Tracking button (VA) to extend the space between all the letters. (See the continuation of this task to add text.)

By placing the strokes on separate layers, you can adjust the opacity of each stroke individually and change the look of the gallery print. You ⌘+click (Ctrl+click) the photo layer to have an active selection the exact size of the photo. You add a new empty layer above the photo layer and, with the selection active, apply a stroke on the new layer. The stroke makes the photo stand out. With the selection still active, you make the selected area slightly wider and higher, add another empty layer, and then apply a stroke on the second empty layer.

Gallery prints often have the name of the gallery, the artist's name or studio, or the name of the image set in a serif-styled font in all capital letters. Type the name and click Window and then Character to open the Character panel. Use the tracking options to increase the space between the letters. Select a script font to sign your work under the outside stroke and add a print number to complete the gallery print look.

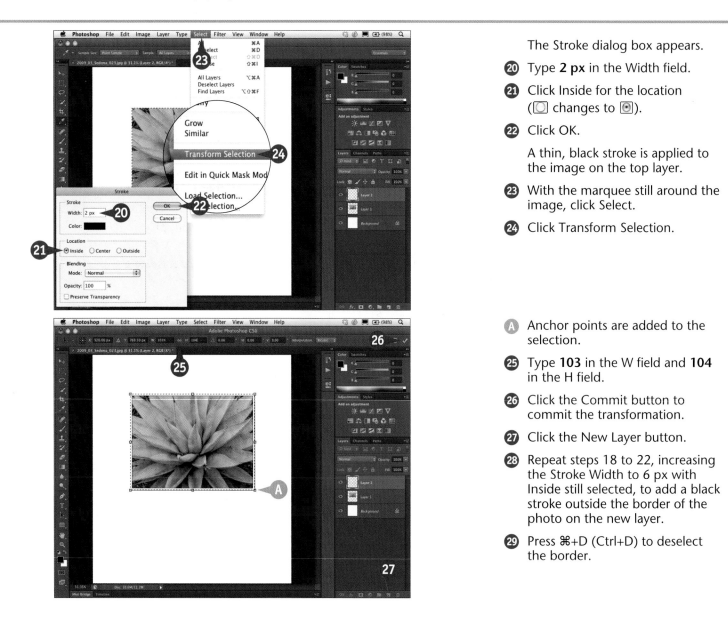

The Stroke dialog box appears.

⓴ Type **2 px** in the Width field.

㉑ Click Inside for the location (◯ changes to ◉).

㉒ Click OK.

A thin, black stroke is applied to the image on the top layer.

㉓ With the marquee still around the image, click Select.

㉔ Click Transform Selection.

Ⓐ Anchor points are added to the selection.

㉕ Type **103** in the W field and **104** in the H field.

㉖ Click the Commit button to commit the transformation.

㉗ Click the New Layer button.

㉘ Repeat steps 18 to 22, increasing the Stroke Width to 6 px with Inside still selected, to add a black stroke outside the border of the photo on the new layer.

㉙ Press ⌘+D (Ctrl+D) to deselect the border.

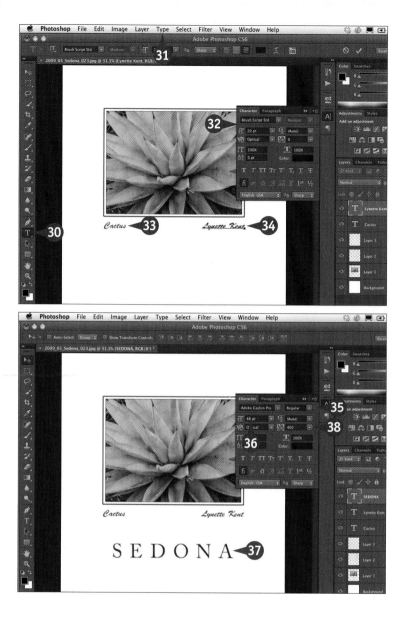

30 Click the Type tool.

31 Click Type ➪ Panels ➪ Character panel.

32 In the Character panel that appears, select a size and a handwriting-styled font.

33 Click one side of the image, type a title, and press Enter (Ctrl+Enter) or click the Commit button.

34 Click the other side of the image, type your name, and press Enter (Ctrl+Enter) or click the Commit button.

35 Select a serif font such as Adobe Caslon Pro and a font style such as Regular.

36 Type a large font size in the field.

37 Click in the center of the gallery frame and type a title, studio, gallery, or print series.

38 Click the drop-down menu to change the space between the letters.

39 Press Enter (Ctrl+Enter) to commit the type.

The image now appears like a traditional gallery print.

TIPS

Did You Know?

The size of the stroke that you apply to the borders depends on the size and resolution of the image.

Important!

Selecting Inside for the stroke location in the Stroke dialog box gives the stroke sharp corners. Selecting Outside applies a stroke with rounded corners.

More Options!

Because each stroke border is on its own layer, you can use different colors for the stroke for different effects. If the photo is light in color, try using a shade of gray to stroke the inner border rather than black, or lower the opacity of the layer if the color of the stroke appears too bold.

Whether you use photos from a digital camera or scans of traditional prints and negatives, the first file downloaded or scanned is the original. You should always keep a duplicate set of the original photos on a separate hard drive or burn a CD or DVD before enhancing or using the photos in projects. You can create and print a contact sheet that fits a CD or DVD case or any other size, to help you identify and keep track of the images on the external drive or other media using the Contact Sheet II Automation in Photoshop CS6. You can also create a photo index of all the images in one project folder to help you identify and catalog groups of images using the same steps.

In the Contact Sheet II dialog box, you select the source files, the document size, the number of columns and rows, and amount of spacing. You can add the filenames as captions and select the font and size. You can even save your settings as a custom contact sheet and apply it to different folders of images.

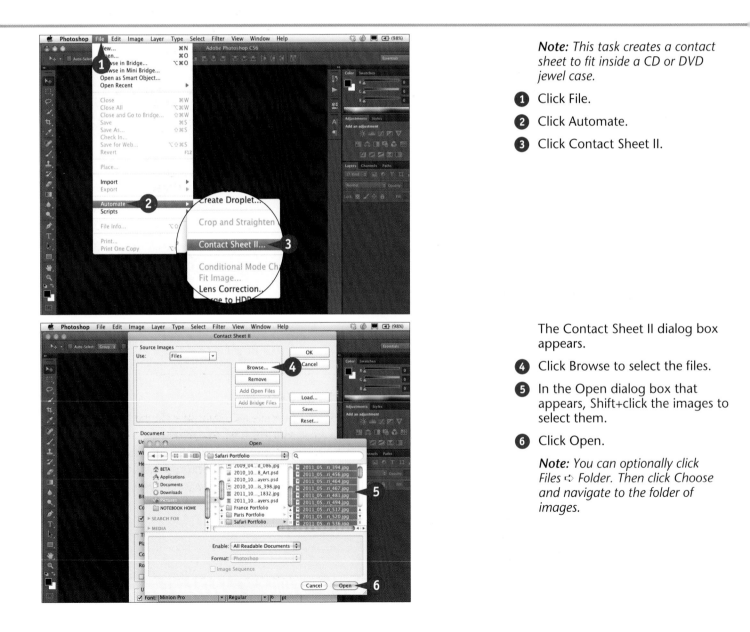

Note: This task creates a contact sheet to fit inside a CD or DVD jewel case.

1 Click File.

2 Click Automate.

3 Click Contact Sheet II.

The Contact Sheet II dialog box appears.

4 Click Browse to select the files.

5 In the Open dialog box that appears, Shift+click the images to select them.

6 Click Open.

Note: You can optionally click Files ➪ Folder. Then click Choose and navigate to the folder of images.

The selected files or folders appear in the list.

7 In the Document section, type **4.688** inches in both the Width and Height fields.

8 Type **100** (pixels/inch) in the resolution field.

Note: Low resolution can be used for printing a contact sheet because the images are very small and only used for identification.

9 In the Thumbnails section, type **5** for both the columns and rows.

10 Click Use Auto-Spacing (☐ changes to ☑).

11 Click the Font drop-down menu and select a font and style.

12 Type **6** for the point size.

13 Click OK.

The Output Preview pane displays the contact sheet.

TIPS

Save It!

If the layout looks good, you can save it as a template. Click File ➪ Automate ➪ Contact Sheet II again. The Previous settings appear. Click Save. Type a name for your contact sheet in the Save Contact Sheet Settings dialog box that appears. Click Save. The custom contact sheet is saved in the Application Support folder. To reapply the template, click Load in the Contact Sheet II dialog box and select your custom template in the dialog box.

Did You Know?

You can also create a Contact Sheet in the Output section of Bridge. Launch Bridge, select the Output tab, select PDF, and select one of the Contact Sheet Templates and your settings. Bridge builds the contact sheet, saves it as a PDF, and launches your default PDF reader.

If you want to e-mail photos to friends or your portfolio to a prospective employer, or send a client some images for review, you can use Photoshop and Bridge to help you create a slide show and save it as a PDF presentation. You can then attach the PDF slide show to an e-mail or burn it to a CD or DVD. You can use any images from Bridge to create the slide show. You determine the layout of the images, and you can add a watermark or copyright to each image. You can

select a complete folder of source images or individually select the images to include in the slide show. You determine the amount of time that each slide appears on-screen and decide if the slide show should stop after the last image or continue in a loop. You can even select from a number of included slide transitions to give your presentation a more professional look.

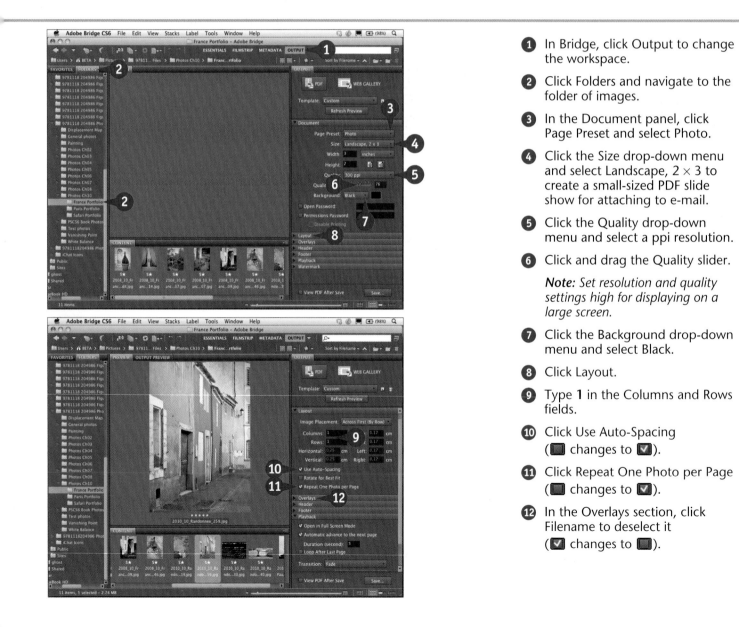

1 In Bridge, click Output to change the workspace.

2 Click Folders and navigate to the folder of images.

3 In the Document panel, click Page Preset and select Photo.

4 Click the Size drop-down menu and select Landscape, 2 × 3 to create a small-sized PDF slide show for attaching to e-mail.

5 Click the Quality drop-down menu and select a ppi resolution.

6 Click and drag the Quality slider.

Note: Set resolution and quality settings high for displaying on a large screen.

7 Click the Background drop-down menu and select Black.

8 Click Layout.

9 Type **1** in the Columns and Rows fields.

10 Click Use Auto-Spacing (■ changes to ☑).

11 Click Repeat One Photo per Page (■ changes to ☑).

12 In the Overlays section, click Filename to deselect it (☑ changes to ■).

13 Click the first two check boxes in the Playback section (☐ changes to ☑).

A You can optionally type a different slide duration.

14 Click the Transition drop-down menu and select Fade.

15 ⌘+click (Ctrl+click) the photos in the Content pane to use in the slide show.

16 Click the Preview tab.

B The thumbnails of the selected images appear.

17 Click Refresh Preview.

The Output Preview pane displays one slide of the slide show.

18 Click View PDF After Save (☐ changes to ☑).

19 Click Save.

The Save As dialog box appears.

20 Type a name for the slide show.

21 Click Save.

Bridge builds the slide show, saves it as a PDF, and launches your default PDF application.

TIPS

Customize It!

You can change the transition style to any of the transition options. You can change how many seconds each image appears on the screen by typing the number in the Duration field in the Playback section. If you want the presentation to repeat in a continuous loop, click Loop After Last Page (☐ changes to ☑).

Did You Know?

You can view the slide show with Acrobat or Acrobat Reader, or even Apple's Preview application, and set the slide show to fill the screen. To stop the slide show presentation, press Esc.

Try This!

To protect the images from being printed without permission, click Permissions Password (☐ changes to ☑) in the Document section. Type the password in the field and click Disable Printing (☐ changes to ☑).

Create a WEB PHOTO GALLERY

In addition to PDF slide shows, you can also build a web photo gallery using Bridge. You can easily create a website home page with your images displayed both as thumbnails and full-sized images. You can select from a variety of web gallery styles and personalize your web page. Bridge includes many different templates, including Filmstrips and HTML galleries. The steps to creating a web photo gallery are similar to those for creating a PDF slide show presentation. You select the images in Bridge, determine a template

and a style, and add a gallery name, your name, your e-mail, and whether or not to display the filenames as image titles. You can select your own set of colors to use on the web gallery to customize your site's appearance even more. You can preview your web gallery inside Bridge as you create it and also preview how it will appear in a web browser. You can even upload your web gallery directly to an FTP server from within the Bridge application.

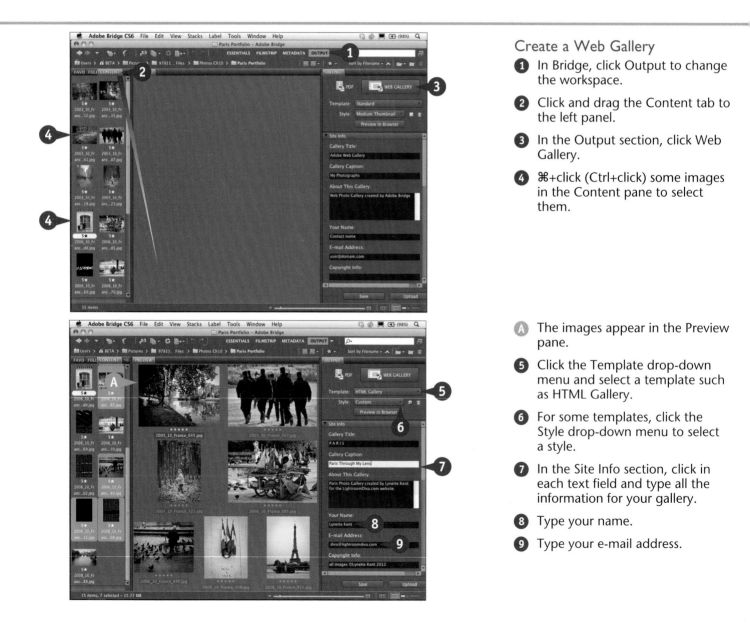

Create a Web Gallery

1 In Bridge, click Output to change the workspace.

2 Click and drag the Content tab to the left panel.

3 In the Output section, click Web Gallery.

4 ⌘+click (Ctrl+click) some images in the Content pane to select them.

Ⓐ The images appear in the Preview pane.

5 Click the Template drop-down menu and select a template such as HTML Gallery.

6 For some templates, click the Style drop-down menu to select a style.

7 In the Site Info section, click in each text field and type all the information for your gallery.

8 Type your name.

9 Type your e-mail address.

10 In the Color Palette pane, click a color box, such as the Text color box.

11 Click a different color In the Colors dialog box that appears.

12 Click here to close the Colors dialog box.

13 Click any of the Appearance options and change the Preview Size and Quality sliders.

14 Click Preview in Browser.

Your web gallery appears in your default web browser.

Upload Your Web Gallery to an FTP Site

15 In Bridge, click the Create Gallery panel.

16 Type the gallery name.

17 Type your FTP server, username, password, and a folder name.

18 Click Upload.

Bridge creates the web gallery and uploads it to your FTP site.

#113

DIFFICULTY LEVEL

● ● ● ◡

TIPS

Try This!

You can design your web gallery and click Save in the Create Gallery section to save it to your hard drive or removable media such as a DVD. You can then upload it to an FTP site or publish it to a WebDAV server when it is more convenient.

Did You Know?

If you include your e-mail in the Site Info section, a viewer can click your name on the web gallery site and automatically open a new mail message with your e-mail address in the address field. Try using an e-mail address you do not use anywhere else to avoid excess spam.

More Options!

The Airtight SimpleViewer, Airtight AutoViewer, and Airtight Postcard Viewer templates all add a white border around each image. You can change both the image border and background colors in the Color Palette options.

Plug In to Photoshop

Photoshop includes all the tools you need to completely edit images and create graphic designs. You can add plug-ins from other software companies to perform some steps for you or even accomplish the image edits more quickly. Certain plug-ins make a variety of changes to one image and display them at once on the screen so you can make visual comparisons of different types of enhancements. Some plug-ins take the Photoshop edits a step further than Photoshop with more advanced and custom algorithms. Other plug-ins perform completely separate and specialized functions.

You can find plug-ins for reducing noise, resizing, adding tonal adjustments, changing color images to black and white, converting photos into artwork, editing portraits, applying custom filters, adding frames, and creating special effects. Plug-ins exist for nearly every project, at every price range, and for every user level.

The best way to know if a plug-in can make your project easier or enhance your image better is to visit the manufacturer's website, look at the examples, and download and test a trial version if available. Trying the plug-in out on your own images is the best way to decide whether to purchase and use a particular plug-in.

The tasks in this chapter illustrate the use of some plug-ins from Nik Software, AKVIS, and Alien Skin that interact with images in a unique way.

In addition to these companies, you can find very effective and often time-saving plug-ins from OnOneSoftware.com, TopazLabs.com, AutoFX.com, Imagenomic.com, Portrait professional.com, TiffenSoftware.com, PostWorkShop.net, and many more.

DIFFICULTY LEVEL

Enhance colors and light selectively with NIK VIVEZA

Nik Software's high-end editing plug-ins are used by many professional photographers because of their powerful algorithms for making changes to images.

You can control the changes to color and light in your images and even target certain areas with Nik Software's Viveza. You can darken the background and lighten the main subject, or modify the tones in specific areas visually using interactive sliders. Viveza, like other Nik Software plug-ins, includes the custom U Point technology. You can add multiple control points in the image and change how the filter is applied to each area individually. As you move the

control point sliders to adjust the brightness, contrast, and saturation, Viveza edits the colors of the objects under the points and automatically blends the tonal changes as it applies them. You can optionally choose to paint the edits directly on the image using the Brush option in the interface.

By applying Viveza to a Smart Object layer, you can fine-tune any edits after they have been applied. Viveza is also available as part of the complete collection of Nik software plug-ins available at www. niksoftware.com.

① With an image open, click Filter ➪ Convert for Smart Filters.

Ⓐ The Background layer is changed to a Smart Object layer.

Note: Nik's Brush option is deactivated when using a Smart Object layer.

② Click Viveza 2 in the Selective tool.

Note: If the Selective tool is not open, click File ➪ Automate ➪ Nik Selective Tool.

Note: You can optionally click Filter ➪ Nik Software ➪ Viveza 2 to open the Nik Viveza interface.

The Viveza 2 interface appears.

③ Click the Side-by-Side preview button to select a before and after preview.

Ⓑ You can also click the Split preview button to display a split preview.

④ Click Add Control Point.

⑤ Click an area in the photo to adjust it.

Ⓒ A control point appears.

⑥ Click and drag the top slider to adjust the circle so it covers the area to be changed.

7 Click and drag the Brightness, Contrast, and Saturation sliders to adjust the tones in the area.

8 Repeat steps 4 to 7 to add more adjustment points.

9 Click Duplicate to duplicate a control point.

10 Click and drag the duplicate control point to another area.

The identical settings are applied to that area.

11 Click OK.

Viveza applies the changes to the colors and light in the image as a Smart Filter.

D You can double-click the Viveza Smart Filter to reopen the interface and readjust the sliders.

114

DIFFICULTY LEVEL

TIPS

Did You Know?
When the main preview window shows the entire image, the Loupe window displays a section of the image at 100%. When you click the Nik Zoom tool (⊕) to preview the image at 100% in the main preview window, the Loupe window shows the entire image and acts as a navigator.

Try This!
You can click the Settings button in the Viveza interface to set how the interface functions. You can select the default zoom size, change the default preview style, change the control point size and the types of sliders, and choose to always have the filter applied to a separate layer.

More Options!
Viveza adds four visible sliders to each control point you add. You can click the arrow below the fourth slider to reveal additional sliders for adjusting the hue, red, green, blue, and warmth of the selected area.

Colorize a black-and-white photo with AKVIS COLORIAGE

You can add color to a grayscale photo in Photoshop using adjustment layers, masks, and brushes; however, the Coloriage plug-in from AKVIS makes colorizing a black-and-white photograph quick and automatic. You can intuitively add color to a variety of images from antique photos to hand-drawn sketches and cartoons and still maintain a very natural look. You can even use Coloriage to replace the colors in a color image.

Your image must be in RGB mode for the Coloriage filters to be applied. Click Image ⇨ Mode ⇨ RGB

before selecting AKVIS Coloriage from the Photoshop filters.

You can colorize an image with Coloriage by clicking different colors from the Colors palette or using the Color Library for difficult colors such as skin, hair, and lips. You then paint over areas in the photo with loose brush strokes. When you click the green forward button, the software determines the borders of the various areas and applies the colors based on the grayscale values.

You can find Coloriage at AKVIS.com.

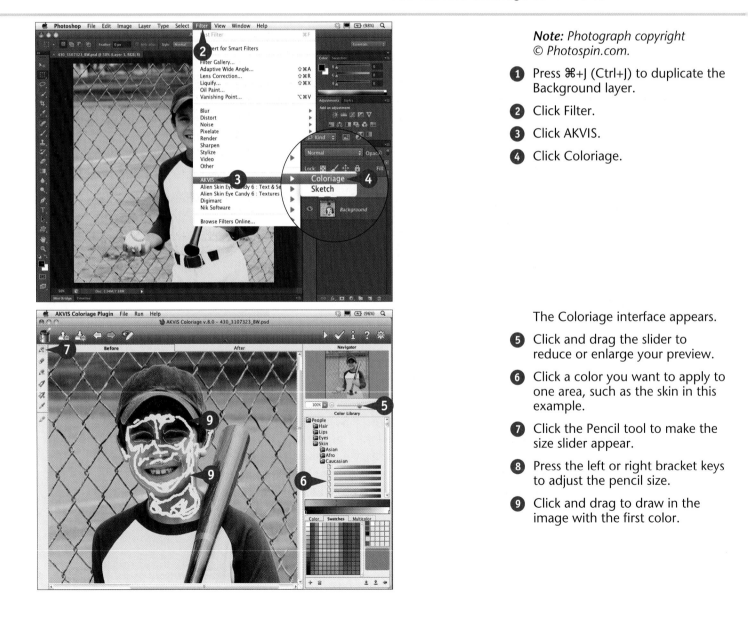

Note: Photograph copyright © Photospin.com.

1. Press ⌘+J (Ctrl+J) to duplicate the Background layer.

2. Click Filter.

3. Click AKVIS.

4. Click Coloriage.

The Coloriage interface appears.

5. Click and drag the slider to reduce or enlarge your preview.

6. Click a color you want to apply to one area, such as the skin in this example.

7. Click the Pencil tool to make the size slider appear.

8. Press the left or right bracket keys to adjust the pencil size.

9. Click and drag to draw in the image with the first color.

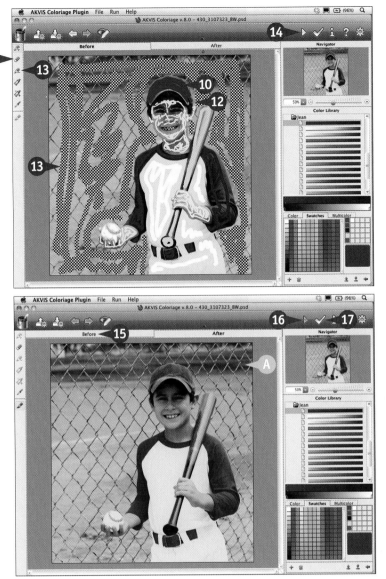

10 Repeat steps 5 to 9 to set all the colors to be used.

11 Click the Eraser tool.

12 Click and drag to correct any stray marks.

13 Click the Keep-Color Pencil tool and click in any areas you do not want to colorize.

14 Click the Run button to see a preliminary colorization.

A AKVIS determines the blends, and the colorized image appears in the After pane.

15 Click the Before tab and repeat steps 6 to 12 to change any colors as needed.

16 Click the Run button again to view the corrections.

17 Click the Apply button.

The final colorization is applied to the image.

Note: If the colors are too vibrant in the Background copy layer, you can lower the opacity of the layer.

TIPS

Did You Know?

If you want to change only one particular color in any color image and not alter the rest of the colors, use the Pencil tool (🖊) and draw on the object. Then use the Keep-Color Pencil tool (🖊) and draw a closed outline around the object.

Try This!

When you colorize a black-and-white photograph, select the less saturated colors in the Color palette to make the colorization appear more natural. The less saturated colors are at the bottom of the palette.

More Options!

You can save the color strokes to edit colors later or vary different colorization schemes. Click the Save Strokes button (🖼) after drawing all the strokes but before applying them and closing the interface.

Convert a photo to a pencil sketch with AKVIS SKETCH

In addition to Coloriage, AKVIS makes a number of other plug-ins to restore, retouch, and enhance images. AKVIS art-styled plug-ins help you create paintings and drawings from photographs while giving your project the look of traditional media.

AKVIS Sketch makes it easy to change a photograph into a pencil or charcoal sketch. The plug-in gives you control over the style and thickness of lines and pencil strokes as well as other artistic attributes in a preview mode. You can change a setting, run a new preview, and continue to make changes before applying the

effects. You can create various natural media versions of your photo on separate layers and then blend them together for different effects. You can achieve unique artistic effects by painting with Photoshop's new Bristle tip brushes and the Mixer Brush tool on the AKVIS Sketch layers.

Using a photo-to-art plug-in from AKVIS alone or in combination with Photoshop's art tools enables you to unleash your creativity, learn to draw and paint, or just improve your artistic skills.

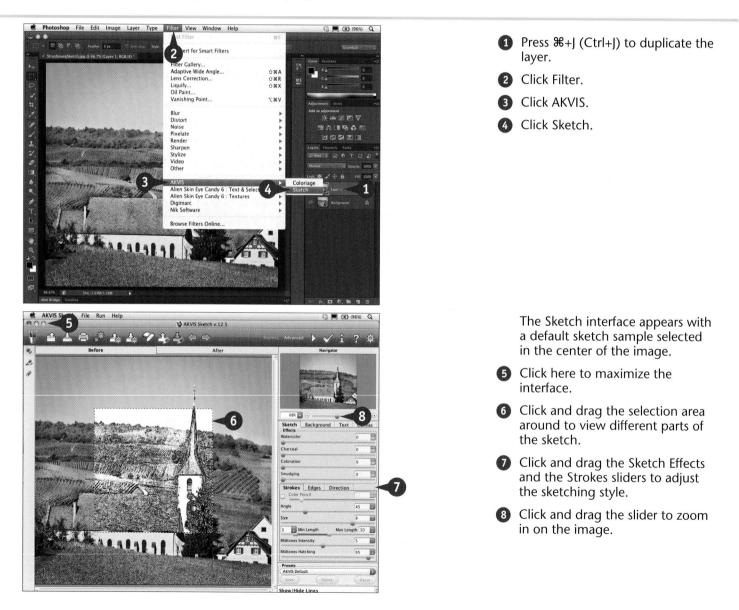

① Press ⌘+J (Ctrl+J) to duplicate the layer.

② Click Filter.

③ Click AKVIS.

④ Click Sketch.

The Sketch interface appears with a default sketch sample selected in the center of the image.

⑤ Click here to maximize the interface.

⑥ Click and drag the selection area around to view different parts of the sketch.

⑦ Click and drag the Sketch Effects and the Strokes sliders to adjust the sketching style.

⑧ Click and drag the slider to zoom in on the image.

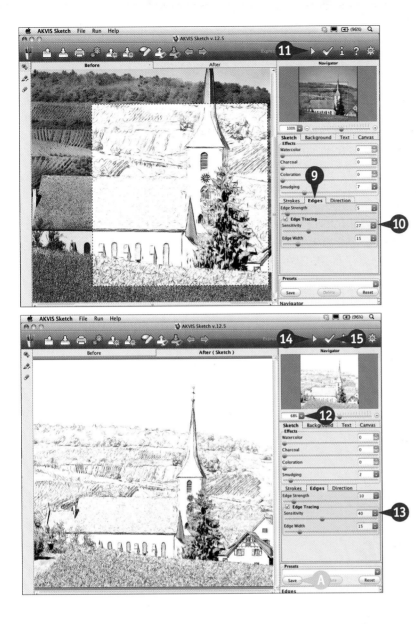

DIFFICULTY LEVEL

9. Click the Edges tab.

10. Click and drag the Edge Strength, Sensitivity, and Edge Width sliders to increase or decrease quality of the lines.

11. Click the Run button to preview the changed settings.

AKVIS redraws the image as a sketch.

12. Click the drop-down menu and select Fit Image to view the whole image at once.

13. Click and drag any of the sliders to readjust the drawing.

14. Click the Run button to preview the new settings.

15. Click the Apply button to apply the sketch to the layer in Photoshop.

A. You can optionally click Save to save the settings as a preset.

TIPS

Try This!

Similar to Sketch, AKVIS Artwork turns a photo into a painting with minimal effort and still produces a creative rendering. The sliders and settings let you select the style of paint and thickness of brush strokes to make your painting look as though it were done with natural media.

Did You Know?

AKVIS and other plug-in software companies not only have examples of the plug-in effects on their respective websites, they also have complete tutorials for their products.

More Options!

Selecting areas and masking are often easier to accomplish with a masking plug-in from one of the software companies. Using technology similar to that of Coloriage, you draw over areas to keep with a blue pencil and then draw with a red pencil to define the areas that should be cut away. The software finds the borders and removes the unwanted areas in the photo.

Create a gold logo with ALIEN SKIN EYE CANDY 6

Eye Candy 6 from Alien Skin helps you create a diverse range of designs and specialty effects. You can easily build glass-like buttons for a web interface, add depth to stylize a logo, design custom titles, or even simulate natural phenomena, such as fire and smoke. You can create metal, gel, or animal fur textures simply by moving the sliders. You can even add a drop shadow to text and make it converge in perspective. Eye Candy 6 includes 30 filters you can use and combine to make designs come to life. The filters perform complex simulations to render detailed images, and the results can be easier to accomplish than using the filters built into Photoshop alone.

You can design a logo that looks like gold with only minimal steps, save it, and then place that golden logo on any image. This task uses a custom shape. You can use your signature, an existing logo, or any other design on a transparent layer as a starting point.

With 1,500 presets that you can use and edit to fit your particular design, experimentation is key to designing with Eye Candy 6.

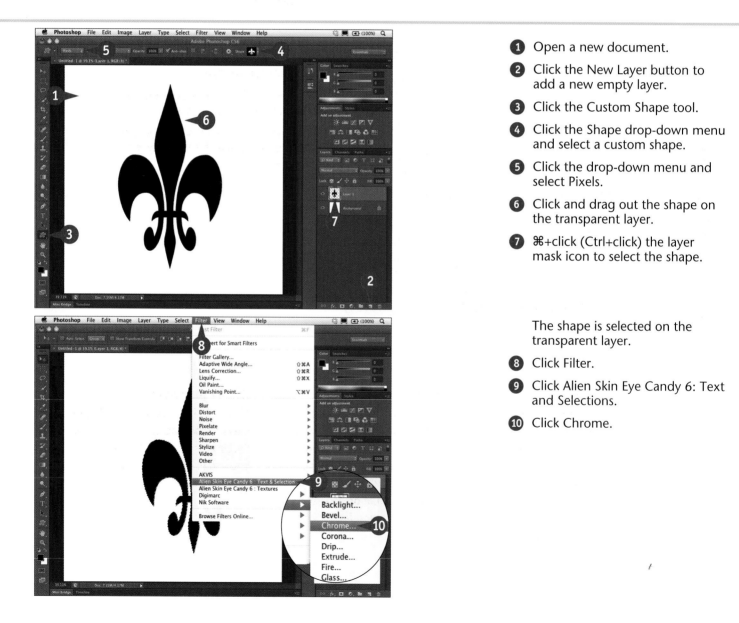

① Open a new document.

② Click the New Layer button to add a new empty layer.

③ Click the Custom Shape tool.

④ Click the Shape drop-down menu and select a custom shape.

⑤ Click the drop-down menu and select Pixels.

⑥ Click and drag out the shape on the transparent layer.

⑦ ⌘+click (Ctrl+click) the layer mask icon to select the shape.

The shape is selected on the transparent layer.

⑧ Click Filter.

⑨ Click Alien Skin Eye Candy 6: Text and Selections.

⑩ Click Chrome.

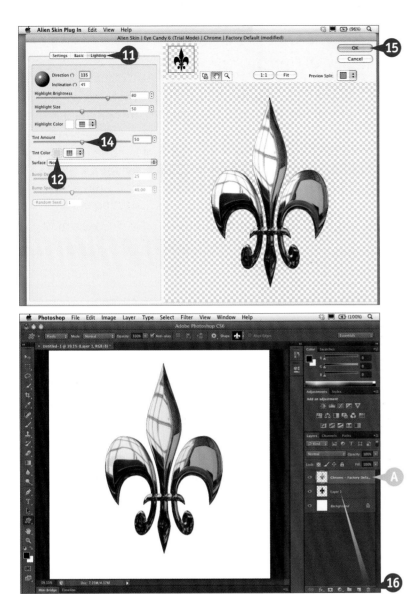

The Alien Skin dialog box appears with the default chrome settings.

⑪ Click the Lighting tab.

⑫ Click the Tint Color box.

⑬ In the Color Picker that appears, select a yellow color such as R:235, G:215, G:35 and click OK.

⑭ Click and drag the Tint Amount slider to about 50 to create a gold look.

⑮ Click OK.

Ⓐ Eye Candy fills the shape with gold and places it on a separate transparent layer.

⑯ Click and drag the original pixel shape layer to the trash.

⑰ Save the file with both layers so you can place the logo layer onto any image.

TIPS

More Options!

You can vary the reflections and bevels in the Basic tab of Alien Skin's Chrome dialog box. Click and drag any of the sliders to change the bevel. Click Inside Selection (◯ changes to ◉) and then click any of the Reflection Maps in the list to apply it.

Important!

The Eye Candy 6 Filters work with CMYK files and 16-bit per channel images. They can even be used on very large files. And because they can be applied to Smart Objects and can be built on separate layers, the filters are nondestructive.

Did You Know?

Alien Skin has a number of plug-in filters for photographers as well as the professional graphic designer. You can find them all at www.alienskin.com.

Index

Index

Index

M

Marquee tools, 58, 213, 247, 248
masks
    clipping mask, 200–201
    color of, changing, 51
    defined, 34
    layer masks, 58–59, 162–163
    selections using, 50–51
    Unsharp Mask filter, 134, 136–137
Match Color command, 120–121
matte, adding to an image, 246, 250–251. *See also* canvas of
image, expanding
Median filter, 226, 228, 234, 240
memory usage, 9
Merge to HDR Pro command, 170–171
Mini Bridge, 16–17
mirror images, adding, 184–185
Mixer Brush Cloning Paint Setup action, 236, 239
Mixer Brush tool
    blending colors with, 222
    Bristle tip brushes, effect on, 223
    for oil painting effect, 236, 238, 239
    for pastel drawing effect, 230
    for sketched effect, 224–225
    for watercolor effect, 243
monitor, calibrating, 30–31
Move tool, 58–59, 164–165, 168, 201, 203, 205
Multiply blend mode, 189, 229, 233, 251

N

NEF files. *See* RAW files
New Action dialog box, 20
New Adjustment Layer option, Layer menu, 158
New option, File menu, 212, 222
New Workspace dialog box, 11, 15
Nik Viveza plug-in, 264–265
noise
    reducing, 155, 214, 226, 228, 232, 234, 240
    sharpening's effect on, 137
    in third channel, not exaggerating, 135
    Threshold values affecting, 136
Notes tool, 29

O

Oil Paint filter, 214–215, 236
oil painted effect, 214–215, 236–239
Oil Pastel-Soft Opaque brush, 230
On-image adjustment tool, 42–43
Open As Smart Object option, File menu, 44
Open option, File menu, 12, 153
Overlay blend mode, 61, 88–89, 101, 128, 129, 137

P

Paint Overlay style, 159
painting effect, 214–215, 236–239
panel groups, 10
panorama, assembling, 80–81
paragraph styles, creating, 206–207
Paste Special option, Edit menu, 58

pastel drawing effect, 228–231
Path Selection tool, 204–205
Pattern Stamp tool, 240–243
patterns
    adding, 25, 229, 240
    Artist Surfaces patterns, 215, 242–243
    Canvas fill pattern, 215
    Colored Paper pattern set, 229
    Custom Patterns, 229
    Gold Parchment fill pattern, 229
    Gold Vellum fill pattern, 229
    Gouache Light on Watercolor pattern, 241
    performance affected by, 9
    for Texture Elements, 205
pen and colored wash drawing effect, 232–235
pen and ink drawing effect, 226–227. *See also* sketched effect
pen and tablet. *See* tablet
Pencil brush preset, 225
pencil sketch effect. *See* sketched effect
Pencil-Soft Opaque brush, 230
people. *See* portraits
Performance Preferences, 8–9
perspective, 74–75, 172–173, 180–181, 198–199
pets, eye color of, 99
Photo Filter adjustment, 158
photo gallery, web, 260–261
photographic designs, 64–65
Photomerge command, 80–81
Photoshop CS6
    new features, 2
    plug-ins for. *See* plug-ins
    preferences for, 6–7, 8–9, 28, 142, 145
pincushion distortion, correcting, 76–77
Place option, File menu, 65, 189, 220
plug-ins. *See also* Camera Raw plug-in
    AKVIS Artwork plug-in, 269
    AKVIS Coloriage plug-in, 266–267
    AKVIS Sketch plug-in, 268–269
    Alien Skin Eye Candy 6 plug-in, 270–271
    benefits of using, 262
    Nik Viveza plug-in, 264–265
Point-Round Long Blender brush, 238
portraits
    adjusting, guidelines for, 84
    eyeglasses, removing glare from, 96–97
    eyes
        brightening, 102–103
        catchlights in, adding, 108–109
        color of, 98–99, 104–105
        depth of, increasing, 104–107
        lightening, 100–101
        sharpening, 110–111
    group shots, 165, 168–169
    lips, color of, 104–105
    skin
        imperfections in, removing, 86–89
        skin tones, selecting, 52–55
        softening, 92–95, 154, 155
        wrinkles, reducing, 90–91
poster effect, 218–221
Posterize adjustment, 218–221
Preferences, Bridge, 15

Index